Blood Cries Out

Pentecostals, Peacemaking, and Social Justice Series

PAUL ALEXANDER AND JAY BEAMAN, SERIES EDITORS

Volumes in the Series:

Pentecostal Pacifism: The Origin, Development, and Rejection of Pacific Belief among the Pentecostals by Jay Beaman

Forgiveness, Reconciliation, and Restoration: Mulitdisciplinary Studies from a Pentecostal Perspective edited by Martin W. Mittelstadt and Geoffrey W. Sutton

A Liberating Spirit: Pentecostals and Social Action in North America edited by Michael Wilkinson and Steven M. Studebaker

Christ at the Checkpoint: Theology in the Service of Justice and Peace edited by Paul Alexander

Pentecostals and Nonviolence: Reclaiming a Heritage edited by Paul Alexander

The Liberating Mission of Jesus: The Message of the Gospel of Luke by Dario Lopez Rodriguez

Pentecostal and Holiness Statements on War and Peace edited by Jay Beaman and Brian K. Pipkin

BLOOD CRIES OUT

Pentecostals, Ecology, and the Groans of Creation

EDITED BY

A. J. SWOBODA

PICKWICK *Publications* · Eugene, Oregon

BLOOD CRIES OUT
Pentecostals, Ecology, and the Groans of Creation

Pentecostals, Peacemaking, and Social Justice Series 8

Pickwick Publications
An Imprint of Wipf and Stock Publishers
199 W. 8th Ave., Suite 3
Eugene, OR 97401

www.wipfandstock.com

ISBN 13: 978-1-62564-462-6

Cataloging-in-Publication data:

Blood cries out : Pentecostals, ecology, and the groans of creation / edited by A. J. Swoboda.

xxiv + 234 p. ; 23 cm. —Includes bibliographical references and index(es).

Pentecostals, Peacemaking, and Social Justice 8

ISBN 13: 978-1-62564-462-6

1. Pentecostalism. 2. Ecotheology. 3. Human ecology—Religious aspects. I. Title. II. Series.

BT695.5 B48 2014

Manufactured in the U.S.A.

For Mark Cartledge.

You Awakened My Mind, Mate. Thanks.

Contents

Foreword

Steven Bouma-Prediger

Few today would doubt the need to care for our home planet. Various ecological problems show up almost every day in the local paper or national newscast, and examples of ecological degradation are painfully evident in our own neighborhoods and cities: polluted air, contaminated water, species extinction, topsoil erosion, toxic waste, acid rain, global warming. The litany of ecological woes is, sadly, much too long. In the past decades many voices have arisen, from all around our home planet, increasing our awareness of our contemporary predicament and advocating change for the better. Some of these voices, not surprisingly, have used the language of religion, since religious beliefs and practices are at the very core of human identity, despite what some sociologists might posit. And some of those people who invoke religious faith to address ecological harm are Christians. Indeed, in the past forty or so years a large and still growing number of Christians have come to see caring for the earth as integral to their faith. They have embraced the ideals and practices of environmental stewardship or care for creation or earthkeeping (this goes by many names) as part and parcel of their Christian faith.

Within Christianity, in all its diversity, many have articulated their understanding of our responsibilities to care for the earth in terms of their particular tradition. We can, of course, do no other. There is no generic Christian faith. We are who we are by virtue of the time and place we live, which includes that branch of the church we call home. So we have contributions from Roman Catholics in Africa and Lutherans in Europe and Reformed folk in South Africa and Anabaptists from Canada and the Orthodox from Greece, among others, each offering the riches of their tradition to the task of doing ecological theology and ethics. Missing in this mix, until recently, have been Pentecostal or Charismatic contributions. While there have been a few essays and articles, there has been no substantive book bringing together these pertinent voices to examine the relationship between Pentecostal and Charismatic theology and the ecological issues of our day. Until now.

In *Blood Cries Out* we have, at long last, a rich treatment of ecological issues by Pentecostal and Charismatic theologians and thinkers. This volume brings together important voices such as Veli-Matti Kärkkäinen, Jay Beaman, Peter Althouse, and A. J. Swoboda to examine how our Pentecostal sisters and brothers have engaged ecological (and ecojustice) issues in the past, to explore how the Bible and Pentecostal tradition can and should inform our theology and ethics in this present age, and to survey how this tradition of Christian faith can support earth-friendly practices and ways of living now and in the future. So whether you are curious about the beliefs of important historical figures such as William Seymour or Aimee Semple McPherson, or are puzzled about how the gifts of the Spirit figure into eco-ethics, or are wondering about what local Charismatic churches are doing to make their buildings and grounds more sustainable, this book is for you.

I commend Dr. Swoboda for gathering these thinkers and their essays into one place and I pray for a wide readership for this book. We have much to learn from each other. So God's blessings to you as you take up and read this stimulating work of timely scholarship. May you—whether Pentecostal or not—be inspired by what you learn. And may the Holy Spirit lead us all in our care of the earth and its amazing plethora of creatures, to bear witness to God's great, good future of shalom.

Introduction

A. J. Swoboda

Not unlike the oversized picture book sitting atop my grandmother's cof-fee table, the narrative of Scripture is divinely placed before us as a kind of storehouse of imagery, pictures, and snapshots of real, day-to-day life.[1] It might be easy, I would think, for the assumption to be made that such images are unbearingly mundane, unavoidably otherworldly, or even yet, achingly antiquated by some inexperienced reader. But surprisingly, this very old book remains in touch with the now, with today, with our world. As such, the Bible continues to be unrelentingly timely to whatever mo-ment its new generation of readers find themselves in. Which, in itself, is quite the feat in the realm of ancient literature. One cannot say the same about the high-minded ancient Greek and Latin poets and philosophers whose metaphors and pictures no longer speak pointedly to today's situ-ations as powerfully as the simple words of a rejected peasant in the first century still do. How, we may wonder, is it possible that the simple stories and parables of a first-century peasant Jew remain in touch with contem-porary human hearts today as much as they did two thousand years ago? The Bible, and truth for that matter, is like that: they can be at the same moment old and timely.

As its title suggests, this volume is built on a biblical image; namely, the repeated image of crying.[2] The blood cries out. Whose blood?, a reader

---

1. Clark Pinnock discusses the Bible in similar terms, as primarily a book of images rather than a set of dry propositions. See his *Scripture Principle*, 48.

2. This is discussed in greater length in my co-authored textbook: Brunner, Butler,

may ask. Wherever found in the Old Testament, the violence of the verb "cry out" (Heb. tsaʿaq) is sure to conjure up one of many unpleasant and oftentimes unbearable human experiences and emotions: Esau "cries out" upon realization that his father's blessing was not to be his (Gen 27:34), God is aroused to action through hearing his peoples' "cries" during their Egyptian bondage (Exod 5:8), and, of course, the Psalmist repeatedly "cries out" to YHWH for divine help (Pss 34:17, 77:1, 88:1). Perhaps most explicit is its use in Deuteronomy whereupon "crying out" appears to be connected to the physical trauma resulting from forced sexual violation (Deut 22:24). While disconcerting at times, the sheer fact that the Bible refuses to side-step these varying nuances of human pain and suffering is telling of the Bible's timeliness; humans have suffered since they took their first steps as humans. And the Bible enters that suffering. Yet, what's more telling is that Scripture similarly describes the suffering of all of creation, not merely of its human inhabitants.

Creation laments in the Bible. Inextricably connected to this image of "crying out" is another central biblical image—"mourning" (Heb. ʿabal). Jeremiah, for instance, describes the destruction of God's "pleasant field" as it "mourns . . . because there is no one who cares" (Jer 12:11). Again, the prophet Hosea prophesies that God's land, the earth, itself "mourns" because of the bloodshed perpetrated upon its fields (Hos 4:3). So while Scripture enters head-on into the varying dimensions of human suffering, it likewise tackles the suffering and oppression of non-human creation— the travail of the birds, the insects, the air, and the soil. Humans cry out; the earth mourns. Lamentation, in Scripture, is therefore anything but an exclusively human affair. Rather, all of creation can mourn. And all of creation does mourn. The New Testament strengthens this theme. As Paul's letter to the Romans would put it, all of creation "groans" (Rom 8:22). Even the "stones" cry out, Jesus says (Luke 19:40). In wrestling with the various "woes" of John's Revelation, Barbara Rossing agrees that it the earth who has a greatest lament to place at the feet of humanity. For it is in the ecological crisis, through creation, that God is crying "in a cosmic lament against the violent conquests and predatory economic system of the empire that has enslaved both people and nature."[3] The eco-crisis,

---

and Swoboda, *Introducing Evangelical Ecotheology*, 61–62. I want to thank Paul Ede for his word study on "crying" throughout Scripture that he provided years ago in email correspondence.

3. Rossing, "God Laments with Us," 123

Rossing suggests, is the voice of a God communicating to our world that our way of doing "life" is not only not life, it is actually a system of murder and death that institutionalizes oppression.

Crying out and mourning are part and parcel of experiencing God's creation. So one is provoked to ponder: How is it that God responds to such crying and mourning in his creation? Over and over—as opposed to stumbling upon some Creator God passively watching (some might say voyeuristically) his creation spin out of control into tribulation and chaos from some safe distance—we're presented with a dynamic, near, vulnerable, and responsive God who not only goes to great pains to bear justice into pain and suffering but actually chooses to enter into pain and suffering through the incarnation of Jesus Christ. God is a God of justice bearing injustice on his back in the form of a wooden cross. And, in that way, the Bible speaks to our present age, an age of unimaginable suffering. Our minds—whether one believes in God or resonates with the message of the Bible—cannot fathom a world minus justice. A Jewish rabbi once explained to me that the idea of a God of justice could not be more important for the Jews than in the years following the holocaust. For without justice, the rabbi pointed out, we are relegated to the despairing and haunting thought that Anne Frank and Adolf Hitler received the same lot in the afterlife. And that does not sit right with any sensible mind.

The truth is, any postmodern, postChristian, intellectually-privileged, secular individual who has rejected the claims of the Bible will at some level believe in and practice their own sense of justice in their world. Admittedly, that sense of justice may not be rooted in any way to Christian theology or Scripture. But one quickly becomes aware that nearly every non-religious Western individual believes wholeheartedly in justice and absolute truth the minute the words "bullying," "rape," "subordination," or "Monsanto" are spoken. Everyone has a sense of justice—religious or not. My friend Dr. Matthew Sleeth has pointed out to me on more than one occasion that the environmental movement points to a move of justice that God is accomplishing outside the walls of the church, and that every environmentalist who gives their life to caring for creation is, whether they know it or not, living the *imago Dei* in their created nature.

And that is because justice is fundamentally built into every string of the fabric of creation. That is precisely why even the non-human, non-rational, non-intellectual, non-"learned" created realm, can "groan" and "mourn" and "cry out" in the same way Israel could in their oppression. Just because it isn't human doesn't mean it doesn't have a voice. Justice is at the heart of all God has made, in the human and non-human realms. In the Christian tradition, no act of evil, injustice, or oppression can be appropriately understood as a private or personal affair, as if something could be done in secret. In fact, secret and creation are mutually exclusive ideas. Everything is laid bare before God. God sees all and knows all. "Nothing," writes the author of Hebrews, "in all of creation is hidden from God's sight" (Heb 4:13; italics mine). This principle of what Donald Gelpi has called the God of "scrutinizing omniscience" comes into play quite early in the Bible as we come upon the Bible's very first instance of "crying out."[4] It is there, one chapter following humanity's fall, that we happen upon the story of Cain and Abel (Gen 4). The tale is well known: Cain, jealous that his brother Abel's sacrifices before God are acceptable while his are not, lures his brother into a field outside the city.[5] There, Cain commits the first murder in the Bible; cutting short his brother's life in a murder of cold blood. It is disturbing that the first murder recorded in the Bible is a religiously motivated murder, the beginning of a precedent we haven't yet managed to stop.

With Abel silenced, Cain very well might have assumed that his "secret" fratricide done away from the human community would have gone unpunished; the murder was seen by no one. Or, perhaps, Cain would not have even considered that murder was wrong in the first place. Keep in mind that previous to Abel's death, no such commandment against murder had been recorded or spoken by God; the Ten Commandments will not come for some time. Murder, then, was assumed to be unjust from creation to the time of Cain. Murder was bad even if God had not gone on record to say it. As if it were unclear from his likely guilty conscience, Cain soon finds out God's opinion on the social deterioration he has initiated. God saw, and God visits Cain.

God bears a weighty message in the form of a simple question, not all that unlike his question to Adam and Eve following the first sin: "Cain, where is your brother?"[6] Cain's response, like Adam and Eve, is

4. Gelpi, *The Divine Mother*, 48.

5. Peck points out that the Cain/Abel narrative intentionally omits the rationale behind God's preference of Abel's sacrifices over Cain's. "This is an important aspect of the story," writes Peck, "since it suggests that the cause for the murder is not external but rather resides within Cain." "From Cain to the Death Camps," 159.

6. It is interesting to compare God's response to Cain with that of Adam and Eve.

deflective: "I don't know. Am I my brother's keeper?" (Gen 4:9). The Lord replies quickly, clearly, and pointedly: "What have you done? Listen! Your brother's blood cries out to me from the ground" (Gen 4:10; italics mine). Abel's blood was tsa`aq; it "cried out" the way Israel would later "cry out" to God in Egypt. The text solicits that God is not only aware of Abel's murder but can actually hear his blood crying out, seeping into the ground as it slowly dries on the grass surface of some field outside the city. And so God curses Cain. His words seem damning: "Now you are cursed from the earth, which has opened up its mouth to receive your brother's blood from your hands" (Gen 4:10–11). This curse is indicative of a new reality in God's creation that had been initiated just one chapter earlier with the fall of humanity; a reality where the once intimate relationship between two brothers has broken down invariably breaking down the murderers relationship to the earth. As Cain killed Abel, Cain was separated from the earth. The breakdown in one relationship led to the breakdown of another.

Abel's blood screams for justice, crying out for rightness, or righteousness. But why must we linger on that point? Because injustice will always cry out. Injustice will not hide. Injustice will cry out until wrongs are righted. And the blood will not shut up until it is. Thomas Dozeman has pointed out that once Abel's blood falls to the earth and is no longer in its proper place, it becomes a kind of pollutant rather than a life force in Abel's body. As Dozeman puts it, blood becomes a "virus" infecting the story of creation from that story on.[7] But the blood of Christ becomes a kind of reversal of this viral hatred. As it often does, the future gospel stories about Jesus of Nazareth not only rely upon such narratives like that of Cain and Abel, but actually build upon them as a kind of narrative backbone.[8] Jesus, like Abel, made religious people squirm—he infuriated

---

God, in the initial sin of humanity, simply asks: "Where are you?" (Gen 3:9). Here, in a similarly simple line of questioning, asks Cain, "Where is your brother?" (Gen 4:9). In two successive chapters, God asks where Adam is and then asks where Cain's brother is.

7. "The Priestly Vocation," 119.

8. The Cain/Abel narrative has many connections to the New Testament narratives. For example, see Luke 11:47–51; Heb 11:4, 12:24; 1 John 3:4–17. Similarly, there remains a long, and rich, history of interpretations of the Cain/Abel narrative among the Jewish and Christian communities. See Byron, *Cain and Abel in Text and Tradition*. Finally, Allison has drawn similar parallels between Jesus' life and teachings to the Cain/Abel narrative, in "Murder and Anger, Cain and Abel (Matt 5:21–25)," in *Studies in Matthew*, 65–78. I would like to express my indebtedness to Stan Saunders of Columbia Theological Seminary for helping point these resources out to me in an

the Jewish leaders with his ability to inspire the crowds and speak of his intimate love of his Father. They grew jealous at him. He infuriated them all the more by instructing them that righteousness embodied was among them. *He* was that righteousness; "I am sending you prophets and sages and teachers. Some of them you will kill and crucify; others you will flog in your synagogues and pursue from town to town. And so upon you will come all the righteous blood that has been shed on earth, from the blood of righteous Abel to the blood of Zechariah . . . whom you murdered between the temple and the altar" (Matt 23:34–35). Jesus' blood would be the most righteous blood of them all.

Jesus, like Abel, was not received by his own (John 1:11). In the end, Jesus was taken outside the city by his Jewish brothers where he would die on a Roman cross, blood dripping into the cracks of the sun-scorched earth. His blood, like Abel's, still cries out. And not unlike Abel's blood, the blood of Jesus cries out to God eternally on behalf of creation. It cries forgiveness, love, peace, and acceptance. And that blood calls out to us as well. It pulls at us. It calls to us. It disturbs us. It whispers to us. Paul describes Jesus' blood as the blood of divine reconciliation, a sacrifice that tears down walls of false separation. We have been, as the Pauline letter to Ephesians says, "[B]rought near by the blood of Christ. For He Himself is our peace, who has made the two groups one and has destroyed the barrier, the dividing wall of hostility" (Eph 2:13–14).

Is it possible that the blood of Christ that fell upon the earth could heal even the enmity between Cain and Abel? It could reconcile us to God, why not Cain to Abel? Could Jesus' blood break down that dividing wall of hostility? Miroslav Volf, in a provocative reflection on the reconciliatory power of the coming age ushered in by the sacrifice of Jesus, argues that it will be in that coming day where enemies will be made right. In that day, righteousness will prevail. It is there, in resurrection reconciliation, that Cain and Abel will once again face each other. Volf writes:

> If Cain and Abel were to meet again in the world to come, what will need to have happened between them for Cain to not keep avoiding Abel's look and for Abel to not to want to get out of Cain's way? . . . If the world to come is to be a world of love, then the eschatological transition from the present world to that world, which God will accomplish, must have an inter-human

unpublished paper, "Salt of the Earth," which he allowed me to read.

side; the work of the Spirit in the consummation includes not only the resurrection of the dead and the last judgment but also the final social reconciliation.[9]

Volf rightly articulates an eschatological vision of Christ's reconciliation that is not only framed in terms of the provision of peace with God, but peace with God leading to peace with the other—in Abel's case, even his murderer. Volf wisely points out that when Karl Barth was asked if we would see our loved ones in heaven, Barth glibly responded: "[N]ot *only* the loved ones!"[10] In the final reconciliation, justice will be served—justice between the oppressors and oppressed, murdered and murderer, perpetrator and perpetrated. Perhaps that is why John's Revelation looks forward to that day as a day when, "He will *wipe every tear* from our eyes. There will be no more death or mourning or crying . . . for the old order of things has passed in hear" (Rev 21:4; italics mine). John knew we would enter the heavenly dimension with many tears from a life of crying and mourning. He also knew, however, they would be wiped away.

I want boldly to take Volf's reconciliatory theology one step further. While one cannot understate the dynamic element of social reconciliation that can easily be traced through the words and work of Jesus Christ and his church as Volf has pointed out, I'm pressed to take it further: to say that the Spirit of Pentecost seeks both to bear reconciliatory healing between human beings (Cain and Abel) and also between humans and earth. As one is healed, the other will be healed. By that, I'm simply arguing that God's Spirit is bringing to fulfillment Isaiah's prophetic promise of the anointed Messiah: when Messiah came, the infant could play by the cobra's den and even put her hand in the viper's nest and all will be well (Isa 11:8). The Spirit is eschatologically healing, reconciling, fixing every broken relationship in creation and is simply unwilling to stop with the human community. Being filled with God's Spirit, therefore, is to open oneself up to the healing process. And it is by that same Spirit that we cease responding to our part of the injustices done unto creation with the deflection of Cain. We'll stop saying we don't know what is going on. We'll stop dodging responsibility. And respond afresh, as we did in Eden, that it *is* we who are tasked as keepers of God's garden. And it is by the Spirit we stop passing the buck to the next generation.

9. Volf, "The Final Reconcilation," 94.

10. Ibid., 91; italics mine.

And so, the blood cries out. This book is an attempt to address head-on the swelling tide of concerns related to environmental degradation, eco-injustice, and creation care from the distinctive perspective(s) of the Pentecostal and Charismatic traditions.[11] Such concerns have yet, for Pentecostals or Charismatics, to be substantively addressed in a way that the crisis itself demands. Although I will allow the chapters themselves to speak to various dynamics of climate change and ecological degradation, I do believe that a laconic statement is in order: a crisis this big demands an equally big theology. And to do so requires great time and energy. Signs are showing that any lingering apathy toward developing such a Pentecostal/Charismatic ecotheology is itself shrinking. And that, for the sake of God's creation, is a good thing. By virtue of a growing network of thoughtful writers, thinkers, theologians, pastors, and practitioners, we are watching first-hand a distinctively Pentecostal/Charismatic ecotheology form before our very eyes. Hence the rationale for this volume.

It is my overwhelming joy to present the following chapters to you—a collection of breathtaking reflections representing the first edited volume of its kind, bringing together disparate voices from varying expressions of the Pentecostal and Charismatic tradition directly addressing ecological concerns. While I present it proudly to the academy and the church for its consideration, it has its shortfalls, as with any writing projects.[12] With all imperfections aside, the text is organized into three main parts (history, theology, and practice) that thematically connect the chapters in each. Part one examines a wide array of historical vignettes from the early formation of Pentecostal imagination regarding creation. In chapter 1, Darrin Rodgers and Nicole Sparks dust off and examine an oft-forgotten historical reality in the early formation of the environmental movement: that of the entrepreneurial work of John S. McConnell Jr. and his Pentecostal faith upon the genesis of Earth Day. One will be

11. This builds on my previous research and writing, which develops a distinctively Pentecostal/Charismatic theology of the Spirit with particular sensitivity to ecological concerns and issues. See Swoboda, *Tongues and Trees*; and Swoboda, "Eco-glossolalia."

12. Most particularly, I am personally uncomfortable with the dearth of female and non-Western voices in this text. I had exceedingly hoped for more willing female and non-Western participants in this project. While I sought to recruit them, willing female and non-Western authors were difficult to find. The personal consternation this caused me was great, but I have come to believe that the lack of diverse scholars who write on the topic of ecotheology among Pentecostals and Charismatics is indicitave of a great need. Even since the completion of this manuscripts, a number of notable resources have come to light that continue to show signs of maturity in the field.

surprised at the role McConnell and his faith played in the formation of Earth Day. Brandon Hubbard-Heitz's piece, chapter 2, examines early Pentecostal interpretations and utilizations of space in their worship gatherings as a springboard to discuss possible Pentecostal excursions into ecotheology. Chapter 3 further develops the theological peace theology of John McConnell with particular reference to his ardent practice of pacifism and how that might play into Pentecostal ecotheology. In the final chapter of Part I, Brian Pipkin draws on the theological and historical tradition of early American Pentecostalism through the story of Aimee Semple McPherson, the founder of the International Church of the Foursquare Gospel, with special attention given to her unique perspectives on creation.

Section II deals more exclusively with contemporary theological reflection on Pentecostal and Charismatic ecotheology. Fuller's Veli-Matti Kärkkäinen, a sensible, trusted, and willing dialogue partner for Pentecostal and Charismatic theological reflection, approaches the conversation from the perspective of the relationship of the Spirit to various environmental issues by outlining the vitality of their convergence in chapter 5. Steve Overman's chapter (chapter 6), in an effort to sustain a deeper Pentecostal appreciation for and dialogue with the rich traditions of the Eastern Church, mines the theology of Maximus the Confessor to create a rich dialogue between the two. In chapter 7, Peter Althouse reexamines Moltmann's theology of the Spirit with particular attention to the kenosis of the Spirit being poured out on the whole world. In a fascinating chapter 8, Robby Waddell tackles Pentecostal eschatology by examining Revelation and 1 Enoch as ways through which a green eschatology might be imagined. Jeffrey Lamp, building on the earlier ecotheological writings of Matthew Tallman, suggests that there may be benefits to looking at the fivefold nature of Pentecostal theology as opposed to only the fourfold paradigm. Finally, in chapter 10, Michael Chan reconsiders the Old Testament texts on "generational sin" in light of current Old Testament studies and a growing awareness of environmental degradation.

The final section, Part III, offers a praxis-oriented conclusion: How can a Pentecostal and Charismatic theology of the earth be lived out? In chapter 11, Matthew Tallman offers the reader a front-row view of his experience of seeing Pentecostals and Charismatics at work in Africa, with special reference to the AAEC (Association of African Earthkeeping

Churches). Paul Ede's chapter 12 is a fitting follow-up, examining what healing of the land might look like in an urban European context. Finally, Richard Waldrop explores the relationship of the Spirit to creation at Pentecost with special attention given to reflecting upon ecotheology as mission in Latin America in chapter 13.

Finally, I wish to thank my wife, Quinn, and my son, Elliot, for all the days away they gave me to finish this project. I love you both dearly. As well, I proudly wish to thank my friend and editor extraordinaire, Paul Pastor, for his willingness to take time away from his busy day-to-day editorial work with *Christianity Today* to help get this book up to scratch. Your editorial eye was uncompromising, and we are all in debt to you for your work. This project would also not have been possible without the generous financial support of the Seminary Stewardship Alliance and its parent organization, Blessed Earth. Its intrepid leaders, Nancy and Matthew Sleeth, and the administrative team of Will Samson, Laura Leavell, and Keith Jagger cannot go unnoticed. They have all been the best team of ongoing supporters of young Christian voices like myself in both the church and the academy. Thank you each for your continuous hard work.

BIBLIOGRAPHY

Allison, Dale. *Studies in Matthew: Interpretation Past and Present*. Grand Rapids: Baker Academic, 2005.

Brunner, Dan, Jen Butler, and A. J. Swoboda. *Introducing Evangelical Ecotheology: Foundations in Scripture, Theology, History, and Praxis*. Grand Rapids: Baker Academic, 2014.

Byron, John. *Cain and Abel in Text and Tradition: Jewish and Christian Interpretations of the First Siblings Rivalry*. Leiden: Brill, 2011.

Dozeman, Thomas. "The Priestly Vocation." *Interpretation* 59, no. 2 (2005) 117–28.

Gelpi, Donald. *The Divine Mother: A Trinitarian Theology of the Holy Spirit*. Lanham, MD: University Press of America, 1984.

Peck, William J. "From Cain to the Death Camps." *Union Seminary Quarterly Review* 28, no. 2 (1973) 158–76.

Pinnock, Clark, and Barry Callen. *The Scripture Principle: Reclaiming the Full Authority of the Bible*. Grand Rapids: Baker Academic, 2006.

Rossing, Barbara. "God Laments With Us: Climate Change, Apocalypse and the Urgent Kairos Moment." *Ecumenical Review* 62, no. 2 (2010) 119–30.

Swoboda, A. J. "Eco-Glossolalia: Emerging Twenty-First Century Pentecostal and Charismatic Ecotheology." *Journal of Rural Theology* 9, no. 2 (2011) 101–16.

———. *Tongues and Trees: Toward a Pentecostal Ecological Theology.* Journal of Pentecostal Theology Supplement 40. Blandford Forum, UK: Deo, 2013.

Volf, Miroslav. "The Final Reconciliation: Reflections on a Social Dimension of the Eschatological Transition." *Modern Theology* 16, no. 1 (2000) 91–113.

Contributors

A. J. Swoboda is a pastor, professor, and author of *Introducing Evangelical Ecotheology* and *Tongues and Trees*, residing in Portland, OR.

Steven Bouma-Prediger is the author of *For the Beauty of the Earth* and professor of religion at Hope College in Holland, MI.

Darrin J. Rodgers is the director of the Flower Pentecostal Heritage Center, Springfield, MO.

Nicole Sparks is an independent scholar in Springfield, MO.

Brandon Hubbard-Heitz is a Master of Divinity and Master of Arts in Education student at Wake Forest University in Winston-Salem, NC.

Jay Beaman is the author of *Pentecostal Pacifism* and administrative faculty at Warner Pacific College, Portland, OR.

Brian K. Pipkin is the Co-Editor of *Pax Pneuma: The Journal of Pentecostals and Charismatics for Peace and Justice*.

Veli-Matti Kärkkäinen is professor of systematic theology at Fuller Seminary, Pasadena, CA, and Docent of Ecumenics at the University of Helsinki, Finland.

Steve Overman is the senior pastor of Eugene Faith Center (Foursquare) in Eugene, OR.

PETER ALTHOUSE is professor of religion at Southeastern University, Lakeland, FL.

ROBBY WADDELL is professor of New Testament and Early Christian Literature at Southeastern University, Lakeland, FL.

JEFFREY S. LAMP is associate professor of Theology and Ministry at Oral Roberts University, Tulsa, OK.

MICHAEL J. CHAN is an associate professor of Old Testament at Luther Seminary in St. Paul, MN.

MATTHEW TALLMAN is director of Church & Community Relations at Open Arms International in Portland, OR.

PAUL EDE is a PhD candidate at the University of Glasgow, UK.

RICHARD E. WALDROP is the Latin American Social Ministries Coordinator for the Church of God World Missions.

PART ONE

Historical Precedents

1

Pentecostal Pioneer of Earth Day: John McConnell, Jr.

Darrin J. Rodgers and Nicole Sparks

Many readers will be surprised to learn that the founder of the original Earth Day was a Pentecostal.[1] John McConnell Jr. (1915–2012) was best known for his zeal for peace and earth-care, but few people realize that his life work arose from his formative experiences in the Pentecostal church. McConnell had an impeccable Pentecostal patrimony—his grandfather (T. W. McConnell) was Spirit-baptized at the Azusa Street Mission, and his parents (John S. and Hattie McConnell) were founding members of the Assemblies of God. Their story provides insight into the lives of entrepreneurial pioneers in the rough-and-tumble world of early Pentecostalism. Perhaps more importantly, the life of John McConnell, Jr. demonstrates that one can both love Jesus and care for His creation.[2]

---

1. McConnell is the founder of the original Earth Day, which is celebrated by the United Nations, among others, on the spring equinox (March 20 or 21). However, another Earth Day, which is celebrated more widely in the United States, occurs on April 22. McConnell came to identify the spring equinox celebration as International Earth Day in order to distinguish it from the event on April 22.

2. This chapter is a revision of Sparks and Rodgers, "John McConnell, Jr. and the Pentecostal Origins of Earth Day," *Assemblies of God Heritage* (2010), 16–25. McConnell's Pentecostal background was briefly noted in *Assemblies of God Heritage* (Summer 2000), 33. A biography of McConnell includes a chapter on his Pentecostal roots: Weir, *Peace, Justice, Care of Earth*, previously published as *Star of Hope: the Life and Times of John McConnell, Founder of Earth Day*. Weir has written extensively about peace, the environment, and spirituality (primarily Eastern religions). Weir's

Pentecostal pedigree

The founder of Earth Day had a solid Pentecostal pedigree. John McConnell, Jr.'s grandfather, Theodore Ward (T. W.) McConnell, was a Baptist minister who identified with the Pentecostal movement at the interracial Azusa Street Revival in Los Angeles in 1906—which was one of the focal points of the emerging Pentecostal movement.[3] The first issue of the *Apostolic Faith*—the newspaper published by the Azusa Street Mission—shared his testimony:

> About 28 years ago, I went into a meeting to break it up, and the Lord broke me up. My conversion I never could doubt. I was called to preach . . . The Lord supplied my every need, and was with me in revival meetings and in healing many that I prayed for. But I heard of people receiving the Holy Ghost and speaking with tongues. I came to Los Angeles to investigate, and found it was a fact, and earnestly commenced to seek the Lord for the baptism with the Holy Ghost. And the Lord, knowing my heart, came and took possession of me and spoke with my tongue. I want to say to every person, test God and you will never deny the baptism with the Holy Ghost.[4]

T. W. and Frances McConnell had five children, the youngest of whom, John Saunders McConnell (1892–1966), answered the call to become an evangelist in 1911 while attending the Stone Church, a prominent Pentecostal congregation in Chicago. One of the first things J. S. McConnell did as he launched into ministry was to purchase and rebuild an "auto express car" into a "gospel car." This ministry-mobile allowed the budding evangelist to venture beyond the reaches of the railroads and provided a home while on the road in the ensuing years.[5]

While holding revival meetings in Shannon, Texas, J. S. McConnell fell in love with the beautiful young woman who was his pianist—Hattie MacLaughlin (1892–1992). They were married on December 15, 1912,

---

meticulously researched book establishes the timeline of McConnell's life but at times reflects the author's unfamiliarity with the Pentecostal tradition. More recently, Regent University professor John Munday edited McConnell's writings and life story: *John McConnell, Earth Day.*

3. Weir, *Peace, Justice, Care of Earth*, 3.

4. "Evangelist T. W. McConnell's Testimony," 3. See also McConnell, "Experience in Trusting God for Needs," 4; and "In Santa Cruz, Cal.," 3.

5. "Sowing the Seed," 21.

on the front porch of her parents' home. She later recalled that they had a working honeymoon: "We left the next day [after the wedding] in his 'gospel car' headed for southern Texas, without appointments—just trusting God to lead us to wherever we could be of service and give the gospel message."[6]

Despite his father's embrace of Pentecostalism at Azusa Street and his own involvement at Chicago's Stone Church, J. S. McConnell apparently had not experienced Spirit-baptism himself until several years into his ministry. J. S. and Hattie began to seek their own personal Pentecost after a doctor's wife—whom Hattie called "a very dear and spiritual lady"—shared her testimony with them a few times while attending revival meetings held by the McConnells at a town near Houston, Texas. This lady just happened to be the daughter of Arch P. Collins, a leading Pentecostal pastor from Fort Worth who later became the second chairman of the General Council of the Assemblies of God. Impressed by this woman's walk with the Lord, J. S. remarked, "I think she has something that we need."[7]

The McConnells headed to Houston to seek the baptism in the Holy Spirit. Hattie remembered, "We were made very hungry for more of God and our hearts were open. Yet we had reservations." One Sunday morning, J. S. was asked to preach at Brunner Tabernacle, just outside of Houston, even though he had not yet received the experience. Hattie was concerned, but these fears were soon allayed:

> I thought, 'Oh, I hope he says nothing to offend.' Instead, he preached the best 'Pentecostal' message I ever heard. At the close of his message he said, 'Now this is what the Bible says.' This experience is for me and as many as our Lord shall call. So I am going to this altar—not to seek—but to receive what God has for me.[8]

J. S. and Hattie were each baptized with the Spirit and spoke in tongues that morning. This experience resulted in rejection by some of their former friends and ministry colleagues, who claimed that the McConnells had accepted heresy. However, J. S. and Hattie found acceptance in Pentecostal circles—ministering in prominent churches such

---

6. McConnell, "Reminiscing at Age 83," 3.

7. Ibid., 3–4.

8. Ibid., 4.

as F. F. Bosworth's Dallas congregation and Chicago's Stone Church, as well as in storefront missions, schools, theaters, and tents.[9] Hattie noted, "As my husband's calling always seemed evangelistic or preaching in new fields where the Pentecostal message had never been heard, we were ready to move on, in a short time."[10] During the next decades, the McConnells would be involved continuously in church planting and town-to-town revivals. In April 1914, the McConnells attended the organizational meeting of the Assemblies of God in Hot Springs, Arkansas. They became founding members of the General Council of the Assemblies of God.[11]

Childhood

On March 22, 1915, less than a year after the Hot Springs meeting, John McConnell, Jr. (John) was born in Davis City, Iowa, where his parents briefly pastored a church. The eldest of six children, John was raised in an environment thoroughly infused with the Christian faith.[12]

J. S. taught his children to memorize Scripture at an early age. John remembers that he accepted Christ at age seven or eight, and shortly afterward experienced the baptism in the Holy Spirit. John recalled that his experience of Spirit-baptism, which occurred during one of his father's tent meetings, was dramatic: "I fell over backwards and began speaking in tongues." John said that this experience changed his life: "I remember my attitude and conversations changed as a result of my baptism." John remembered that his mother agreed: "My mother later on said I was a changed person. She said I was doing much better and taking care of the dishes and things. She thought my experience was real."[13]

During their years of ministry, the senior McConnells lived from offering to offering, trusting God to provide, as evidenced by their life-style—living out of a donated automobile. J. S. McConnell never passed an offering plate to collect money, preferring instead to utilize a box in the back of the church where individuals could give discreetly. On one

9. Ibid., 5–6.

10. Ibid., 7.

11. The McConnells were pictured in the well-known photograph of participants at the founding General Council, April 2–12, 1914, Hot Springs, Arkansas. Gohr, "Known Persons Who Were at Hot Springs," 22.

12. Weir, *Peace, Justice, Care of Earth*, 5.

13. John McConnell Jr. and Anna McConnell, interview by Darrin Rodgers, Timberline Church, Fort Collins, Colorado, June 15, 2009.

occasion, the family was in need of one hundred forty dollars to pay a bill. Rather than requesting help, he instructed his family to pray, because the recent offerings had been averaging only twenty-five dollars. When the young John collected and counted the money after the service, it was—to the penny—the amount for which they had prayed. Nostalgically and with a hint of challenge, he remarked, "I wish we had the faith that was demonstrated back in those times."[14]

In addition to counting offering money, "Johnnie" and his sister Grace were actively involved in their parents' ministry. The family of four sang as a quartet in many of the services, and Grace even sang gospel songs on national radio. Additionally, the children preached on occasion, revealing their early intelligence and—in at least one specific instance— quick wit. In one town, Grace and John were speaking at a local theater on the topic of "The Devil's Partner," but Grace had arranged the words on the sign to read, "The Devil's Partner: John McConnell." "Everybody laughed about that," he ruefully admitted.[15]

The children's early mastery with words reflected the talents of their parents. Both John and Hattie wrote prolifically across a wide field of genres: tracts, books, and hymns. When the airplane was invented, J. S. McConnell composed a song comparing Christ's return to a "heavenly airoplane":

> One of these nights about twelve o'clock,
> This old world's gonna reel and rock,
> Sinners will tremble and cry for pain,
> And the Lord will come in his airoplane.
>
> Ho! Ye Weary of every tribe,
> Get your ticket for the airoplane ride,
> Jesus our Savior is coming to reign,
> And take us up to glory,
> In the heavenly airoplane.[16]

Though he had seen photographs of airplanes, young John had never seen a real one until he was six. After it flew overhead, he ran inside the

---

14. John McConnell Jr. and Anna McConnell, telephone interview with Nicole Sparks, Darrin Rodgers, and Martin Mittelstadt, April 3, 2009.

15. Ibid.

16. McConnell recounted all five verses of "The Heavenly Airoplane" in a letter to the editor published in *Assemblies of God Heritage* (Summer 2000) 33.

house to announce to Hattie, "Come quick, Mommy! Jesus is here!"—a story that she retold with a laugh many times throughout her life. J. S. McConnell's acknowledgment of contemporary scientific progressions, as evidenced in the above song, proved to have a profound impact upon his son's later focuses.[17]

During one church meeting, young John joined with a few other young boys in forming a chain with their hands and grasping a live wire to feel the divine "spark." John remembered this shock of electric current vividly and relates it to the work the Spirit was performing in revival meetings—"sawdust and people falling and . . . being healed," he recalled.[18]

John recalled another instance from this period in his life that deeply influenced him. After arriving in a new town, his father was full of the Spirit and began preaching in German, a language he neither spoke nor had studied. Afterward, a group of individuals remarked to him, "We didn't know you spoke German. You spoke perfect German to us!" Such events strengthened the McConnells' faith and encouraged them in their traveling evangelism. For John, such obvious miracles reinforced his childhood faith and belief in the miraculous.[19]

J. S. McConnell Sr.'s ministry

John recalled that his father, more than anything else, emphasized the teachings of Jesus. John stated that his father summarized his beliefs in a book, *The New Covenant*, which largely consisted of Scripture verses containing Christ's teachings, organized thematically.[20]

17. John McConnell Jr. and Anna McConnell, telephone interview, April 3, 2009.

18. Ibid.

19. Ibid.

20. The purpose of the book, McConnell wrote, was "to bring to light and to empha-size 'the principles of the doctrine of Christ' as revealed in the commandments of the Lord Jesus, and to restore to God's people the standard of true discipleship which can be found only in the new covenant; believing that if the people of God will make the commandments and words of Jesus the foundation for all doctrine, and the all sufficient basis for fellowship and holy living, it will bring them everywhere into a perfect unity of the faith as well as the Spirit (Eph 4:11–16), and will establish them upon the rock which the gates of hell cannot prevail against (Matt 7:24–25, 16:18), and will restore to them that full power which will enable them to do the works that Christ did and greater works than he did, just as soon as they all come into perfect obedience to all of the commandments of the Lord Jesus Christ (Jn 15:7, 14:12)." McConnell, *The New Covenant*, 17–18.

J. S. McConnell's emphasis on the teachings of Jesus became of central importance to John. He stated, "While in his book, Dad had catalogued 147 commandments of Jesus . . . there was one commandment that fired my soul. This stood out in my mind at that time and as I grew older sustained me in times of trouble and uncertainty. This commandment of Jesus was: 'Seek ye first the kingdom of God, and His righteousness . . .'"[21]

J. S. McConnell regularly submitted revival reports to the *Pentecostal Evangel* and preached at an afternoon service at the 1925 General Council on the subject of love.[22] He became a fixture on the Pentecostal evangelistic circuit. J. S. McConnell was known as "the fighting, fiery Irishman" who presented, as one advertisement declared, "scorching, scathing, liquid lumps of burning truth to meet present needs."[23]

The charismatic J. S. McConnell possessed a strong mind and was a gifted communicator. However, these giftings, combined with a strong independent streak, prophetic personality, and a tendency to question various cultural and doctrinal shibboleths, resulted in friction between himself and leaders within the Assemblies of God.

McConnell allowed his ministerial credentials to lapse in 1928. When he reapplied for credentials in 1929, the Southern California District did not give their immediate approval, citing concerns regarding McConnell's character and beliefs. Correspondence reveals that church officials were uncertain how to react to McConnell. His positions on various doctrinal issues were hard to pin down—he defied simple explanations. General Secretary J. R. Evans described McConnell this way: "he is very full of notions and always has some big project in his mind."[24] Helen Stewart, a concerned church member, expressed confusion after hearing McConnell's silver-tongued preaching that offered rebuke to Pentecostal and non-Pentecostal alike. She described his appeal, "[He] had such a wonderful flow of speech. He seemed to have a power over the people."[25]

21. McConnell, "A Testimony of Faith," 2.

22. General Council Minutes, 1925, 60.

23. Various newspaper clippings announcing McConnell Sr.'s meetings at the Portland Rose Tabernacle, New York City, June 1935.

24. J. R. Evans, letter to Robert A. Brown, May 20, 1929. J. S. McConnell ministerial file.

25. Helen B. Stewart, letter to J. R. Evans, April 30, 1931. J. S. McConnell ministerial file.

Responding to Stewart, Evans offered a candid appraisal of McConnell, noting that he suspected the difficulties with McConnell did not stem from doctrine: "I really believe that Brother McConnell's main trouble is that he considered himself to be a very popular evangelist and in the ordinary sense of the word we would say that he got a swell head."[26] McConnell continued his ministry independently, although he still maintained fellowship with some Assemblies of God churches and members. The complex issues and strong personalities of McConnell and the church leaders make it difficult to ascertain whether McConnell's departure from the Fellowship could have been avoided.

After his credentials lapsed with the Assemblies of God, McConnell spoke in a variety of churches—indeed, anywhere that would provide a platform—as he preached his fiery sermons with titles including: "The Greatest Love Story Ever Told," "God Loving His Enemies," and "The New Covenant."[27] The denominations of churches in which he spoke varied broadly: Assemblies of God, Methodist, Presbyterian, Baptist, Christian and Missionary Alliance, and Church of God in Christ. McConnell strove to minister to a broad cross-section of Christians, not just to Pentecostals. John described his father's attitude: "people should come together . . . on what they agree on and accommodate their differences . . . [H]e didn't stress the differences; he stressed the gospel." McConnell frequently attracted crowds of hundreds, and sometimes thousands, of people.[28]

One church that John remembered fondly is Philadelphia's Tindley Temple Methodist Church, the world's largest African American church at the time, where his father was invited to preach in the 1930s. When asked whether his father spoke at both black and white churches, John responded, "Oh, yes. My goodness . . . He was, of course, totally against segregation."[29]

J. S. McConnell, like most early Pentecostals, maintained that the Christian's heavenly citizenship far outweighs earthly citizenship, and that it is not morally justifiable for a Christian to kill on behalf of the State

26. J. R. Evans, letter to Helen B. Stewart, May 8, 1931. J. S. McConnell ministerial file.

27. Various newspaper clippings announcing McConnell Sr.'s meetings at the Portland Rose Tabernacle, New York City, June 1935.

28. John McConnell Jr. and Anna McConnell, telephone interview, April 3, 2009.

29. Ibid.

in war.[30] This pacifist position, which the Assemblies of God endorsed until 1967, proved costly for people such as John McConnell when they tried to adhere to it during wartime.

War woes

John McConnell felt conflicted when World War II broke out in 1939. He wanted to be a "loyal American," but his father instilled in him a strong belief that Christians were not supposed to kill, even in war. John enlisted in the Merchant Marine in the summer of 1942 as a way to serve his country but to avoid fighting. Ministry was the only way of life that John had known, so it was quite natural that John would see his time in the Merchant Marine as an opportunity to minister. He held prayer meetings aboard the vessels, and also preached ashore in Brazil. He received an honorable discharge in August 1943. John returned to California, where he met and married Mary Lou Clark in 1944.[31]

Soon after his marriage, John was drafted to serve in the army. He asked for an exemption as a conscientious objector and as a minister; however, the draft board did not accept his request, apparently because McConnell had lectured draft board members on the need to promote peace and not war. McConnell stated, "They got angry, stopped the deferment and drafted me."[32]

The army sent John to Texas for basic training, where he was required to participate in target practice. While lying on the ground preparing to shoot at an image of a man, John had a shocking vision flash through his mind: "When I would look at it, the figure changed into the figure of Jesus." John recalled Jesus' words, "Inasmuch as ye have done it unto one of the least of these my brethren, ye have done it unto me" (Matt. 25:40). John laid down his weapon and walked off the rifle range. He later reflected, "Boy, if the soldiers would see Jesus every time they killed an enemy, we wouldn't have any more wars."[33]

John's refusal to shoot the target landed him in the stockade. Always willing to speak his mind, he began lecturing his guards about their

30. Weir, *Peace, Justice, Care of Earth*, 24–25; McConnell, *The New Covenant*, 64; Frodsham, "Our Heavenly Citizenship," 3.

31. Weir, *Peace, Justice, Care of Earth*, 24–27.

32. Weir, *Peace, Justice, Care of Earth*, 27.

33. John McConnell Jr. and Anna McConnell, telephone interview, April 3, 2009.

participation in the war. As a result, he was placed in solitary confinement, called "The Black Box." His new quarters consisted of an iron bed
and nothing else. He refused to eat, spending his time reading his Bible,
praying, and singing hymns. During his time in solitary confinement,
John's hair turned prematurely white. While working in a base office for
several months, John yearned for freedom. After he overheard a sergeant
say, "McConnell's file [seeking discharge] is going under the pile and
won't come up again until after the war," he knew he had to find a way of
escape.[34]

John escaped from the military compound, bought a 38-foot sailboat with Mary Lou, which they christened *The Christian*, and fled the
country. They landed on Roatán, a small island off the coast of British
Honduras, where they found an idyllic, remote town with a nice church
but no minister. John, along with Mary Lou, settled into the community
and became known as "Reverend Miracle."

At this point, John held ministerial credentials with the International
Fundamental Christian Association, a Pentecostal organization head-
quartered in Washington, DC, which had been founded in 1943 by former
Assemblies of God evangelist Guy Shields. It did not take long until the
US Federal Bureau of Investigation heard about the McConnells. The FBI,
according to a communiqué, found that McConnell "occupies himself by
preaching and maintaining himself by the collections he makes as a minister of the Gospel." FBI records reveal that, after a six-month-long investigation, FBI Director J. Edgar Hoover decided to leave the McConnells
alone because they were not engaged in subversive activities.[35]

The McConnells left their island paradise in late 1946 because Mary Lou,
who was pregnant, wanted their child to be born in the United States.
When John faced another draft during the Korean Conflict, he again
asked to be exempted as a conscientious objector and as a minister. As
a result, he was given a psychiatric examination. The psychologist diag-
nosed John as "unfit for the army." The psychologist later explained, "He

34. John McConnell Jr. and Anna McConnell, interview, June 15, 2009; Weir, *Peace, Justice, Care of Earth*, 27–28.

35. Weir, *Peace, Justice, Care of Earth,*, 28–31; Flower, "Statement concerning Withdrawal of Brother Guy Shields," 14. McConnell was listed as an ordained minister in the International Fundamental Christian Association's ministerial roster for 1945. The roster listed two addresses: one in Oakland, California, and another in Guatemala City, Guatemala. He is not listed in the 1948 ministerial roster. Constitution and Bylaws of the International Fundamental Christian Association, 1945 and 1948, FPHC.

was questioning everything. That's why he didn't fit in . . . It was boot training. What do you do? You obey orders. You just take all the guff they hand out and you do it, that's all. Well, he couldn't do that. He was too brilliant for the Army."[36]

Mary Lou, unable to cope with John's difficulties with the military, filed for divorce in 1954 and left their two children—Constance and Cary—with him. John's pain from his struggles with the military was now compounded by his divorce. Seeking a new start, in 1956, he moved to North Carolina and became co-publisher of two local newspapers.[37]

Seeking peace

While in North Carolina, John began to more fully devote himself to the cause of peace, which arose from his desire to be faithful to the Prince of Peace. John spearheaded two nationally recognized peace movements: the Star of Hope (1957) and the Minute for Peace (1963–present), and served as a leader in another: Meals for Millions (1961–1963).[38] In his Star of Hope campaign, John encouraged the United States to launch a satellite as a symbol of peace. This was in response to the concerns over possible Soviet aggression inspired by the launching of its satellite, Sputnik.[39] In 1961, John left his newspaper job in North Carolina and moved to San Francisco, California, to start a chapter of Meals for Millions, a non-profit organization "dedicated to the relief and prevention of starvation."[40]

John often thought about the link between prayer and peace. He recalled the miracles that occurred in response to prayer, which he witnessed as a child while traveling on the evangelistic circuit. From his Pentecostal background, he knew that "There have been times of great spiritual awakenings, when people are awakened in their hearts and in their minds to true values, when more people pray and more people do the right thing." With these thoughts in mind, in 1963 John launched the Minute for Peace, an initiative that encouraged people to spend a minute in meditation or prayer each day. The Minute for Peace was first held

36. Weir, *Peace, Justice, Care of Earth*, 32.

37. Ibid., 32–33, 36.

38. To learn more about these and McConnell's other projects, visit his websites: www.earthtrustee.org and www.earthsite.org.

39. Weir, *Peace, Justice, Care of Earth*, 35–56.

40. Ibid., 57–62.

on December 22, 1963, one month after John F. Kennedy's assassination, and has since been widely observed. Short Minute for Peace messages, read by various heads of state, United Nations leaders, and other globally respected people, were broadcast by CBS, NBC, on shortwave radio, and on other stations around the world.[41]

In 1965, John moved from California to New York, which offered more opportunities to network with leaders and to promote peace. A friend of John's—local Lutheran pastor Richard John Neuhaus—was aware of John's Pentecostal background and encouraged him to introduce the Minute for Peace to a charismatic prayer group that met at St. Mark's Lutheran Church in Brooklyn. The pastor, Ervin Prange (Neuhaus's uncle), was a charismatic renewal leader in the Lutheran Church-Missouri Synod. At the prayer group, John met Anna Zacharias, the principal of an inner-city Lutheran school. They married two years later—on Christmas Day 1967. He was 52, and she was 36. Within the next few years, they had two children: John Paul (who had Down Syndrome and died at age 14 months) and Christa Marie.[42] Anna would become John's most important confidant and advisor, believing in his idealistic visions, even when others did not. Equally supportive, John joined his wife's church, the Lutheran Church-Missouri Synod, soon after their marriage, though he still claimed to be faithful to his father's Pentecostal teachings. In a 2009 interview, he stated, "I definitely still believe what my father taught and preached."[43]

Earth day

John McConnell, Jr. coined the name "Earth Day"—now internationally recognized—in 1968. John's vision for Earth Day arose from his passion to promote peace. He wanted to find a tangible symbol around which people from various backgrounds could come together in peace and unity, and the earth fit the bill as universally important. He began searching for a suitable date for the new holiday. In 1969, after praying for guidance, the spring equinox (March 20 or 21) sprang to his mind as the most vi-

41. Ibid., 63–91.

42. John McConnell Jr. and Anna McConnell, interview, June 15, 2009; Weir, *Peace, Justice, Care of Earth*, 92–96.

43. John McConnell Jr. and Anna McConnell, interview, June 15, 2009.

able day, a time already internationally acknowledged and linked to the concepts of rebirth and renewal.[44]

On October 3, 1969, McConnell proposed his Earth Day concept to San Francisco city officials, who placed it on the Board of Supervisors' agenda. On February 3, 1970, the board voted to celebrate Earth Day on March 21, 1970—the first governmental recognition of Earth Day. Celebrations of Earth Day on March 21, 1970 were held in San Francisco, Berkley, New York, and in others cities and universities across North America. Politicians soon began promoting Earth Day. California congressman Charles Teague introduced a bill before the House of Representatives to establish Earth Day as a national day of reflection. California Senator George Murphy presented the idea to President Richard Nixon. The United Nations adopted the holiday the following year and has been celebrating Earth Day on the spring equinox since 1971.[45]

This original Earth Day was quickly eclipsed in prominence, however, by a second Earth Day (celebrated on April 22). McConnell described how this second Earth Day came to be:

> I announced Earth Day at a UNESCO conference in San Francisco in November 1969. Present were people connected with Senator Gaylord Nelson. Gaylord Nelson had a wonderful program called Environmental Teach-In and he had called April 22 Environmental Teach-In Day. When I announced Earth Day for the March equinox, a representative from Gaylord Nelson came up to me and said, 'This is a wonderful idea but you should change the date to April 22. We already have our Environmental Teach-In Day then and we can change the name to Earth Day.' I said, 'Absolutely not. Earth Day on nature's event is too important for this global occasion.'
>
> So the next thing I knew they stole my name 'Earth Day,' and they used it for April 22. I was urged to sue, but I didn't. I didn't believe in suing. [Anna McConnell interjected: And that comes from his Pentecostal background.] San Francisco kicked it off and later on we had the United Nations. The Secretary General, who had backed my Minute for Peace, thought Earth

44. John McConnell Jr. and Anna McConnell, telephone interview, April 3, 2009.

45. Weir, *Peace, Justice, Care of Earth*, 125–133.

Day was a great idea and the United Nations celebrates Earth
Day on the March equinox.[46]

McConnell's biographer, Robert Weir, has documented the sequence of events that led Nelson to adopt the name Earth Day for his
Environmental Teach-In on April 22, 1970. According to Weir, Nelson
admitted that he got the idea from others, but he did not specify from
whom. In time, Nelson began to publicly claim full credit for the founding of Earth Day.[47]. Weir described how McConnell and Nelson had
different purposes and agendas for their respective Earth Day events.
McConnell's purpose was to promote "a climate of peace and justice as a
prerequisite for ecological preservation," and he sought to achieve this by
working with the United Nations. Nelson's purpose was a political protest
against pollution—he saw Earth Day as a means to force the environment
onto the national agenda by mass demonstration. While McConnell was
an idealist, Nelson was a pragmatist.[48]

In the end, Senator Nelson achieved fame, fortune, and political action to preserve the environment through the successful promotion of
Earth Day on April 22. In contrast, Weir noted in 2007 that John and
Anna McConnell were "living their senior years in relative obscurity,
poor in money, yet unflinchingly rich in spirit and unyieldingly strong in
determination to demonstrate, as John continued to say, 'April 22 is not
Earth Day.'"[49]

While McConnell lamented that the Earth Day celebration on the
spring equinox did not gain the widespread traction of the April 22
holiday, he nonetheless recognizes the latter day's value in promoting
awareness of earth-care. However, he feels the April 22 observance is too
politicized, which alienates many people, including conservatives and
Christians, whom John wanted to include in the Earth Day celebration.
In addition, John noted that April 22 was the birthday of communist
leader Vladimir Lenin. John maintained that the spring equinox was a
preferable date, because it was politically neutral and more likely to unite
people.[50]

46. John McConnell Jr. and Anna McConnell, interview, June 15, 2009.

47. Weir, *Peace, Justice, Care of Earth*, 125–51.

48. Ibid., 149.

49. Ibid., 151.

50. For a detailed account of the sequence of events concerning McConnell's
founding of the original Earth Day and Nelson's later adoption of the name for his

There is no doubt that John McConnell, Jr.'s lifework sprang from the influence of his parents and their faith. He boldly declared, "If there had been no Christian experience in my life there would be no Earth Day—or at least I would not have initiated it."[51]. In addition, he noted, "I'm a peacemaker, and part of the reason was my father, who was, without question, the greatest influence in my life."[52]

John McConnell, Jr.'s interest in earth-care developed in part from his own lifelong study of Scripture. In a 2009 interview, he explained his simple logic, stating, "We love God . . . [and therefore should] have an appreciation for his creation." To clarify and define this logical "appreciation," McConnell, Jr. cited Psalm 115:16, "The earth has been given to the children of men." He connected this promise to the command in Genesis 1:28, that humanity is to "subdue" the earth. "We're caretakers upon earth. . . . 'Subdue the earth'—I think that meant to take care of it. . . . In other words, if you take care of it, it's not going out of control."[53] McConnell's call is not for earth-worship but for responsible stewardship of the earth that all people share.

John often found the Christian response to the call for earth-care and environmental responsibility, however, to be less than encouraging. Challenging the apathy and dismissal of environmental concerns, he wrote:

> Don't most evangelicals neglect responsibility and care of Earth because they are taught that Earth will soon pass away and is of relative unimportance in comparison with heaven and eternity? Wouldn't a more Christ-like view be to recognize Earth as a precious gift that is our responsibility to protect and nurture?[54]

Later in life, John believed that churches were becoming more receptive to the concept of earth-care as a Christian responsibility. He even viewed Christian participation in Earth Day as an opportunity to be a witness: "While Earth Day is non-sectarian and non-political (people of all religions and no religion participate), it provides a great opportunity

---

Environmental Teach-In, see Weir, *Peace, Justice, Care of Earth*, 125–51. See also John McConnell Jr. and Anna McConnell, telephone interview, April 3, 2009; John McConnell Jr. and Anna McConnell, interview, June 15, 2009.

51. McConnell, "A Testimony of Faith," 1.

52. Quoted in Weir, *Peace, Justice, Care of Earth*, 25.

53. John Jr. McConnell and Anna McConnell, telephone interview, April 3, 2009.

54. McConnell, "To Die Is Gain," 1.

for Christians to show the power of prayer, the validity of their charity and their practical concern for Earth's life and people."[55] McConnell encouraged Christians to lead the way in living out the kingdom of heaven on earth and observed, "The cutting edge of freedom and order has often been people with a strong love for Jesus and what he taught."[56]

The story of Earth Day's Pentecostal origins has remained obscured for various reasons. John McConnell, Jr.'s part in the founding of Earth Day was marginalized by historians as the April 22 celebration became more prominent than the original event on the March equinox. Those within the environmental movement who recognized McConnell's role tended to view his Pentecostal background as out-of-place within the broader environmental movement, which had become identified with non-Christian and left-wing political agendas. Both J. S. McConnell and John McConnell, Jr. were highly articulate visionaries whose independent personalities and views did not always mesh well with other Pentecostal leaders. After J. S. McConnell parted ways with the Assemblies of God in 1928, he seemed to fade from view in the mainstream Pentecostal press. When John McConnell, Jr. came into prominence through the Star of Hope and Minute for Peace, he had already ceased his active involvement in Pentecostal ministry. By the time he came up with the idea of Earth Day in 1968, he had already joined his wife's Lutheran church.

To some observers, it might seem improbable that a Pentecostal would play a role in the founding of Earth Day. However, when one considers some of the other themes that flowed out of the early Pentecostal worldview of full consecration to Christ and His mission—such as racial reconciliation, women in ministry, and a critique of war—it becomes easier to see how John McConnell, Jr.'s desire to promote peace and stewardship of the earth could flow from his Pentecostal roots. John's upbringing in an entrepreneurial, idealistic Pentecostal environment set him on a trajectory that would meld heart-felt faith with a desire to address pressing issues in the broader society. McConnell believed that, above all, he must be fully devoted to Christ and His teachings. He found that trying to live as a citizen of heaven earned him scars while in this earthly kingdom.

McConnell's call toward peace and care of the earth is not an entreaty to fanaticism; rather, it is a fusing of belief with appropriate action. Connecting belief with action is of second nature to the McConnells, and

55. McConnell, "A Testimony of Faith," 1.

56. John McConnell Jr., unpublished introduction to *The New Covenant*.

this mystery of faith and works is reflected in an early hymn, written by John's mother, Hattie McConnell:

Oh, the faith that works by love
Will move mountains when we pray.
Oh, the faith that works by love
Will turn darkness into day.[57]

In recent years, John McConnell's role in the founding of Earth Day has been noted by increasing numbers of scholars. McConnell's 2007 biography by an environmentalist insider, Robert Weir, shed light on the movement's internal tensions. Some purists such as Weir view the April 22 Earth Day as having been co-opted by politicians and marketers, preferring McConnell's original vision of an Earth Day that would be less commercialized and that could be shared by all. Pentecostals have also discovered McConnell. Nicole Sparks and Darrin Rodgers, in the 2010 edition of *Assemblies of God Heritage*, shared the story of McConnell and the Pentecostal origins of Earth Day.[58] The magazine, which was distributed to 33,000 ministers and subscribers, surprised many Pentecostals by showing that an iconic environmentalist celebration grew from roots within their own tradition. John Munday, Professor of Natural Science and Mathematics at Regent University, formed a friendship with McConnell over a number of years and edited a 569-page compilation of McConnell's life story and writings, which was published in 2011.[59]

In addition to recent scholarly publications about McConnell, researchers may access primary source materials in two archives. McConnell deposited his papers relating to his work promoting peace, justice, and care of earth at Swarthmore College, a Quaker school, where it is part of the Swarthmore College Peace Collection. The McConnell collection at Swarthmore primarily covers the years 1950 to 2006. McConnell deposited personal papers which related to himself and his family, including correspondence, publications, photographs, scrapbooks, and ephemera from the ministry, at the Flower Pentecostal Heritage Center. The McConnell collection at the Flower Pentecostal Heritage Center primarily covers the years 1912–1987.

57. Weir, *Peace, Justice, Care of Earth*, 9.
58. Sparks and Rodgers, "John McConnell, Jr. and the Pentecostal Origins of Earth Day," 16–25.
59. McConnell, *Earth Day*.

John McConnell passed away on October 20, 2012, and his funeral was held at St. John's Lutheran Church (Lutheran Church-Missouri Synod) in Denver, Colorado, on November 2, 2012. His wife, Anna, continues to live in Denver. John McConnell, Jr.'s story provides a glimpse into the lives and worldview of early Pentecostals; it also gives an intriguing example to Pentecostals from within their own tradition of how one man loved Jesus and cared for His creation.

BIBLIOGRAPHY

Alexander, Paul. *Peace to War: Shifting Allegiances in the Assemblies of God.* Telford, PA: Cascadia, 2009.

Apostolic Faith (Los Angeles). "Evangelist T. W. McConnell's Testimony." September 1906.

Apostolic Faith (Los Angeles). "Experience in Trusting God for Needs." September 1906.

Apostolic Faith (Los Angeles). "In Santa Cruz, Cal." February–March 1907.

Assemblies of God Heritage. Summer 2000.

Constitution and Bylaws of the International Fundamental Christian Association. 1945 and 1948. FPHC.

Earth Trustee. www.earthtrustee.org (accessed August 29, 2014).

Evans, J. R. "Letter to Helen B. Stewart." May 8, 1931. J. S. McConnell ministerial file.

———. "Letter to Robert A. Brown." May 20, 1929. J. S. McConnell ministerial file.

Flower, J. Roswell. "Statement concerning Withdrawal of Brother Guy Shields." *Pentecostal Evangel*, October 23, 1943.

Frodsham, Stanley H. "Our Heavenly Citizenship." *Weekly Evangel*, September 11, 1915.

General Council Minutes. 1925.

Gohr, Glenn. "Known Persons Who Were at Hot Springs." *Assemblies of God Heritage*, Spring 2004.

Latter Rain Evangel (Chicago). "Sowing the Seed." November 1911.

McConnell, Hattie. "Reminiscing at Age 83." Typewritten manuscript. FPHC.

McConnell, John, Jr. Letter to the editor. *Assemblies of God Heritage*, Summer 2000.

———. "A Testimony of Faith." Typewritten manuscript. FPHC.

———. "To Die is Gain." Typewritten manuscript. FPHC.

———. Unpublished introduction to *The New Covenant.* 1987. FPHC.

McConnell, John, Jr., and Anna McConnell. Interview by Darrin Rodgers. Personal interview. Timberline Church, Fort Collins, Colorado, June 15, 2009.

McConnell, John, Jr., and John C. Munday. *Earth Day: Vision for Peace, Justice, and Earth Care: My Life and Thought at Age 96.* Eugene, OR: Resource, 2011.

McConnell, John, Sr. *The New Covenant.* Walla Walla, WA: Self-Published, 1920.

Sparks, Nicole, and Darrin Rodgers. "John McConnell, Jr. and the Pentecostal Origins of Earth Day." *Assemblies of God Heritage*, 2010.

Stewart, Helen B. "Letter to J. R. Evans." April 30, 1931. J. S. McConnell ministerial file.

Various newspaper clippings announcing McConnell Sr.'s meeting at the Portland Rose Tabernacle, New York City, June 1935. FPHC.

Weir, Robert M. *Peace, Justice, Care of Earth: The Vision of John McConnell, Founder of Earth Day.* Kalamazoo, MI: Press On, 2007.

———. *Star of Hope: The Life and Times of John McConnell, Founder of Earth Day.* Pine Plains, NY: Swan, 2006.

2

The Devil's Suicide:
Early Pentecostal Hermeneutics of Space
and Their Ecotheological Implications

Brandon Hubbard-Heitz

Introduction

On May 10, 1959 John Osteen, a newly Spirit-baptized pastor, stood in an abandoned feed store that he had turned into a meeting space and welcomed a small group of people to Lakewood Church for the first time. Forty-six years later, his son, Joel Osteen, would stand on a stage in the middle of the former Compaq Center, which had served as the Houston Rockets' home arena for 28 years, and welcome the Lakewood Church congregation to their newly transformed home.[1]

Lakewood Church and the Osteens are not the only religious group with a proclivity for taking over formerly nonreligious settings and transforming them into houses of worship. Beginning with the Second Great Awakening evangelists and then congregations began to look to secular spaces in order to both accommodate large crowds and appeal to the masses that preferred the entertainment offered to them by the sort of establishments that operated in secular spaces. Charles Grandison Finney was, in fact, one of the first preachers to utilize theaters for revivals.[2] For the next century prominent evangelists like D. L. Moody and Billy Sunday

---

1. Martin, "Prime Minister," 67; Lakewood Church, "Our Story," http://www.lake-woodchurch.com /Pages/new-here/Our-History.aspx (accessed April 9, 2013).

2. Loveland and Wheeler, *From Meetinghouse to Megachurch*, 22.

would hold services in settings as varied as dance halls, saloons, theaters, opera houses, and tobacco warehouses.[3]

Like their revivalist forebears, early Pentecostals also regularly converted secular space or, in the words of one Pentecostal pastor, "places of darkness" into settings for revivals or permanent churches.[4] While they never acquired a sports arena quite as ostentatious as the Compaq Center, denominational periodicals and personal biographies indicate that there were over one hundred distinct occasions from 1901 to 1925 of North American Pentecostals utilizing buildings and locations for revivals and Sunday worship that had been used for what they defined as illicit or immoral purposes. The number is high enough to be significant and suggestive of a tacit Pentecostal hermeneutic of space.

Early Pentecostalism was a grassroots movement that lacked a centralized hierarchy or bureaucracy, so it is difficult to generalize about the movement as a whole, especially in light of the lack of critical reflection about their use of space; yet, there are enough similarities to construct a two-pronged thesis about early Pentecostals' approaches to space. (1) Most frequently—and like other nineteenth and early twentieth century revivalists—Pentecostals occupied secular spaces for pragmatic purposes. Such spaces were large enough to accommodate the extraordinary crowds they expected to attend their meetings or the rent was low enough to suit their budgets. (2) On the other hand, some Pentecostals, including those who utilized secular locations out of practicality, found a deeper meaning in their physical location.[5] The occupation of formerly "immoral" or "dark" space speaks to some early Pentecostals' belief that such locations needed to be transformed—a process best understood through the Pentecostal categories of salvation, healing, and the baptism in the Holy

3. Ibid., 83, 272n5.

4. Werda, "Full Gospel Assembly, Persian Mission," 14. All subsequent references to early Pentecostal periodicals are drawn from Consortium of Pentecostal Archives, "Digital Collections," http://www.pentecostalarchives.org/ (accessed February 27–April 22, 2013).

5. I first became aware of this trend among early Pentecostals through the work of Grant Wacker. In his opinion, Pentecostal appropriations of secular space represented an affirmation of "their ability to transform disordered zones into ordered ones." Though I am appreciative of Wacker's identification of this trend, I disagree with his conclusion. "Disordered" and "ordered" zones are not categories early Pentecostals would have employed. I think the categories of salvation, healing, and Spirit baptism are much more faithful to the language and the experiences of Pentecostals who occupied these spaces. Wacker, Heaven Below, 112.

Spirit.[6] These categories have important relevance in the development of an incipient Pentecostal ecotheology in response to the human threat to the natural environment and its inhabitants.

Early pentecostal conceptions of space

Early Pentecostals were not so interested in developing any sort of systematic hermeneutic of human-occupied space as they were in soul-winning, healing, and Spirit-baptism. Not until the 1930's did Pentecostals begin to develop any sort of systematized theology of their faith.[7] Even so, their periodicals betray a dualistic understanding of physical space. According to the authors of the periodicals, human-occupied space is either oppressed by the devil or rightly controlled by God. Those places devoted to entertainment are especially dominated by demons. One author argues, "for the most part the devil has a great big mortgage on all amusements," including theaters, dance halls, and skating rinks.[8] Though some felt that there was nothing intrinsically wrong with places of amusement except for the devil's possession of them, in general, Pentecostals believed such places were demonic in and of themselves. Other Pentecostals went so far as to contend that the whole world belonged to the devil already.[9]

People's patronage of immoral sites explicitly claimed by the devil revealed their alliance with Satan: people either belonged to the world of the devil or to the kingdom of God. Any location that promoted amusements that might distract from one's commitment to God was a "place that is purely of this world."[10] Thus, Christians had to maintain "a clear-

---

6. While the fivefold formulation is common to Pentecostals who maintain Holiness roots, I am here drawing on a fourfold gospel formulation shared by many Pentecostals. Land, *Pentecostal Spirituality*, 6. I stand within the tradition of the Assemblies of God and emphasize the fourfold gospel pattern as more befitting of Pentecostal theology. There is no reason why, however, my argument could not be adapted to a fivefold gospel formulation. On the fourfold pattern, see Dayton, *Theological Roots of Pentecostalism*, 21–23.

7. Jacobsen, "Knowing the Doctrines of the Pentecostals," 90.

8. Piper, "Giving Heed to Seducing Spirits," 6.

9. Boddy, "The Christian's Relation to World Reform," 4. See also Anderson, *Vision of the Disinherited*, 199–200.

10. Glover, "Contrasting Wisdom," 8. Glover argues that Christians cannot even attend religious events that are held in such places because to do so offers the location "a cloak of righteousness" when it remains under the dominion of the devil. See also Piper, "Giving Heed to Seducing Spirits," 5.

THE DEVIL'S SUICIDE 25

cut separation," if they were to retain their identity as Christians.[11] The concern to avoid those buildings and other spaces that are operated by the devil was not only religious, but also humanitarian. Time and time again Pentecostals warned that patrons of such places were susceptible to alcoholism, drugs, and prostitution. Pentecostals cautioned that theaters taught young women to sexualize all forms of romantic love. After these women left home they would begin to put into action what they had learned at the theatre, namely through prostitution.[12] A more lurid urban myth circulated among Pentecostals at the same time. They preached that young women who attended movie theaters were often secretly injected with sleep-inducing drugs. The girls would only feel a pin pick, before falling sleep, at which point they would be kidnapped and sold into sexual slavery.[13]

Even as they recognized specific places to be the domain of the devil, many Pentecostals disputed the devil's right to occupy them uncontested. Though they had renounced the amusement offered in such places, they had not abandoned the places themselves or the people within. Pentecostals were willing to return to such places so that they could preach the gospel.[14] They had a strong sense not only of their ability but also their calling to cast Satan out from those places. Prior to a revival she held in San Diego, Aimee Semple McPherson climbed into the boxing ring of the venue where she planned to preach and declared she would "Meet His Satanic Majesty on His Own Ground."[15] Pentecostals, like McPherson, understood themselves to be engaged in spiritual warfare against the forces of hell. One author with an exemplary set of spiritual eyes remarks, "The very atmosphere presses heavy with the multitude hosts of darkness that are arrayed against the children of light."[16] Like the desert fathers and mothers before them, Pentecostals girded themselves for battle, ready to exorcise demons from persons and places. They fought

11. Smith, "The World Beats a Path to Her Door," 23.

12. Pope, "Morphine Tablets of Hell," 5.

13. "White Slave Craft," 3. While the tale of theater-going women sold into sexual slavery is probably nothing more than an urban myth, the early Pentecostals concern for human trafficking displays a progressive ethic that remained untapped in the church at large until the latter half of the twentieth century.

14. McPherson, "The Bridal Call Family Visits the Angelus Temple Revival," 7.

15. McPherson, "In Dreamland Arena, San Diego, Cal.," 13.

16. Flower, "Daily Portion From The King's Bounty," 7.

by prayer and worship, demonstrating the power of the church to control its territory. When one Pentecostal community discovered that someone had set up a fortunetelling shop not far from their house of worship, they determined to "pray it out" for "it is an abomination that the church of Jesus Christ is not strong enough to keep such hell-holes as that out of its vicinity."[17] Clearly, there was an expectation that Christians had a duty to patrol the land, casting out demons and their hellholes in order to take back the land in the name of Jesus Christ.

While Pentecostals expected to win the battles in which they engaged the enemy, they did not expect to win the war. As long as Jesus tarried, they recognized that the devil would continue to lure people into his lairs. Their victories were often seen as proleptic representations of an eschatological reality that would not be inaugurated until the second coming. Thus, they looked forward to the eschaton when there would be "no need of theaters, parks, shows, festivals, or picnics," because everyone will see God face-to-face.[18] In their minds, Jesus' *parousia* would coincide with the fulfillment of his promise "to cast out all that doth offend, and to set up His own rule and reign of universal peace."[19]

Pragmatic transformations of space

Most Pentecostals did not express such lofty hopes when they occupied immoral or secular spaces. Despite their fervent denunciations of dance halls, gambling dens, theaters, roller skating rinks, and the like, Pentecostals were often all too happy to move into any space that would accommodate their needs.[20] Grant Wacker convincingly argues that despite their commitment to a stringent interpretation of biblical morality, "Pentecostals proved remarkably willing to work within the social and cultural expectations of the age."[21] The Pentecostals who denounced a

17. Piper, "Giving Heed," 4.

18. Juillerat, "The Coming of the Great City," 2.

19. Boddy, "The Christian's Relation to World Reform," 4.

20. Because of the disparate nature of the movement, there are, of course, exceptions to this observation. For example, on a trip to Corona, Long Island, Sister Aimee could not secure a place in which to hold a revival. A saloonkeeper offered the parlor behind his business because it could hold several hundred people, but Sister Aimee refused to hold a service in such a disreputable location. McPherson, "The Story of My Life," 16.

21. Wacker, Heaven Below, 13.

place as the devil's den had no qualms about moving into that same place when it suited their interests.

Pentecostals' pragmatism in many ways mirrored that of the evangelists and revivalists of the nineteenth century who emphasized their message and its promulgation much more than the trappings of the institutional church setting. It is important to remember, however, "a building acts as a vehicle of meaning even if it is supposed to be meaningless."[22] Thus, there is good reason to analyze the early Pentecostals' settings for worship. Several important conclusions arise out of such an exegesis.

First, such religious sects prioritized their messages above their settings. Louis Nelson explains, "The careful attention given by revivalists to the reception of their message meant that in most cases, preachers selected or constructed spaces that best facilitated the delivery of their message."[23] Revivalism placed a significant emphasis on the preaching of the word, because the word is what brings salvation. As a result, space was designed or chosen with the message in mind. Early Pentecostals prioritized souls above structures.

Of course, Pentecostals did not always have much of a choice when it came to locations of their revivals. Like their Holiness counterparts, Pentecostals were not typically wealthy or celebrated by society at large. Robert Mapes Anderson's analysis of the demographics of early Pentecostalism led him to conclude, "The Pentecostal faithful everywhere were drawn from the humbler orders of society."[24] While some have disputed the accuracy of Anderson's judgment, it is true that Pentecostals, like most Americans, were generally poorer than they were richer.[25] This is reflected in their selection of physical spaces in which to worship. The revival that began on Los Angeles's Azusa Street in 1906 exemplifies this trend. Though an African Methodist Episcopal congregation initially built and used the building, it had largely been abandoned by 1906, serving only as a storage area for planned renovations. The floor was dirt and the building displayed the scars of an arsonist's fire from 1904. In short, "the place was a disaster."[26] While not all Pentecostal houses of worship

---

22. Klotz, *The History of Postmodern Architecture*, 3; see also Jones, "Monumental Occasions," 21–37.

23. Nelson, "Architecture and Revivals," 28.

24. Anderson, *Vision of the Disinherited*, 114.

25. For example, see Wacker, *Heaven Below*, 202–12.

26. Robeck, *The Azusa Street Mission and Revival*, 69–73; and Dorries, "Azusa Street

were as primitive as the one on Azusa Street, in general "pentecostals studiously disregarded society's notions of aesthetic attractiveness."[27] Ostensibly, they claimed their interest was not in architecture, but in souls; however, the ostentatious buildings that they began to build as the movement gained fame and funds indicate otherwise.[28]

The Pentecostal emphasis on the message over the setting and their generally lower socioeconomic status were both worked out in the specific situations in which Pentecostal congregations pragmatically occupied immoral spaces. First, and most commonly, Pentecostals moved into locations of disrepute because those were the only places available to them. One Church of God congregation in Brooklyn had rented a theater for a meeting and "failing to find any other suitable building . . . [continued] to hold it for [their] church services."[29] A "Colored Mission" that held tent meetings during the summers was forced to move indoors for the fall and winter campaign and rented "a hall which had been used for a theater."[30] Sometimes unexpected situations arose and groups that had not planned to use secular space had to make do with what was available to them. On one occasion Aimee Semple McPherson arrived in Orlando to discover that her tent had been held up. Driving through town Sister Aimee spotted a large brown tent, quickly discovering that the tent stood over an old skating rink. Plans were made to hold her revival there.[31]

Entangled in the issue of availability is the question of finances. The prosperity gospel had not arisen and early Pentecostals did not have much money to spend. One congregation in Leavenworth, Washington found their meeting hall was too small to accommodate their needs, so when someone donated a downtown theater to them they jumped at the chance to expand their ministry.[32] A church in Knoxville, Iowa was

Revival," 38.

27. Wacker, *Heaven Below*, 112. Wacker does not capitalize "pentecostal" throughout his text.

28. An early example of this trend is Aimee Semple McPherson's *Angelus Temple*. For more contemporary examples of this architectural extravagance, see Loveland and Wheeler, *From Meetinghouse to Megachurch*, 127–260.

29. Tomlinson, "Notices," 2.

30. *The Latter Rain Evangel* 13, no. 10 (1921) 11.

31. McPherson, "Orlando, Florida," 15.

32. McPhee, "Reports from the Field," 14.

forced to meet at a large skating rink until they could raise the money to construct their own building.[33]

In fact, most congregations that met or held revivals in immoral places did not plan to remain; they frequently wrote of their desire to move on or out. These congregations had no interest in converting the space into something holy; many of them wanted to build their own churches. One group in Chicago met in a former saloon. In their words, "It is a small [sic], and not a very good location, but it is the best the brethren could do for this winter." They did not stop there, though, looking ahead to the spring when they hoped to either a better place or begin building their own church.[34] Another congregation in Cincinnati met in an old theater until they were able to move into a building they describe as "lovely, bright, cheerful."[35] One gets the sense that these Pentecostals did not find the prospect of worshiping in immoral spaces to be appealing—perhaps they considered the locations to be ugly, dark, cheerless—and thus they embodied the escapism that continues to define many popular premillennial eschatologies to this day.[36]

Secondly, Pentecostals, especially those with grand ambitions, selected locations that would seat the greatest number of people, regardless of that setting's intended use. Pentecostals have always been prone to boasting about the extraordinary number of converts or inquirers they were able to attract to their meetings. A local pastor reflected on a revival McPherson had held in Denver and could not help but brag that the meetings had to be moved to a partitioned portion of the city auditorium due to the large crowds. Even the initial seating capacity of four thousand was too small and they had to remove the partitions to accommodate an audience double that size. "The great building was packed to capacity. Not only were the seats occupied, but the standing room on the main floor and in the balconies and galleries gave footing to the multitudes."[37] One evangelist in Idaho announced an upcoming revival with the simple notice, "Will conduct a return campaign in the Gooding Roller Skating rink seating 1,500, Dec. 6-20."[38] Location, size, and date were the only relevant

33. Richardson, "Knoxville, Iowa, Feels the Power of God," 14.
34. Evans, "Reports from the Field," 14.
35. Brann, "The Work and Workers," 14.
36. Wacker, *Heaven Below*, 256–59.
37. Peck, "Dean Peck Reviews Work Accomplished in Denver Revival," 18.
38. Argue, "Forthcoming Meetings," 14.

information this evangelist saw fit to include. A casino housed a revival in Vandergrift, PA, because "it has a large seating capacity." Pentecostals played the numbers game and large gathering places, immoral or not, enabled them to testify to the success of their ministries and the blessings of God upon them.[39]

Finally, Pentecostals intentionally sought out secular spaces in order to attract the greatest number of potential converts possible. Prior to Sister Aimee's trip to the boxing match to advertise her revival, her friends objected. She responded to them in her message to the boxing spectators,

> 'Why, if I go fishing I would not go into the mountains and sit upon the top of Mount Baldy expecting the fish to come to me; I would go to the ocean,' so here I am [at the boxing ring]. I consider this a good fishing ground—better than the churches and cathedrals from which I have just come . . . I am in the ring for [Christ] and wage a different kind of fight; it will be against sin, uncleanness and evil . . . I want you all here to see the devil take the count for many a heart, life and home; he will get a knockout blow.[40]

McPherson was not the only Pentecostal to search out the most disreputable establishments in town in order to reach the unconverted masses. As early as 1906, there are stories of Pentecostals going to saloons and holding street meetings outside.[41] In a similar vein, a group of American Pentecostals stopped at "The Revival Mission" in Vancouver, B.C. and discovered the congregation employed a thirty-piece orchestra in the street and in the theater in which the American Pentecostals held their campaign. The musicians argue, "Satan uses music to allure people downward and hellward in the picture shows, cabarets and theaters; why

39. Walker, "Fellowship," 14.

40. McPherson, "In Dreamland Arena," 13. Sister Aimee had a habit of picking particularly reprehensible sites at which to preach. While on vacation in France she preached at a Parisian Café. When visiting Denver's Chinatown, she held services in "the former most famous gambling den in Hop Alley." See both Cornell, "Evangelists Preaches in Dance Halls, Calling for Recruits for Christian Army," 13, and O'Connor, "Denver Express Writes of Chinatown Meeting," 17.

41. See "Street Meetings," and Arnold, "Walking in the Light," 19. The second example offers an interesting insight into one strand of Pentecostal conceptions of space: "We preached [before a saloon] . . . and a man came out of the saloon and said, 'Mister, this is no church.' I said, 'This is the devil's den and you belong to him. Get out of it.'" This particular evangelist had apparently already ceded the saloon to hell.

should not God's people use their musical talents to His glory in the salvation of souls?"[42] This impulse to seek out the sinners of this world in their natural environment serves as an important transition between the purely pragmatic motivations of Pentecostals who simply occupied secular space and the Pentecostals who, consciously or unconsciously, played a part in the rehabilitation of places stained by immorality. If one goes to the place where sinners reside to seek those sinners' conversion, it is no longer inconceivable to speak of the conversion of the place itself.

Theological transformations of space

Pragmatic or not, some Pentecostals looked beyond the human experience of revivals and considered the environmental impact of their spiritual work. To begin, it is important to again look to the master storyteller, Aimee Semple McPherson. In 1922, Sister Aimee traveled to San Francisco to hold revival meetings. Because she could not secure the opulent Civic Auditorium, she looked instead to the Coliseum, a former boxing venue that could seat 12,000-15,000 people. When McPherson visited, the Coliseum had been reduced to a weather-beaten roller skating rink. In the May issue of *The Bridal Call* she records a conversation she had with the personified "Mr. Coliseum" prior to the revival. After Mr. Coliseum recounts his glory days, Sister Aimee tells him, "I think it is high time you were converted, had a complete change of heart and begin to undo some of the guilty past of which you speak." After some convincing, Mr. Coliseum responds, "And though it is pretty late in life to begin, I guess I'll try to slick myself up a bit and make myself respectable. I've heard by reputation of the crowds that come to hear you lift up the Christ ... and I'll do my best to be converted and help."[43]

Not all Pentecostals were as forthright or creative in the occupation of formerly immoral space, but there are numerous other examples of Pentecostals doing exactly what Aimee Semple McPherson did in San Francisco. One congregation in Juneau, Alaska found their current meeting place to be too small and "asked the Lord to give them a better loca-

42. Frey, "The Work in Vancouver, B.C.," 9. Larry Norman, who had experienced Charismatic Christianity in the 1970s, advanced a similar argument in his song "Why Should the Devil Have All the Good Music," *Only Visiting This Planet*, Solid Rock, CD, 1972.

43. McPherson, "Within the Golden Gate of San Francisco," 6–7.

tion." One would not expect them to rejoice at the opportunity to rent "a leaky, filthy saloon where many souls had been dragged down to ruin," but they excitedly turned the place into "a lighthouse for the saving of precious souls for the full Gospel of Jesus Christ."[44] In Chicago, the Full Gospel Assembly met in what had "been a saloon, a place of darkness, an open door straight to hell." Once the group had occupied the building they boldly proclaimed, "The devil can go and commit suicide, for in this place Jesus is lifted up and the Holy Ghost manifested."[45]

These Pentecostals understood their occupations of immoral spaces to be victories in the cosmic war between God and Satan, a war Satan was losing. In Montreal, "the saints" took a theater. The author notes, "The devil tried to hinder but God overruled and we had a tremendous victory."[46] McPherson led a revival in San Diego in competition with a jazz dance club that operated on another floor in the same building. The setting was obviously "very undesirable for the holding of a revival meeting." Yet, even though the place had "resounded in the past with the Devil's language, it has been made to resound with shouts of praise from God's people and the weeping supplications of seeking penitents."[47] Elsewhere, "a young people's meeting was instituted in the framework of an abandoned dance hall, and mighty battles were fought, mightier victories obtained there."[48]

The battles Pentecostals fought exorcised the devil and his demons, leaving the space empty and open to the manifestations of God. "God came in the first service after [a Pentecostal group] took possession" of a former saloon and theater in a revival that was held in Olney, Illinois.[49] "God wrought in filling" a converted theater in Oakland.[50] A Salt Lake City boxing arena stained with the blood of fighters was similarly filled with "the glory of God."[51] In taking a place for a revival and casting the devil out by prayer and worship, Pentecostals made it possible for God to reclaim that space as God's dwelling place. It is important to note

44. "In the Regions Beyond," *The Weekly Evangel*, no. 233 (March 30, 1918) 11.
45. Werda, "Full Gospel Assembly, Persian Mission," 14.
46. Urshan, "Montreal, Canada," 14.
47. Wood, "As in the Days of Old," 16.
48. Sisson, "Incidents of Elm Grove Campmeeting [sic]," 2.
49. Trim and wife, "Olney, Illinois Visited with Great Outpurings of the Spirit," 2.
50. Wigglesworth, "Keeping the Vision," 3.
51. Feick, "The Etter Meeting at Salt Lake City," 15.

that Pentecostals would have understood any experience of God to be a manifestation of the Holy Spirit. Sister Aimee's experience of the Spirit of the Almighty God coming down and filling a building that was "usually the constant scene of dancing, carnivals, and merry-making" epitomizes many of the movement's meetings.[52] Pentecostals in their services and tarrying rooms prayed, "Come, Holy Spirit."

A hermeneutic of salvation, healing, and spirit-baptism

In these cases—and perhaps in others that are not discussed in periodical literature—it seems reasonable to apply the framework of salvation, healing, and Spirit-baptism to the ways in which Pentecostals came to occupy formerly secular spaces. These three categories along with the imminent second coming of Jesus make up the four cardinal beliefs or fourfold gospel of Pentecostalism and offer a common language for Pentecostals across the spectrum.

Like other Evangelical Protestants at the time, Pentecostals emphasized the importance of conversion in order to receive salvation offered to them by Jesus. While buildings and places obviously cannot exert or exercise a conscious will to convert, it is possible to discuss the conversion of specific places precipitated by human action. In all of the above cases Pentecostals chose to move into a place and convert it to godly purposes. In some cases, individual salvation was literally linked to the conversion of space. For example, "an uptown worldly hotel proprietor" attended a revival with his wife and son. He converted and was filled with the Holy Spirit along with the rest of his family. When they returned to the hotel, "they immediately transformed part of their hotel into what is known today as the Christian Hall for Jews and Gentiles." The transformed space had previously hosted a variety of dances, but it was "*converted* into one big Chapel Hall where Gospel meetings are being regularly held."[53] The conversion of a building or space, thus, presupposes the conversion of those who plan to occupy or remake the space.

Healing was, and is, an essential Pentecostal belief and practice. The very first issue of William Seymour's *Apostolic Faith* identifies healing as an indisputable reality for Christians as a result of Jesus' atonement. "Now

52. McPherson, "The Bridal Call Family," 11.
53. Sidersky, "The Lord's Doing," 14; italics mine.

if Jesus bore our sicknesses, why should we bear them?"[54] Healing minis-tries abounded and many people happily cast aside their crutches, wheel-chairs, and other physical testaments to their frailties. It is important to note "healing and 'casting out demons' were almost synonymous terms in Pentecostal vocabulary."[55] Indeed, in the same article on healing and Jesus' atonement, Seymour promises that the Christian body is "free from sickness, disease and *everything of the devil*."[56] Likewise, as has already been discussed, Pentecostals regularly conceived of their occupation of certain piece of property to be victories in the spiritual war between God and the devil. By taking over formerly immoral spaces, Pentecostals were bringing healing to the places as much as they brought healing to human bodies.

Finally, the transformation of immoral spaces can be understood through the lens of Spirit-baptism. Much has been made of this phenom-ena. When McPherson experienced Spirit-baptism as a teenager, she felt like a battery that "hummed and shook and trembled under the power of electricity."[57] Often people fell to the ground, laughed, cried, jumped up and down, etc. The phenomenon of tongues quickly became the initial physical evidence that one had been filled with the Spirit. Though many made much of these signs, the signs themselves only signified the inward reality of the Holy Spirit's presence and possession. One Pentecostal rhetorically asks, "Beloved is it possession or profession?"[58] Similarly, McPherson further elaborates upon her baptism: "There was the Third Person of the Trinity coming into my body in all His fullness, making me His dwelling, 'the temple of the Holy Ghost.'"[59]

An understanding of Spirit-baptism as possession fits well with the testimonies the realization of the Spirit's presence in formerly immoral spaces. Descriptions of God or God's glory coming in and filling the place can be used interchangeably with descriptions of people's experiences of Spirit-baptism. Just as a converted Christian can be baptized in the Holy Spirit, so too can a converted space be baptized in the Holy Spirit.[60]

54. Seymour, "The Precious Atonement," 2.

55. Anderson, *Vision of the Disinherited*, 95.

56. Seymour, "The Precious Atonement," 2; italics mine.

57. McPherson, "The Story of My Life," 18.

58. *The Pentecost* 1, no. 1 (August 1908) 8.

59. McPherson, "The Story of My Life," 18.

60. These three frameworks ought not be confused with a Pentecostal *ordo salutis*.

Ecotheological implications of theological transformations of space

Dispensational pre-millennial rapture theologies have flourished in Pentecostalism from its very beginning. The startling number of conversions, healings, and Spirit-baptisms were taken to be the Latter Rain sent by God to humans in anticipation of Jesus' second coming and the end of time. Pentecostals anticipated their rapture from earth, leaving behind the rest of humanity—not to mention the rest of creation—to suffer the Great Tribulation and the destruction its brings.

There are some obvious pitfalls to this type of eschatology. A.J. Swoboda argues that Pentecostal theology as a whole has suffered from "an undeniable overemphasis on the process of the Spirit's role in individual salvation, regeneration, and empowerment to the neglect of ecological, social, and political soteriology."[61] He develops the metaphor of a Spirit-baptized creation in order to expand the previously anthropocentric theology of Pentecostalism to include all of creation. Drawing upon pneumatological connections between God and earth within Scripture, Swoboda expands upon the role of the Spirit, picturing her as "the life-giving power to both humans and nonhumans."[62] In this way, the eschatological goal of God's salvific work in creation is not merely the rapture of God's people, but the salvation, healing, and Spirit-baptism of all creation, people and places, flora and fauna. I believe the early Pentecostal practice of transforming formerly immoral places into houses of worship offers a historical precedent for such a move.[63]

Though they have been presented here as a linear progression, none of the cases examined in this study evidence an understanding of a sequential morphology of spatial transformation. These divine encounters can be understood as concomitant or gradual. The novelty of this system is not in the order but in the extension of the anthropocentric understanding of God's salvific work beyond humans to places as well.

61. Swoboda, *Tongues and Trees*, 193.

62. Ibid., 203. While Swoboda focuses upon the metaphor of Spirit baptism in the development of his "green Pentecostal pneumatology," I think it is proper to extend any divine activity accomplished for the sake of humanity to creation as a whole. Thus, I speak not only of the Spirit baptism of space, but also of its salvation and healing.

63. I am not the first to propsose a Pentecostal ecotheology that draws on the framework of the foursquare gospel. Matthew Tallman has also extended the Pentecostal doctrines of salvation, healing, Spirit baptism, and eschatology to creation. Tallman, "Pentecostal Ecotheology," 135–54. My approach, however, is novel, because I utilize a historical, rather than theological, method. Tallman begins with the foursquare gospel, while my starting point is the first generation of Pentecostals from whom I extrapolate

The earth faces an unparalleled and incontestable ecological crisis on account of uninhibited and unconscionable human practices that pay no attention to the planet's health and the finitude of natural resources. The rise of the earth's temperature has been widely reported and linked to the human production of greenhouse gases and relentless deforestation. The reality of climate change is wreaking death and destruction across the globe. Polar ice caps are melting, contributing to rising sea levels that will soon drown coastal communities throughout the earth, while also destroying numerous habitats that will endanger countless species of animals and plants. Already earth's flora and fauna face decline and mass extinction not seen since the disappearance of the dinosaurs. At the same time, humans are orchestrating the even more rapid destruction of the earth as they seek out new pollutants with which to fuel the deleterious and technologically obsessed lifestyles of citizens of the economically affluent nations. In Appalachia, miners have leveled mountains and filled valleys on account of their practice of mountaintop removal in order to extract coal from deep within the earth. Aside from defacing the Appalachian topography, mountaintop removal has also polluted streams, rivers, and headwaters and led to the rise of birth defects and all manner of health problems. More widely spread, "fracking" has become a preferred method for extracting natural gas from the earth, irrespective of the danger it poses to the water table and human health.

There are, of course, manifold crises that the earth faces that are beyond the scope of this paper. What is important to note is that the origin of all of these problems can be traced to human activities that betray their perpetrators' selfishness, egotism, and disregard for life that is not human (and often human life as well). Early Pentecostals labeled particular places as immoral because of the sinful human activities that took place in those locations. The places themselves did not sin, but had instead been harmed by the sin of humans. While early Pentecostals were only concerned with particular places of entertainment and amusement, it is impossible to deny that the harm done by people to nature is anything but the result of human sin. Rosemary Radford Ruther contends, "We alone can 'sin.' We alone can disrupt and distort the balances of nature and force the price for this distortion on less fortunate humans, as well as the nonhuman community."[64] In view of the long-term consequences

---

an ecotheological ethic.

64. Ruether, *Sexism and God-Talk*, 88. McFague presses this point further, arguing

THE DEVIL'S SUICIDE 37

of human sin for the natural environment, it would seem sins of an ecological nature have marred the earth to a much greater degree than the
immorality of all the dancers, alcoholics, and roller skaters combined.

If indeed the earth has been tainted by sinful human activity, then
the Pentecostal practice of transforming immoral places into sacred
space seen through the hermeneutic of salvation, healing, and Spirit-
baptism offers a path forward. First, by acknowledging the sin of ecological domination and oppression that stains the earth, it becomes possible
to affirm that Jesus' atonement was necessary not only for humans but
for the entire created matrix of life—not merely dance halls, saloons, and
theaters. Human sin affects not only constructed sites of sin, but sprawls
out to pollute every nook and cranny of the earth. If salvation for the
earth is possible, then Pentecostals can look to the model of the movement's founders in order to invite and enact earth's transformation. The
transformation of buildings used for illicit purposes is a clear analogue to
the redemption of degraded creation.

Possessing a broader understanding of salvation, Pentecostals can
then move towards claiming polluted or at risk places and converting
them into clean and redeemed spaces. This process of conversion would
no doubt lead to healing for the land by means of clean up and the adoption of a cooperative and symbiotic relationship with the earth. Finally,
as the land heals, it will naturally bloom as a dwelling place for the Holy
Spirit. If an empty and littered lot in a city or a desolate strip-mined stretch
of land suggests the earth's God-forsakenness, then an urban community
garden or a reforested area surely invites one to experience the presence
of God's Spirit in creation. The Spirit-baptized earth will surely beam with
the proleptic glory of God. In this way, the salvation, healing, and Spirit-
baptism of the earth naturally culminate in the final cardinal doctrine of
Pentecostalism: eschatology.

Whereas Pentecostal eschatology has long been dismissive of creation, this process of transforming the land looks forward to the day when
God's presence will visibly permeate and saturate the whole of creation. If
one follows this line of thought, then "Pentecost becomes a symbol, not

---

that all sin has "an ecological dimension" insofar as sin consists in the human tendency
to operate beyond one's place in God's creation. In consequence, sin not only affects
one's relationship with God but also spills over to created order, for sin disrupts environmental relationships between humans, other animals, and nature. See McFague, *The
Body of God*, 112–29.

only of the divine breath filling and charismatically empowering God's people, but also indwelling all of creation one day."[65] The repurposing of secular space, whether tainted by immoral acts of human society or human pollution, speaks to the Christian mission to ensure that all people and places, flora and fauna experience salvation, healing, and Spirit-baptism in advance of Jesus' return. Thus, this practice embraces the hope of the eschaton, when God will be all in all—a characteristically Pentecostal hope that unites the movement's past, present, and future.

BIBLIOGRAPHY

Anderson, Robert Mapes. *Vision of the Disinherited: The Making of American Pentecostalism*. New York: Oxford University Press, 1979.

Argue, A. Watson. "Forthcoming Meetings." *The Pentecostal Evangel*, no. 626 (December 12, 1925) 14.

Arnold, A. "Walking in the Light." *The Latter Day Rain* 3, no. 11 (August 1911).

Boddy. "The Christian's Relation to World Reform."

Cornell, Carolyn. "Evangelists Preaches in Dance Halls, Calling for Recruits for Christian Army." *The Bridal Call* 3, no. 11 (April 1920), 13.

Consortium of Pentecostal Archives. "Digital Collections." http://pentecostalarchives. org/collections/ (accessed February 27–April 22, 2013).

Dayton, Donald W. *Theological Roots of Pentecostalism*. Grand Rapids: Baker Academic, 1987.

Dorries, David. "Azusa Street Revival." In *Encyclopedia of Religious Revivals in America*, edited by Michael McClymond. 2:37–42. Westport, CT: Greenwood, 2007.

Evans, J. R. "Reports from the Field." *The Pentecostal Evangel* 420–21 (November 26, 1921) 14.

Feick, August. "The Etter Meeting at Salt Lake City." *The Weekly Evangel* 163 (November 4, 1916) 15.

Flower, A.R. "Daily Portion From The King's Bounty." *The Weekly Evangel* 177 (February 17, 1917) 7.

Frey, Mae Elaenor. "The Work in Vancouver, B.C.." *The Pentecostal Evangel* 482–83 (February 3, 1923) n.p.

Glover. "Contrasting Wisdom."

"In the Regions Beyond." *The Weekly Evangel* 233 (March 30, 1918) 11.

Jacobsen, Douglas. "Knowing the Doctrines of the Pentecostals: The Scholastic Theology of the Assemblies of God, 1930–55." In *Pentecostal Currents in American Protestantism*, edited by Edith L. Blumhofer, Russel P. Spittler, and Grant A. Wacker, 90–110. Urbana, IL: University of Illinois Press, 1999.

---

65. Macchia, *Baptized in the Spirit*, 102–3; see also Swoboda, "Eco-Glossolalia," 113.

Jones, Lindsay. *Monumental Occasions: Reflections on the Eventfulness of Religious Architecture*. Vol. 1 of *The Hermeneutics of Sacred Architecture: Experience, Interpretation, Comparison*. Cambridge, MA: Harvard University Press, 2000.

Juillerat, Howard L., "The Coming of the Great City." *Church of God Evangel* 9, no. 16 (April 20, 1918), 2.

Brann, O. P. "The Work and Workers." *The Pentecostal Evangel* 593 (April 18, 1925) 14.

Klotz, Heinrich. *The History of Postmodern Architecture*. Translated by Radka Donnell. Cambridge: MIT Press, 1988.

Lakewood Church. "Our Story." http://www.lakewoodchurch.com/Pages/ne w-here/ Our-History.aspx (accessed April 9, 2013).

Land, Steven Jack. *Pentecostal Spirituality: A Passion for the Kingdom*. Cleveland: SPT Press, 2010.

The Latter Rain Evangel 13, no. 10 (September 1921).

Loveland, Anne C., and Otis B. Wheeler. *From Meetinghouse to Megachurch: A Material and Cultural History*. Columbia: University of Missouri Press, 2003.

Macchia, Frank. *Baptized in the Spirit: A Global Pentecostal Theology*. Grand Rapids: Zondervan, 2006.

Martin, William. "Prime Minister." In *Southern Crossroads: Perspectives on Religion and Culture*, edited by Walter H. Conser Jr. and Rodger M. Payne, 63–88. Lexington: University Press of Kentucky, 2008.

McFague, Sallie. *The Body of God: An Ecological Theology*. Minneapolis: Fortress, 1993.

McPhee, M. "Reports from the Field." *The Pentecostal Evangel* 444–45 (1922) 14.

McPherson, Aimee Semple. "In Dreamland Arena, San Diego, Cal." *The Bridal Call* 4, no. 9 (1921) 13.

———. "The Bridal Call Family Visits the Angelus Temple Revival." *The Bridal Call* 7, no. 1 (1923) 7.

———. "The Story of My Life." *The Bridal Call* 9, no. 1 (1925).

———. "Orlando, Florida." *The Bridal Call* 1, no. 12 (1918) 15.

———. "Within the Golden Gate of San Francisco." *The Bridal Call* 5, no. 12 (1922) 6–7.

Nelson, Louis. "Architecture and Revivals." In *Encyclopedia of Religious Revivals in America*, edited by Michael McClymond, 1:28–32. Westport, CT: Greenwood, 2007.

Norman, Larry. "Why Should the Devil Have All the Good Music." *Only Visiting This Planet*. Solid Rock. CD. 1972.

O'Connor, Elleen. "Denver Express Writes of Chinatown Meeting." *The Bridal Call* 5, no. 3 (1921) 17.

Peck, Dean. "Dean Peck Reviews Work Accomplished in Denver Revival." *The Bridal Call* 5, no. 5 (1921) 18.

The Pentecost 1, no. 1 (August 1908).

Piper, William. "Giving Heed to Seducing Spirits." *The Latter Rain Evangel* 4, no. 1 (1911) 2–6.

Pope, W. H. "Morphine Tablets of Hell." *The Latter Rain Evangel* 11, no. 3 (1918) 2–6.

Richardson, H. J. "Knoxville, Iowa, Feels the Power of God." *The Weekly Evangel* 159 (1916) 14.

Robeck, Cecil M., Jr. *The Azusa Street Mission and Revival: The Birth of the Global Pentecostal Movement*. Nashville: Nelson, 2006.

Ruether, Rosemary Radford. *Sexism and God-Talk: Toward a Feminist Theology*. Boston: Beacon, 1993.

Seymour, William J. "The Precious Atonement." *Apostolic Faith* 1, no. 1 (1906) 2.

Sidersky, Philip. "The Lord's Doing." *The Weekly Evangel* 183 (1917) 14.

Sisson, Elizabeth. "Incidents of Elm Grove Campmeeting [*sic*]." *The Latter Day Rain* 6, no. 12 (1914) 2.

Smith, Oswald. "The World Beats a Path to Her Door." *Tabernacle News* (1925).

Swoboda, A. J. "Eco-Glossolalia: Emerging Twenty-First Century Pentecostal and Charismatic Ecotheology." *Journal of Rural Theology* 9, no. 2 (2011) 101–16.

———. *Tongues and Trees: Toward a Pentecostal Ecological Theology.* Journal of Pentecostal Theology Supplement 40. Blandford Forum, UK: Deo, 2013.

Tallman, Matthew. "Pentecostal Ecotheology: A Theological Paradigm for Pentecostal Environmentalism." In *The Spirit Renews the Face of the Earth: Pentecostal Forays in Science and Theology of Creation*, edited by Amos Yong, 135–54. Eugene, OR: Pickwick, 2009.

Tomlinson, Homer, A. "Notices." *Church of God Evangel* 12, no. 23 (1921).

Trim, H. L. "Olney, Illinois Visited with Great Outpourings of the Spirit." *Church of God Evangel* 13, no. 14 (1922) 2.

Urshan, Andrew D. "Montreal, Canada." *The Weekly Evangel* 210 (1917) 14.

Wacker, Grant. *Heaven Below: Early Pentecostals and American Culture.* Cambridge, MA: Harvard University Press, 2001.

Walker, R. D. "Fellowship." *The Weekly Evangel* 161 (1916) 14.

Werda. "Full Gospel Assembly, Persian Mission." 14.

"White Slave Craft." *Word and Witness* 10, no. 1 (January 20, 1914) n.p.

Wigglesworth, Smith. "Keeping the Vision." *The Pentecostal Evangel* 533 (1924) 3.

Wood, John. "As in the Days of Old–A Story of 20th. Century Christianity." *The Bridal Call* 4, no. 11 (1921) 16.

3

The Pentecostal Pacifism of
John S. McConnell Jr., Founder of Earth Day

Jay Beaman

In April, 1917, the U.S. government declared war on Germany. Within months, one of the largest ever transformations of American society took place as every male of fighting age was required to sign up for the Selective Service System (SSS). The "war to end all wars," as it was known in the U.S., had begun. The new SSS required all men aged 21–29 to register for the draft.

A small group out of the approximately ten million men in the draft—about sixty-five thousand—asked for exemption as conscientious objectors to war, most of them for religious reasons.[1] Mennonites had a four hundred year history of resistance to killing in war. Quakers had resisted war nearly as long. Both groups constituted a large part of the religious resistance to World War I, though neither of these two groups was numerically large in American religion. A fair amount of resistance also came from numerous other small sectarian groups. Groups founded in the nineteenth century, such as Seventh Day Adventists and Churches of Christ offered some objection. However, a number of upstart sects and recent arrivals made a name for themselves as religious objectors. Quite a number were millennial sects from the late nineteenth and very early twentieth century, such as Jehovah's Witnesses. Most of the sects that resisted the war were brand new but became influential beyond

1. Keith, *Rich Man's War, Poor Man's Fight*, 1–4.

their numbers in resistance to the war. Among these new sects were the
Pentecostals.

Pentecostals' narrative of one reconciled humanity

The Pentecostals believed the Spirit of Jesus ruled their lives. Thus, they
could not kill in good conscience.[2] Their reasons varied but nearly always
included some reference to the teaching of Jesus in the Sermon on the
Mount to love and even reconcile with enemies. They saw their role in the
world as reconcilers, active agents of God's reconciliation of humanity.
Central to this reconciliation across national boundaries was the work of
Christian missions which sought to bring the message of God's love and
forgiveness to all nations.

The Pentecostals' founding story was one which they considered
a recapitulation of the founding narrative of the Christian community
on the ancient day of the feast of Pentecost (Acts 2). On that occasion,
the Jewish Diaspora from around the Roman Empire was worshipping
in Jerusalem. They heard the small community of followers of the crucified Messiah speaking in the "tongues" or languages of the pilgrims from
various ethnic regions around the Mediterranean. They heard the Jewish
God being praised in their own tongue and came to believe that God's
Spirit was prophesying a new age of God's presence and that humanity
had become reconciled to God through the crucifixion of Jesus, whom
they worshipped as Messiah and Lord. Early in the twentieth century,
Pentecostals quickly came to interpret their place in history in millennial
terms. This millennial interpretation included living in an age of reconciliation where lion and lamb fed together, presumably on grass. Implicit
in this rendition, is a view reminiscent of a creation narrative of humanity
living in peace with each other and with the created world.

In April, 1917, the *Weekly Evangel* reported that two young
Pentecostal evangelists were holding meetings in Colorado Springs,
Colorado, when the U.S. government declared war on Germany. One was
Clarence Henry Erickson of Kansas City, Missouri, and the other was John
S. McConnell who was reported to have "built a tabernacle in Denver that
will hold a thousand people." The article, by Rev. Mark Thomas Draper,
gave witness to the very physicality of the religious experience the early
Pentecostal revival in Colorado Springs elicited. This religion was not just

2. Beaman and Pipkin, *Pentecostal and Holiness Statements on War and Peace*; and
Beaman, *Pentecostal Pacifism*.

about ideas and beliefs—it was about fighting the forces of evil in one's earthly body. The account titled, "Victory in Colorado Springs," used militant language. Draper noted that there had been a "sweeping victory" begun when R. L. Erickson "opened fire . . . on March 4." The battle language was metaphor, or was it? The battle took place in the hearts of those attending, but also literally and physically in the prayer room next-door to the meeting. One young man "had been under awful conviction." He prayed for the ability to overcome addiction to tobacco. After taking his cigarettes to the preacher to burn, and after praying for an hour, there was serious wrestling with God, the devil, and those in the room.

> . . . the devil told him it was too late, that God would not save him and he decided to go home. But we just got hold of his arm and hung on to him, and finally he got down on his knees again. He was there about three minutes and the power of God struck him. He leaped and shouted and grabbed me and jumped me all over the prayer room. He now testifies that if it is feeling you want, just wait on God, and He will give a person all the feeling they can handle. He told me that he believed that he smoked upwards of thirty cigarettes a day, but God took the desire out of him in a flash, and today he is shouting happy.[3]

This religion involved changes in the man's concrete life in this world, which were interpreted as setting him free in body and soul. The worship was physical as well as spiritual. The evangelists and the man were doing battle in his body and in the room. If they had to, they wrestled him down and in doing so, they fought the devil. They were at war too.

Months later all three young evangelists would have to answer to the U.S. government what their intentions were regarding the SSS. Would they be willing to fight on the battlefields of Europe? They would not. They were currently engaged in another kind of battle and they would not kill another human being in warfare. They were Pentecostals. They might fight the devil and wrestle with other believers, but they would not agree to carry arms to kill other people in human warfare. Pastor M. T. Draper of Colorado Springs registered as a "Minister of religion," and likely received a ministerial exemption from the draft[4] R.L. Erickson's

---

3. Draper, "Victory In Colorado Springs," 16. For this and other Weekly Evangel magazines, see the AG Publications pre-WWII CD (Springfield, MO: IFPHC.org, 2006). All magazine articles referenced in this chapter were found by searching this CD, which used OCR technology to find such names as "McConnell."

4. WWI draft registration card, Mark Thomas Draper, born October 21, 1884,

23-year-old son, Clarence Henry Erickson, "the boy preacher," registered in Los Angeles.[5] Clarence listed his occupation as traveling evangelist, but did not claim ministerial exemption. On line 12 of his draft registration card, he requested exemption based upon "religion." To request religions exemption, he would have to be a part of a denomination officially on record as disallowing members going to war, that is, a peace church. He was a Pentecostal, and almost all Pentecostal denominations at the time were on record against going to war.[6] They were peace churches. The other young preacher in the revival meeting in Colorado Springs was 25–year–old John S. McConnell.

First-generation pentecostal peace church witness

McConnell was a teenager in 1907 when his father, T.W. McConnell, wrote to the *Apostolic Faith* magazine, telling them, "Pentecost has fallen in Santa Cruz."[7] T.W. was a Holiness evangelist turned Pentecostal at the Azusa Street revival. The 1906–1907 revival meeting in Azusa, Los Angeles, was considered the birthplace of the modern Pentecostal movement. When John S. McConnell filled out his draft registration card, he listed his occupation as "Minister—Assemblies of God, employed in Chappell, Nebraska." As mentioned, he was known for recently building a tabernacle in Colorado that seated 1,000 people. He could have requested the standard ministerial exemption. Instead, he requested exemption as a husband and father and for religious belief. The Assemblies of God (hereafter, "AG") was officially on record against members killing in war.[8] Moreover, McConnell was not unusual for having requested religious exemption. I have currently found thousands of draft cards of World War I men listing Pentecostal or their related Holiness denominations as the reason for religious exemption. In 1915, before U.S. entry to the

---

Seattle, Washington. Online: http://search.ancestry.com/cgi-bin/sse.dll?indiv=1&db=WW1draft&h=27090377. Registration State: Washington; Registration County: King; Roll: 1991889; Draft Board 3.

5. Draper, "Victory in Colorado Springs," 16; Online: http://search.ancestry.com/cgi-bin/sse.dll?indiv=1&db=WW1draft&h=28630567. Registration State: California; Registration County: Los Angeles; Roll: 1530899; Draft Board 17.

6. Ibid.; Beaman and Pipkin, *Pentecostal and Holiness Statements*, 5.

7. Vol. 1, no. 6, p. 3. CD, Assemblies of God Publications Pre-WWII (Springfield: MO; Flower Pentecostal Heritage Center) 2006.

8. Beaman and Pipkin, *Pentecostal and Holiness Statements*, 143.

World War I, the *Weekly Evangel* summarized "The Pentecostal people, as a whole, are uncompromisingly opposed to war, having much the same spirit as the early Quakers, who would rather be shot themselves than that they should shed the blood of their fellow–men."[9]

McConnell's local draft board treated him as a ministerial exemption, even though he asked for exemption for family dependents and religious beliefs. An examination of his draft card shows the number 28, seen near his occupation. The number 28 was often inserted by the local draft board in red pencil to designate a decision to exempt based upon ministerial exemption. McConnell frequently appeared as an evangelist in the *Weekly Evangel*.[10] His draft board had taken his exemption request for religious objection to war seriously, but they found it more palatable to focus on his socially-acceptable status as a minister with dependents and avoid the controversy generated by conscientious objection to war.

John S. McConnell's June 5, 1917 draft registration card.

9. "Pentecostal Saints Opposed to War," 1.

10. McConnell, "A Wide and Ready Field," 11. Here we find John McConnell in Chappell, Nebraska, after having been given a car in Omaha, they preached on the street in a completely new field for Pentecostals. As war was declared, he was in Colorado Springs, Colorado. On January 19, 1918 (p. 14) he was found in Renton, Washington. CD, Assemblies of God Publications Pre-WWII (Springfield: MO; Flower Pentecostal Heritage Center) 2006.

After the war, McConnell gained even more notoriety as a leading evangelist in the AG preaching around the Pacific Northwest, Texas, and Canada.[11] He wrote articles for the *Pentecostal Evangel*, with his address as Glad Tidings Tabernacle, San Francisco, California.[12] In 1924, when advertised as keynote speaker for the seventeenth annual Pentecostal Convention at Glad Tidings Tabernacle in New York he was dubbed the "fiery Irish evangelist."[13]

During the war, Glad Tidings and one of its pastors, Robert A. Brown, had been investigated for possible violations of espionage and accused of sedition. The investigation was prompted by articles in the New York press about Glad Tidings being a pacifist organization. When that was taken to mean that they used pacifism to recruit members who wished to avoid warfare, Brown appeared to take the complete opposite point of view. Brown referred people to the peace statement of the AG, which while requiring members to refuse killing in war, also pledged complete loyalty to the U.S. government. Brown said men trying to join the organization to avoid the draft would be rejected. He resented the notion that members and ministers were cowards and asserted they would do anything they could for the government—even to their own peril. Brown noted that their church prayed for the American side of the war, and even had a member fighting at the front who was decorated for valor.[14]

11. In Ferndale, Washington, *Christian Evangel*, 28 June 1919, 6; In Boise, Idaho, *Christian Evangel*, 6 September 1919, p. 14; In Cedar Hill, Texas, *Christian Evangel*, 20 September 1919; In Harrington and Ritzville, Washington hereafter, *Pentecostal Evangel*, 1 November 1919, 29. In Pendleton, Oregon, one follower was jailed and placed in the state mental asylum for some time after converting to the Pentecostal faith (PE:26 June 1920, p.11). They encountered similar police intervention in Walla Walla, Washington (PE: 18 Sept. 1918, p 11), held meetings in Watsonville, California (PE: 19 May 1923, p. 11; 26 May 1923, p. 15; 21 July 1923, p. 10), Lodi, California (PE: 22 Dec. 1923, p. 9), San Jose, California (PE: Jan. 12, 1924, p. 15), Pembroke, Ontario, Canada (PE: 2 Aug. 1924, p. 14), San Jose, CA (PE: 7 Feb. 1925, p. 7). CD, Assemblies of God Publications Pre-WWII (Springfield: MO; Flower Pentecostal Heritage Center) 2006.

12. McConnell, "The Will of God," 2. CD, Assemblies of God Publications Pre-WWII (Springfield: MO; FPHC) 2006.

13. "New York Convention," 14. CD, Assemblies of God Publications Pre-WWII (Springfield: MO; FPHC) 2006.

14. "Assembly of God is Loyal, says Pastor; Asserts Church is not Pacifist Organization, but Supports Government," *Brooklyn Daily Eagle*, 6 July 1918. Charley Grazer is no doubt Charles P. Graeser whose draft card notes that he had no request for exemption from war. Record URL: http://search.ancestry.com/cgi-bin/sse.dll?h=33821 847&db=WW1draft&indiv=try.

Investigator R.W. Finch of the Bureau of Investigation asked Draft Director Robert Conboy to have Brown and his publication, *Midnight Cry*, investigated in October 1918. Stuart Pilcher, assigned to read the documents, seemed unable to see any substantial evidence, and said as much. He also noted that this was probably nothing more than sincere conscientious objection being framed as something more. One agent attended a meeting at Glad Tidings Assembly where members, including Mrs. Brown prayed for the American side in the war and for the safety of American soldiers.[15] Brown was trying to distance himself and Glad Tidings Assembly from the kind of associations that were being made at the time between anarchists and International Workers of the World (IWW) and other pacifists. The term pacifist was often used synonymously with socialist and anarchist, and anyone resisting the government's war effort. R. W. Finch, who was investigating Brown, was also investigating a particularly violent anarchist sect in New York City at that very time, and only months later received a bomb in the mail.[16] Accusations were being made that lumped Glad Tiding Assembly into the larger stereotype.[17] Brown may have gone overboard to distinguish his group as loyal. In November 1925, long after the war, at the Pentecostal Convention at Glad Tidings, where McConnell was to speak, Brown celebrated burning the mortgages on Glad Tidings Assembly, marching in from a rear door in the platform, "With 'Old Glory' draped over his shoulder and a missionary's helmet on his head with the great African spoon in his right hand."[18] There was no mistaking that Pentecostal saints were loyal to the U.S. government.

John S. McConnell, Sr. and Jesus-centric theology

The previous year, the AG met for their eleventh General Council in Eureka Springs, Arkansas. One of the hopes from the executive group had been to put in place a more formal and robust constitution and bylaw to

15. Stuart Pilcher, "In RE: 'Midnight Cry,' Robert A. Brown, Editor, Draft Matter," National Archives Research Administration, Publication Number M1085, Old German Files, 1901–1021, Case Number 125865.

16. http://apushredscare.weebly.com/index.html. Accessed 11 Nov. 2013; see also Kornweibel, "Investigate Everything," 183–84.

17. Ibid.

18. McDowell, "The Convention at New York," 5. CD, Assemblies of God Publications Pre-WWII (Springfield, MO: FPHC) 2006.

replace the very brief 1914 document.[19] The founding General Council in Hot Springs, Arkansas, was controversial for its nearly all white member- ship, and for its formation as an official organization, a denomination one might call it. Many of its members and ministers felt they had suffered in being removed from other denominations or alternately had "come out" of other denominations to purify the church. The statement in 1914 tried to resonate with their concerns. Most sects form with a certain amount of sleight of hand and will be forgiven such. The formula might be stated "we are forming an organization which is not really an organization." The AG stated, "[We] do not believe in identifying ourselves as, or establish- ing ourselves into, a sect, that is a human organization that legislates or forms laws and articles of faith and has unscriptural jurisdiction over its members and creates unscriptural lines of fellowship and disfellowship and which separates itself from other members of the General Assembly . . ."[20] Less than two years later, AG leaders felt that a creed was required given the movement of congregations and leaders in promoting the "new issue"—baptism in Jesus' name. Associated with this new baptism was the re-baptism of previously baptized members of recent Pentecostal sects and an apparently innovative view of God, a kind of modalist view or a rejection of the Trinity. The discussion and adoption of the creed was very heated and in some cases disrespectful. G. T. Haywood, a black pas- tor from Indianapolis, already risking racist intolerance by meeting with this nearly all white group in St. Louis, Missouri, was mocked for his "oneness" position. Glenn Gohr summarizes, "T.K. Leonard facetiously referred to the Oneness doctrine of Haywood and his colleagues as 'hay, wood and stubble,' with the further remark: 'They are all in the wilderness and they have a voice in the wilderness' (referring to Haywood's periodi- cal called *A Voice in the Wilderness*)."[21] The divisive set of "Fundamental Truths," was passed by simple majority vote. One–fourth of the ministers walked out never to return.

19. Gohr, "The Historical Development of the Statement of Fundamental Truths," 60–65. IFPHC.org.

20. Combined Minutes of the General Council of the Assemblies of God in the United States of America, Canada, and Foreign Lands, 1914–1917, 12–8, Digital Version, AG Publications Pre-WWII (International Flower Pentecostal Collection, Springfield, MO: Gospel, 2008).

21. Gohr, "The Historical Development of the Statement of Fundamental Truths," 60–65.

At the 1925 General Council, this division was still painful to many who remained in the house. McConnell must have represented them when he stood up in the evening meeting after a pamphlet describing the new constitution and bylaws was passed out to every minister. He asked to speak to the gathering for a few moments before prayer. He spoke for what must have been one half–hour on the essential quality of love that is the centerpiece of salvation and all mission. For some, it must have seemed a triumph of simplicity and love over organization and doctrinal heavy–handedness. Who could disagree? The altars were filled with ministers weeping and praying. Most of the discussion the next evening was against the new changes. They were tabled and a committee was appointed to study them, the classic organizational move, and two years later they passed somewhat unceremoniously.[22] McConnell failed to renew his credentials as a minister of the AG the following year and operated as an independent Pentecostal evangelist.[23]

Instead of the Fundamental Truths, most of which he surely believed, McConnell liked to point to a set of "Commands of Jesus," that he published in his book, *The New Covenant*, in 1920 and shortly thereafter as a tract.[24] The commands of Jesus were 148 commands culled from the Gospels. Twenty–three of them were from the Sermon on the Mount.[25] The commands were organized into 21 topics, each with seven commands. Each command was a scriptural "one–liner," in the words of Jesus, with citation. The twenty–one section titles are as follows:

    I.   Repentance
    II.   Belief
    III.   The new birth
    IV.   Receiving the Holy Spirit
    V.   Following Jesus
    VI.   Prayer
    VII.   Faith
    VIII.   Searching the Scriptures
    IX.   Letting your light shine

22. Ibid.

23. Note on John Saunders McConnell, Sr. Personal Papers at FPHC (accessed October 2, 2013).

24. McConnell, *The New Covenant*; McConnell, "The Commandments of Jesus," Appendix, in McConnell, *Earth Day*, 431–38.

25. Matthew 5–7.

    X.   The second coming of Christ
    XI.   Supreme love to God
    XII.   Our duty to God and man
    XIII.   Our duty to our neighbor
    XIV.   Covetousness
    XV.   Hypocrisy
    XVI.   Meekness
    XVII.   Our love to the brethren
    XVIII.   Perfect love
    XIX.   Faithful unto death
    XX.   Preaching the Gospel
    XXI.   Wisdom

Even the commands which were not direct citations of the Sermon on the Mount, were in a section whose topic is a major theme within the Sermon on the Mount.

XVI. Meekness

"Take my yoke upon you . . . for I am meek and lowly in heart" Matt 11:29.

"The princes of the Gentiles exercise dominion over them . . . but it shall not be so among you" Matt 20:25–26.

"Whosoever of you will be the chiefest, shall be servant of all" Mark 10:43–44.

"Be not ye called Rabbi" Matt 23:8.

"Sit not down in the highest room" Luke 14:8–11.

"Rejoice not, that the spirits are subject unto you" Luke 10:20.

"Say, we are unprofitable servants" Luke 17:10.

None of these commands of Jesus is from the Sermon on the Mount, but in the Beatitudes, at the outset of the Sermon, Jesus' radical claim is "the meek shall inherit the earth."

Pentecostals were known for emphasizing what was called the four-fold gospel: salvation, Spirit-baptism, healing, and the second coming of Jesus.[26] McConnell believed these, and was known in his ministry for introducing converts to the Pentecostal style of the receipt of the Spirit

---

26. Dayton, *Theological Roots of Pentecostalism*, 21.

with demonstrative signs like speaking in tongues. He was known for dramatic healing when he prayed for people. Because his main teaching was the commands of Jesus, the book of Acts was not cited. His treatment of the coming of the Spirit was largely Johannine: "Receive the Holy Ghost," from John 20:23. His only treatment of healing in the commandments, was one line under preaching the gospel, "'Heal the sick,' Matthew 10:8." The second coming section is a series of commands that remind one to be vigilant, for example, "'Take heed . . . lest . . . your hearts be overcharged with surfeiting, and drunkenness, and cares of this life,' Luke 21:34."[27] There is nothing speculative about when, or prediction, or metaphysics. There is no mention of the millennium, rapture, heaven or hell. The section on faith is largely about living simply and carefree in close connection to God. But God is never defined; theology is implicit, even anthropocentric. There is no mention of justification or imputed righteousness, or progressive sanctification.

What one is left with are commands relating to living lovingly, peacefully, and justly with a loving Creator. Special attention is given to the poor, the broken, and the conflicted. "'Be ye therefore merciful, as your Father,' Luke 6:36; 'Agree with thine adversary quickly,' Matt 5:25; 'When thou makest a dinner . . . call not thy friends, nor thy brethren . . . but . . . call the poor,' Luke 14:12–13; 'Make yourselves friends of the mammon,' Luke 16:9."[28]

McConnell apparently lived quite consistently with what he preached. For at least twenty years he and his wife and children lived on the road, somewhat carefree, telling the good news from town-to-town, praying for people to come to know God and find healing and well-being. They were not buying a home or farm, but living out of a homebuilt camper known as a gospel car and later a Pierce–Arrow bus. Often, the children's only education was studying in public libraries. No sponsoring organization gave provisions, but those finding help along the way gave gifts to support the evangelist's family.[29]

27. McConnell, *The New Covenant*; McConnell, "The Commandments of Jesus," appendix, in McConnell, *Earth Day*, 431–38.

28. Ibid.

29. McConnell, *Earth Day*, 42–46.

XXI. Wisdom

"Be ye therefore wise as serpents, and harmless as doves" Matt 10:16.

"Beware of men'" Matt 10:17.

"Let (the blind leaders) alone" Matt 15:12–14.

"Give not that which is holy unto the dogs, neither cast ye your pearls before swine" Matt 7:6.

"Consider the lilies . . . how they grow" Matt 6:28.

"Whatsoever city . . . ye shall enter, inquire who is worthy; and there abide . . . Go not from house to house" Matt 10:11–13; Luke 10:5–7.

"Whosoever will not receive you . . . shake off the very dust from your feet for a testimony against them'" Luke 9:5; Luke 10:10–11.

XIX. Faithful Unto Death

"Be thou faithful unto death" Rev 2:10.

"When men shall revile you, and persecute you, . . . rejoice, and be exceeding glad" Matt 5:11–12; Luke 6:23.

"When they persecute you in this city, flee ye into another" Matt 10:23.

"When they deliver you up, take no thought how or what you shall speak" Matt 10:19.

McConnell put one part of the whole of the "Commandments of Jesus" at the very center: meekness. Meekness, with its meanings of humility and identification with the lowly, and alternately as gentleness, brought together peacemaking and social justice for the poor. McConnell was involved in a time of soul searching and seeking renewal in 1920 when he compiled his list of commandments of Jesus. In this period, he had a series of vision–like experiences where he saw specific scriptures of the sayings of Jesus dropping down on rays of light from heaven. Evangelizing in Colorado and Nebraska he worked in towns unreached by previous Pentecostal evangelists. After gaining notoriety in Denver and Colorado Springs, he spent a great deal of time in more rural Nebraska and later in the Pacific Northwest. He wrestled with staying in the difficult rural areas or going to the more productive and hence reliably larger offerings of the urban areas like Seattle. Meetings in Pendleton and Walla Walla were disrupted by interference from citizens and authorities alike.[30] McConnell retold the story as evangelists living with deprivation and want and being tempted to choose ease and prosperity and refusal to follow Jesus.

> We had been used to fairly good success in the Middle West and the South, and our needs were always supplied. Unconsciously spiritual pride had been creeping up in my heart; and hardships, short finances and meager results grated on that pride. The enemy began to tell me how my time was being wasted, and how little I was being appreciated in these hard places. . . . Scores of towns in this country had never heard the full Gospel; the need was great. To continue meant sacrifice. Why had not the saints on the Coast evangelized this territory? They were better able to do it than I was. I could have things more comfortable for my family if I preached among the saints too; more money, more popularity, more souls saved, etc. Why should I drag down my family through hardships when unmarried preachers were hanging around the large centres doing nothing? Why should I waste my time preaching to small crowds in these new fields, when I could be preaching to hundreds? Oh, how subtle the enemy is! Brethren, beware of spiritual pride! How deceitful it is!
>
> I ran away from the call of God and went to Seattle, and after a successful meeting among the saints, where numbers were saved and baptized, spiritual pride grew bigger. The saints loved us. We had things comfortable. Plenty of money. Lots of souls getting saved. Then they wanted us to hold a meeting in Portland, and we were about ready to go. But the Christ who loves us, and knows what we need best, even though it be a chastising, would not suffer us to go. He knew we were getting on dangerous ground so for our sakes He began to bring me down. The way up is down.[31]

McConnell compiled "The Commandments of Jesus," as part of the book, *The New Covenant*, during this time of returning to humility and identifying with the lowly; in short, a return to the centrality of meekness. The publication, of "The Commandments of Jesus," as a stand-alone

---

30. *Pentecostal Evangel*, 26 June 1920, 11; *Pentecostal Evangel*, 18 September 1920, 11.

31. McConnell, *The New Covenant*, first page of introduction.

tract, was a way to highlight that the central feature of the gospel was following Jesus as Lord. Meekness, including humility and peacemaking were considered central to who Jesus is and what following Jesus means. For McConnell, compiling the commandments of Jesus was important because following Jesus was the center of his faith.

McConnell's oldest son, John McConnell, Jr., like his father, was born at the right time to be of draft age for war. John, Sr. was a religious objector to World War I and his son John Jr. would be called up for the national selective service system in World War II. What choice would he make? He was a Pentecostal. His father's tract was in his possession with its commands of Jesus.

XII. Our Duty to God and Man

"Render to Caesar the things that are Caesar's, and to God the things that are God's" Mark 12:17.

"Swear not at all" Matt 5:34–37; Mark 4:22.

XIII. Our Duty to God and Neighbor

"Thou shalt love thy neighbor as thyself" Matt 19:17–19.

"Thou shalt do no murder" Matt 19:18.

XVIII. Perfect Love

"Love your enemies" Matt 5:44; Matt 26:52.

"Do good to them which hate you" Luke 6:27–28.

"Resist not evil" Matt 5:39–41.

McConnell, Jr. decided that he could not sit the war out, not taking risks and not helping out. He joined the Merchant Marines to avoid taking life. He claimed he selected ships transporting only nonmilitary materials. He served as a pastor to every ship he was on, conducting religious services and ministry, beyond his actual work shoveling coal in the boiler room. In 1943, on a visit home to Oakland, he was seized by authorities and inducted into the military. His draft board was not impressed with his arguments and refused his plea for conscientious objection to war. McConnell, Jr. refused to take the oath, train, or fire a rifle. "The target was the figure of a man. I was supposed to get as many bullets as possible into the figure. Suddenly that figure turned into the face of Jesus, who said, 'Inasmuch as you do it to them, you do it to me.' I decided that soldiers, whenever they kill, they're killing Jesus."[32]

McConnell, Jr. was placed in the stockade and preached to the guards. Then, in solitary confinement for eleven days in darkness and cold he refused to eat the bread from the diet of bread and water. After losing forty pounds he was released and charges were dropped. He remembered how he kept his sanity during this ordeal. He remembered the testimony of Katie Booth, evangelist and daughter of the founders of the Salvation Army. Katie Booth had practiced civil disobedience in Europe in the late nineteenth century, by doing street preaching. Since this was illegal, she was jailed. She took consolation in this great hardship, in the presence of Christ, as she put it, "Blest beloved of my soul. I am here alone with thee. And my prison is a haven, since thou sharest it with me."

McConnell, Jr. was then moved temporarily to an office job and he applied for a discharge thinking he had already done merchant marine duty. Realizing he was going to be reassigned to military duty, he and his young wife headed for Florida, purchased a sailboat and sailed to Honduras, intentionally "going absent without leave" (AWOL) to avoid military service. They spent the last two years of the war being pastors to villagers in Honduras. He was hiding from the draft board and U.S. federal authorities. After the war they returned to the U.S. where he served some months in prison for desertion.

J. S. McConnell, Jr.: reconciliation to all creation

In the end, McConnell, Jr. would be known for founding Earth Day in San Francisco in 1970, having coined the idea as early as 1968.[33] What was it about his father's belief in peacemaking, his father's conscientious objection to World War I, and his father's teaching about the sayings of Jesus that led him to his deep concerns for the earth? At the center was peacemaking as he saw it. His convictions were prompted by the teachings of Jesus in the Sermon on the Mount, and the connection was largely the idea of meekness. Jesus said: "The meek shall inherit the earth," and this was McConnell, Sr.'s central thread aligning peacemaking, economic

32. McConnell, *Earth Day*, 47–49.
33. Ibid., back cover.

justice, and earthkeeping.[34] McConnell, Jr. believed that peacemaking was a form of favoring the needs of the humble of the earth over the powerful and greedy. He thought that human survival and well–being would be based upon recognizing that each person had a stake in their locality, in having some rights derived by birth and being related to the earth. Each person had an inherent birthright and inheritance in the earth. He foresaw the need for legal changes that gave recognition to this birthright, resulting in either literal giving land to each person on earth, or more likely, a share of earth's resources. Conversely, greed and covetousness, the cause of destruction to our biosphere, would have to be legally curbed and culturally delegitimized.

An analysis of McConnell, Sr. and his son McConnell, Jr.'s roles in the beliefs and practices that led to Earth Day, especially peacemaking and the ownership of the earth by the humble, remind us that these men were Pentecostals and something central to their experience of that religious subculture contributed to this creative concern for earthkeeping. An analysis of the role of Earth Day or its overall effect on earthkeeping is perhaps another matter entirely. At the very least, the larger environmental movement may find ways to include the particularistic spirituality of Pentecostal–style Christians, who are often ignored by academic and cultural elites as irrelevant. Conversely, Pentecostal and evangelical Christians might reassess their role in contemporary peacemaking, eco–justice and earthkeeping or perhaps, in the very least, a part of their concern for saving the earth.

BIBLIOGRAPHY

"Pentecostal Saints Opposed to War." *Weekly Evangel* (1915) 1.

Beaman, Jay. *Pentecostal Pacifism: The Origin, Development, and Rejection of Pacific Belief among the Pentecostals.* Eugene, OR: Wipf & Stock, 2009.

Beaman, Jay, and Brian K. Pipkin. *Pentecostal and Holiness Statements on War and Peace.* Eugene, OR: Pickwick, 2013.

Dayton, Donald W. *Theological Roots of Pentecostalism.* Grand Rapids: Baker Academic, 1987.

Draper, M. T. "Reports from the Field." *Pentecostal Evangel* (July 21, 1923).

———. "Reports from the Field." *Pentecostal Evangel* (May 19, 1923).

34. McConnell, *Earth Day*, 110–16; "Living the Beatitudes," 400–403.

————. "Reports from the Field." *Pentecostal Evangel* (May 26, 1923).

————. "Victory In Colorado Springs." *Weekly Evangel* (April 28, 1917). AG Publications pre–WWII CD, Springfield, MO: iFPHC.org, 2006.

Gohr, Glenn W. "The Historical Development of the Statement of Fundamental Truths." *AG Heritage* (2012). IFPHC.org.

Keith, Jeanette. *Rich Man's War, Poor Man's Fight: Race, Class, and Power in the Rural South During the First World War*. Chapel Hill: University of North Carolina Press, 2004.

Kornweibel, Theodore. *"Investigate Everything": Federal Efforts to Compel Black Loyalty during World War I*. Bloomington: Indiana University Press, 2002.

McConnell, John, Jr., and John C. Munday. *Earth Day: Vision for Peace, Justice, and Earth Care: My Life and Thought at Age 96*. Eugene, OR: Resource, 2011.

McConnell, J. S. [Sr]. "A Wide and Ready Field." *Weekly Evangel* (June 10, 1916).

————. "Pendleton, Oregon." *Pentecostal Evangel* (June 26, 1920).

————. "Reports from the Field." *Christian Evangel* (September 6, 1919).

————. "Reports from the Field." *Pentecostal Evangel* (November 1, 1919).

————. "The Will of God." *Pentecostal Evangel* (April 7, 1922).

————. "Walla Walla, Wash." *Pentecostal Evangel* (September 18, 1920).

————. *The New Covenant*. Self-published, 1920.

McDowell, D. H. "The Convention at New York." *Pentecostal Evangel* 2 (January 1926).

Note on John Saunders McConnell Sr. Personal Papers at Flower Pentecostal Heritage Center, accessed October 2, 2013, iFPHC.

Pilcher, Stuart. "In RE: 'Midnight Cry,' Robert A. Brown, Editor, Draft Matter." NARA, M1085, OGF, 1901–1921, Case Number 125865.

The Red Scare. http://apushredscare.weebly.com/index.html. Accessed November 11, 2013.

Shields, S. G. "Reports from the Field." *Christian Evangel* (September 20, 1919).

4

The Environmental Theology
of Aimee Semple McPherson

Brian K. Pipkin

My initial investigation into Aimee Semple McPherson—founder of The International Church of the Foursquare Gospel—and ecology was bleak: every word search returned a spiritual metaphor. "Garbage" came back as "garbage can of Satan," "pollution" came back as "pollution of the soul," "plants" came back as "plants of faith," and "dumping" came back as "dumping ground for gossip." But eventually, persistence paid off.

Popular pastor and author Rick McKinley writes, "Margins are those clear spaces along the edge of a page that keep the words from spilling off. Every book has them. You might jot notes in the margins, but for the most part they go unnoticed. They don't represent the book, and they don't define its message. They're simply there."[1] McKinley's analogy describes McPherson's engagement with nature. McPherson made comments, not commentaries, about nature. She had strong opinions—some radical by today's standards—yet most remained underdeveloped. Moreover, her theology was largely anthropocentric. People, not the environment, occupied the center of her doctrine.[2] While nature, theologically, occupied the margins for McPherson, politically, it took center stage, especially during her anti-war expositions. Thus, environmental concern ultimately found expression in her patriotism.

1. McKinley, *Jesus in the Margins*, 11.

2. McPherson, "The Inter-World Bridge of Earth and Heaven," 5; McPherson, "Ship That Bore the Healer," 3.

McPherson spent little time theologizing about nature's relationship to humans. She believed in a good creation, and there remain some comments alluding to nature, but nothing expanding on Scriptures used by contemporary green theologians. This is not to say she was apathetic, but living between two World Wars, she had more immediate impending issues to consider. The earth, she believed, was on the verge of self-extinction, not through environmental degradation, but through weapons of mass destruction. She believed war and ecological destruction were one package. Thus, her opposition to war was also her opposition to ecological destruction. The war-earth-destruction combo is summed up in her commentary on needlessly destructive scorched earth tactics in war. Within, she introduced a cast of characters and systems responsible for the scorched earth—greedy politicians, war manufacturers, demons, armament, and over-funded military budgets. The consequences of scorched earth as foretold in the Bible provided her the context to criticize politics, unjust laws, institutions, and the people who perpetuate the destruction of earth.

The world aflame

McPherson believed in the dual-use of nature. She believed nature pointed to God's provision as well as God's judgment. God blessed humanity with a "heating and lighting system overhead," a "sprinkling system," and a "cooling system." God gave us "beautiful granaries of fields of weather and orchards of fruit. He has given us the coal and oil, the emeralds of diamonds, the precious treasures that have never been fully discovered."[3] Yet, God also used the elements, namely floods and fires, to purge the world. In her message, "The World Aflame," she referenced her favorite end-time narrative, the Noah doctrine, and reminded listeners that God would not destroy humanity again through flood—instead, God will use fire. The earth, she argued, was being scorched by none other than humanity itself through the institution of war. She blamed munitions factories, arsenals, and the death-dealing instruments of war.[4]

The risk weapons posed to the earth and its inhabitants were a problem for McPherson. Drawing on Joel, she connects tanks (war) to the devouring and destruction of land, animals, and vegetation. McPherson

3. "Debate between Aimee Semple McPherson and Charles Lee," 21.
4. McPherson, "The World Aflame," 5–7.

quotes Joel 2:1: "How do the beasts groan, the herds of cattle are perplexed because they have no pasture: yea, the flocks of sheep are made desolate." She believed war was responsible for destroying Earth—pastures, trees, rivers, vegetation, and cattle.[5] Because of poisonous bombs "nothing shall ever grow again where they fall, for the poisonous gases will destroy all vegetation."[6] Not only were toxins bad for the environment, they were bad for people. She described how people's "lungs were tortured with every breath" from poisonous gases that covered battlefields like a blanket of death.[7]

McPherson believed the U.S. was guilty of fueling this fire. She was far from blind to the imperfections of America. Though she embraced the God-and-country Christianity of her generation, it did not prevent her from questioning the notion of a "Christian American." She once asked, "Why should God bless America when America curses God?" Additionally, she linked America's turning away from God with a laundry list of sins including cross-dressing and war-making. The prospect of America calling itself a "Christian nation" while it manufactures explosives, poisonous gases, and stockpiles long range guns, disturbed McPherson.[8] She appealed to other nations to stop rolling out "barrels" of hunger, poison, hate, and munitions.[9]

Self-extermination

As mentioned, McPherson affirmed the goodness of God's creation. God created a "perfect world" with "perfect people" and placed them in a "perfect spot." The fall, she believed, introduced a host of problems like revenge, disease, and patriarchy in the world.[10] Moreover, she interpreted the "groans of creation" (Rom 8:22) as earth waiting to be delivered from wars, bloodshed, and earthquakes.[11] McPherson's greatest concern, however, was one that threatened human existence—war. New weapons

5. McPherson, "Today in Prophecy," 14.

6. McPherson, "The Ancient Mariner," 3; McPherson, "Sunset Hour," 3–4.

7. McPherson, "The Hub of The Universe," 23.

8. McPherson, "The World Aflame," 6, 48.

9. McPherson, "Roll Out The Barrel," 3.

10. McPherson, "Double Cure," 6–7; McPherson, "Little Women," 2; "Foursquare Program Proves Women Should Preach," 7.

11. McPherson, "Today in Prophecy," 14–15.

technologies created a moral challenge for clergy following World War I. Poisonous bombs, in particular, contributed to the pacifist sentiment of the 1920s and 1930s.[12] McPherson echoed these moral concerns by consistently rejecting the invention and use of poisonous bombs.[13] She believed these new poisonous gases would make World War I look like a child's play toy.[14] She also protested new war inventions, namely the technological sophistication of airplanes. Nations were deploying their "messengers of death" (airplanes) to destroy people, land, and cities.[15]

McPherson believed humanity was on the verge of self-extermination, not through environmental deterioration, but by weapons of mass destruction. Her self-extermination discourse sounded a lot like biologist Ernst Mayr who believed human intelligence was a lethal mutation. Mayr argued the more you move up the scale of intelligent life, survival begins to steadily decline. Life at the bottom of the biological pyramid, like bacteria and beetles, have a greater survival rate than mammals and humans.[16] In other words, humans possess the intelligence and technology to exterminate themselves. Similarly, McPherson suggested that instead of using the "engineering skill of the world" for peaceful purposes, minds were being devoted to "devise more deadly arms, gases, and aerial bombs" to destroy life.[17] She described the intellectuals of her day as "giants of thought" who, filled with violence, were responsible for the "mechanical and demon-inspired inventions for [the] destruction of humanity."[18] Thus, McPherson's view is succinctly expressed by President Kennedy who warned, "If mankind does not put an end to war, war will put an end to mankind."[19]

12. Yoder, *Christian Attitudes to War*, 334.

13. McPherson, "Hold Your Horses," 24–5; McPherson, "Humpty Dumpty," 1, 3.

14. McPherson, "Behold He Cometh!," 5.

15. McPherson, "Sherman Is Still Right," 2.

16. Chomsky, "Human Intelligence and the Environment." See also Challenger, *On Extinction*. Challenger shows how our human drive to exploit resources is leading toward extinction. She quotes George Perkins, who wrote, "Man is everywhere a disturbing agent . . . Whenever he plants his foot, the harmonies of nature are turned to discords." Challenger, *On Extinction*, 13.

17. McPherson, "The Blood Bank," 6; "Church Faces World Chaos," 3.

18. McPherson, "The Ancient Mariner," 3; McPherson, "God's Clock Strikes," 1; McPherson, "Blue Beard Stalks," 1.

19. Frost, *John F. Kennedy in Quotations*, 158.

Natural disasters

Following natural disaster, the inevitable question arises: Who is responsible? McPherson had many explanations, but unlike her contemporaries,
she did not exploit tragedy for evangelistic gain. She was not in the guilt-
producing business. McPherson believed in hell, but not for advertising
purposes.[20] Although McPherson's sermons were incredibly emotional,
she scorned preachers who exploited the range of human emotion for
the wrong reasons. She verbalized her opposition to the hell-fire and
brimstone techniques of old-style evangelicalism, and labeled the tactics
used by these theater-evangelists as "pulpit-pounding"—the use of "fear,
abuse, touching stories, a tear in the voice, and visions of hell" in order
to "coerce people into making a decision" to follow Jesus.[21] Moreover, it
was uncharacteristic of her to blame victims of natural disasters; instead
she generally attributed natural disasters to the preordaining of events,
prophecy, or fate—not individual lifestyles. With that said, I have no
doubt she would agree people play a key role in perpetuating natural
disasters (e.g., the Dust Bowl). Her xenophobia did, occasionally, lead
to name-calling.[22] However, she tried to distinguish between opposing
evil from the people committing it. Her enemy was poverty. "You can
blame it on whatever you want, but it is here." She described her enemy in
suprapersonal terms like squalor, hunger, and crime.[23]

When disaster struck, rather than playing the blame-game,
McPherson chose practical Christianity as evidenced in her disaster response such as the 1925 Santa Barbara earthquake, the 1938 Los Angeles
flood, and the 1930s Dust Bowl. She used these tragedies constructively as
talking points to (1) remind her people of the temporal nature of life, (2)
to give to the poor, and (3) to call the nation back to God. She sermonized
her gospel-in-overalls ethic in a message titled, "Practical Christianity"
where she argued for a "whole gospel" that was "practical for the poor."[24]
Historian Edith Blumhofer notes that McPherson's practical response to
crisis reflects her desire to help the needy.[25] McPherson also applauded

20. Sutton, *Resurrection of Christian America*, 47.

21. McPherson, "Conformed or Transformed," 2.

22. McPherson, "Three Blind Mice," 1; McPherson, "The Trojan Horse," 2.

23. McPherson, "Angelus Temple And It's Needy," 2.

24. McPherson, "Practical Christianity," 1.

25. Blumhofer, *Aimee Semple McPherson*, 269.

the Public Works Administration for assisting "a million ruined farmers" and "starved cattle" caused by drought. The Dust Bowl, which caused major ecological, agricultural, and economic havoc for farmers, concerned McPherson. She voiced interest over the soil quality of the corn belt as "plows turn over only ashes instead of moisture."[26]

Whodunit?

So "whodunit?" Who is responsible for natural disasters? McPherson believed Satan was the primary cause of ecological destruction. Satan, she argued, was the "arch-conspirator venting his wrath on the world by creating havoc among the powers and the laws of nature." Satan was plummeting earth towards ecological Armageddon through "tribulation, sorrow, pestilence, and famine."[27] Satan was also responsible for war, the "hidden hand" pulling the "political and economic strings" of nations in an attempt to "defeat their plans for peace."[28] Satan, she argued, occupied every war council while "war-mad demons" were "perched on the shoulders of every military commander riding in the cockpit of every bombing plane."[29]

Although she blamed Satan for ecological destruction and war, she was not an archetype of the demon-behind-the-bush brand of Pentecostalism.[30] The Achilles heel of Pentecostal political theology—the personalization of evil—was common for her Pentecostal contemporaries, but nevertheless rejected by McPherson. She challenged systemic sin, though she was careful to frame political criticism in theological terms.[31]

Lifeboats

Influenced by D.L. Moody, McPherson commonly used lifeboats, a sectarian symbol of escapism, to symbolize her ministry. Although she did not fully embrace Pentecostal sectarianism, she routinely swayed

---

26. McPherson, "Stunned Nation Prays as Drought Devastates," 1; McPherson, "Flood Brings Death and Destruction," 1.

27. McPherson, "Distress of Nations," 2.

28. McPherson, "The Hidden Hand," 2.

29. McPherson, "Sherman Is Still Right," 2.

30. Wink, *Engaging the Powers*, 9.

31. Sutton, "Clutching to 'Christian' America," 337.

between critical pessimism and hopeful activism. Understandably, given her context, McPherson's depression-era editorials communicated a defeatist perspective, embracing a kind of ecological predeterminism. "No need to pray for better times as they are not in the cards." Abandoning wishful thinking, she advised readers to "accept the inevitable and get ready for the coming of Jesus."[32] What can we do for this sinful world? "Nothing so far as changing it is concerned. She is like an old sinking ship. There's no use to put upon her any patches of reformation or improvement movements; for she is doomed to go down, patches and all."[33] Destruction was imminent. Jesus was coming. Souls needed to be saved. Her eschatology is sprinkled with doomsday fatalism, interpreting end-times Calvinistically—a fate in which humanity cannot change world events. Consequently, this lifeboat portrait has mistakenly led historians to overlook McPherson's political activism.[34]

However, we should not judge her lifeboat ethics too harshly or anachronistically. First, pessimism and optimism coexisted for McPherson. Her defeatist everything-is-hopeless-I-quit sayings were published simultaneously with columns encouraging readers towards contributing to here-and-now social reforms. For example, the *Foursquare Crusader* praised the church's activist role in diplomacy between nations, sanitation and health, better wages and living conditions, and peace over militarism.[35] Second, lifeboat ethics was only a small part of her larger here-and-now social justice ministry. While McPherson shared the Assembly of God's doomsday eschatology, she also embraced a "this worldly" focus.[36] Third, McPherson believed in Augustine's total depravity doctrine. Everything was fallen, declining, and decaying. However, her doctrine of depravity did not lead to inaction. As Matthew Sutton notes, McPherson interpreted the Bible as a directive to engage the nation's political systems and institutions to create a more Christian nation.[37] Her life provides a critique of the partisan direction in which subsequent Pentecostal movements traveled.[38] Finally, while lifeboat doctrine may have fueled pessimism, it

32. McPherson, "Distress of Nations," 2.

33. "Churches Faces World Chaos," 8.

34. Sutton, "Clutching to 'Christian' America," 332.

35. "What the Church Has Done for our Nation," 3; "Toward World Peace," 24.

36. Sutton, "Clutching to 'Christian' America," 309.

37. Sutton, *Resurrection of Christian America*, 215.

38. Sutton, "Clutching to 'Christian' America," 330–31.

also fueled her protest. She questioned the notion of human progress, lamented violence, and denounced the worldliness of American culture.[39] While ecological destruction and the foreordaining of events was inevitable in McPherson's theology, it did not result in passivity or inaction. Her depression-era editorials were indeed despairing, but pessimism did not trump her political engagement.

Conservation

In the 1930s, McPherson, a Democrat, supported Franklin D. Roosevelt's liberal New Deal reforms which included regulatory reforms protecting natural resources.[40] She believed in environmental patriotism—the belief that a country's greatness is defined by its environment.[41] For example, she equated the greatness of America with its abundance of resources such as fruitful fields, forests, powerful rivers, water systems, mines, and quarries of gold and silver.[42] She also said California was Uncle Sam's favorite child as it offered the best in resources.[43] McPherson, I believe, scratched the surface of what historian Ronald Wright argues in *A Short History of Progress*. Wright believes a culture is no better than its woods. In other words, the health of land and water and woods can only be the lasting basis for any civilization's survival and success. "If civilization is to survive, it must live on the interest, not on the capital, of nature."[44]

McPherson observed state conservation laws. For example, her Temple Welfare Department re-routed commissary items to conserve

39. Ray, "Aimee Semple McPherson and Her Seriously Exciting Gospel," 163. Ray notes McPherson's rejection of violence and human progress stemmed from her embrace of Calvinism's total depravity doctrine.

40. McPherson, "The Boston Revival," 11; "Index to Register of Voters Precinct No. 1145"; Sutton, *Resurrection of Christian America*, 234.

41. Todd, *Communicating Environmental Patriotism*, 6. I'm using Todd's definition of environmental patriotism.

42. McPherson, "The Prodigal Son Called Sam," 11, 14.

43. McPherson, "Los Angeles Marches On," 5.

44. Wright, *A Short History of Progress*, 105, 129. Wright argues that civilizations fall suddenly because as they reach full demand on their ecologies they become more vulnerable to natural fluctuations (84). Wright argues the first eyewitness accounts of a human-made environmental catastrophe is in the Genesis story. Not only did Adam and Eve drive themselves from Eden by exploiting this natural paradise, but the eroded landscape they left behind set the stage for Noah's flood (67–68, 75).

rubber and gas.[45] She also exchanged her vehicle for a buggy to conserve gasoline.[46] McPherson was no Mark Driscoll, who, when defending his choice of gas-guzzling cars, argued that the one who made the environment is coming back to destroy it.[47] Although McPherson had moments of despair, she did not advocate a theology that views the world as disposable (i.e. "Throwaway Theology").

McPherson supported both peacetime and wartime environmental regulations. Although it is difficult to be certain, her support for conservation was possibly inspired by patriotism more than theology given most of her references to conservation took place during World War II. In other words, while theology inspired her to reflect on God's good creation, patriotism inspired her action to conserve.[48] Moreover, war also provided her the occasion to prove her patriotism to U.S. officials. By World War II, Foursquare leaders encouraged churches to integrate "patriotic programs" into Sunday morning worship. This included buying war bonds and conserving rubber.[49] What began as a genuine effort to protect resources in the 1930s transformed into an occasion to market her movement as patriotic in the 1940s.

Pulpit politics

Because political offense can be costly, McPherson's strategy was to keep the pulpit politically neutral, although she believed the church and government worked hand-in-hand and frequently used the pulpit to advance patriotic politics. In 1936, McPherson clarified her approach to faith and politics when she learned her associate pastor, Rheba Crawford, criticized Roosevelt's liberal reforms. In an article titled "Pulpit and Politics," McPherson laid out her separatist policy explaining, "Our motto concerning politics and religion is that 'never the twain shall meet.'"[50] In 1942 she reiterated her policy advising, "Do not talk politics; talk Jesus."[51]

45. "Commissary Need Growing," 1.

46. "Sister in Great San Jose Meeting," 20.

47. Pierson, "Gas-Guzzlers a Mark of Masculinity."

48. McPherson, "The New Birth," 6–7.

49. "Forthcoming Convention to be Spiritual 'Call to Arms,'" 3.

50. McPherson, "Pulpit and Politics," 4; Sutton, "Clutching to 'Christian' America," 337; Epstein, Sister Aimee, 406.

51. Foursquare Annual Convention Records, 5.

Though McPherson argued separatist rhetoric, she was the worst offender of her own policy as she continued supporting New Deal reforms, peace, disarmament, conservation, and women's rights. Despite her promotion of liberal reforms, some scholars have failed to acknowledge the depth of McPherson's political activism.[52]

Some have likely misjudged the extent of McPherson's politics because she masterfully disguised political speech with theological metaphor. Grant Wacker's book, *Heaven Below*, suggests that McPherson was more apolitical than political, and that her politics was not conspicuous enough to merit comment.[53] Others like Sutton, however, insist McPherson was far more politically active than historians have admitted.[54] In documenting her support for progressive reforms, Sutton believes it was McPherson's political activism that distinguishes her from her Pentecostal counterparts who argued separatist doctrine.[55] In *Pentecostalism in America*, Roger Robins writes that McPherson's group was far more culturally assimilated, more socially and politically engaged, and less bound to the moralistic heritage of Holiness than the average Pentecostal.[56] In fact, by World War II, The Foursquare Church was the only major white Pentecostal denomination to disavow separatism from political engagement.[57]

Furthermore, McPherson's displays of patriotism may have led some scholars to overlook her more radical teachings, confusing flag waving with conservatism and uncritical obedience to government.[58] In *The Vine and the Branches,* Foursquare historian Nathaniel M. Van Cleave highlights McPherson's patriotic credentials and obedience to government during war. However, Van Cleave presents McPherson's relationship to war starting in 1942, after she abandoned peacetime pacifism and deleted the Foursquare Bylaw recognizing conscientious objectors. There

52. Sutton, "Clutching to 'Christian' America," 332.

53. Wacker, *Heaven Below*, 222.

54. Sutton, "Clutching to 'Christian' America," 332.

55. Sutton, *Resurrection of Christian America*, 215.

56. Robins, *Pentecostalism in America*, 62.

57. Sutton, "Clutching to 'Christian' America," 330.

58. McPherson's sermons were saturated with metaphors of war and civic responsibility. Her patriotism was often expressed in the triplets of conservation, citizenship, and peacemaking. Moreover, her patriotic speech consisted of political polarity by blending the U.S. flag with diplomacy and military might. She did not, however, always equate the flag with militarism.

is brief mention (two sentences) on Foursquare opposition to war, while entire paragraphs are devoted to Foursquare loyalty and patriotism.[59] Consequently, McPherson's objections to large-scale communal sin like violence, war, arms production, and capital punishment are absent from the official narrative.[60] Omissions like these may be due to inattentional blindness—our failure to notice the unexpected. We become so fixated on our preconceived ideals of McPherson that we block out other possibilities even when they are visible. In this case, patriotism becomes the red herring. Researchers who assume the more patriotic one is, the less radical they must be, should be cautious. As Jay Beaman reminds us, patriotism does not always equal uncritical allegiance to all war.[61]

To this day, McPherson's political views exceed the standards of many conservative Pentecostals. For example, how many pro-military, flag-waving, patriotic Pentecostals are, like McPherson, supporting global disarmament, calling for reducing military spending, opposing capital punishment, and supporting labor and welfare reform? Moreover, McPherson's political speech challenges the assumption that she accommodated and compromised herself to mainstream conservative politics and theology. She crossed conservative boundaries by incorporating both social gospel and Salvation Army themes into her ministry.[62] Nevertheless, acknowledging these views can be a struggle. Some are resistant to the possibility that the founder of their movement was anything but loyal and unquestioningly patriotic to their country.[63] It is uncomfortable to be reminded of such counterculturalism within your denomination, especially if you adhere to an alternative ideology.[64]

59. Van Cleave, *The Vine and the Branches*, 157–58. Edith Blumhofer, McPherson's biographer, likewise highlights McPherson's hyper-patriotism during both World Wars while omitting her interwar peacetime appeals to nonviolence. See Blumhofer, Aimee Semple McPherson, 252–53. For a history of early Foursquare attitudes on peace and war, see Pipkin, "The Foursquare Church and Pacifism."

60. Ray, "Aimee Semple McPherson and Her Seriously Exciting Gospel," 162–63.

61. Beaman and Pipkin, *Pentecostal and Holiness Statements*, 30.

62. Sutton, *Resurrection of Christian America*, 186–87.

63. I experienced this resistance when I attempted to interview a former coworker of McPherson. Because I suggested the possibility that McPherson was something more than the stereotypical patriot and pro-war theologian, she denied my interview and expressed her disdain that I would dare suggest she was anything but loyal to her country.

64. McPherson's liberal leanings are seldom highlighted and typically presented as haphazard or an exception to the Foursquare metanarrative. The McPherson I experienced in Foursquare Bible College was charismatic, conservative (except in relation to

Joseph in america

Despite McPherson's separatist policy, by the early to mid-1930s, she began to integrate politics more explicitly into her writings.[65] Some of her boldest criticisms of U.S. economic policies were editorialized in a column titled "Joseph in Egypt" in which she compared the unjust policies of Joseph with the unjust policies of the U.S. McPherson's commentary on Joseph is similar to Walter Brueggemann's "Food Fight of Faith." Brueggemann and McPherson identified a similar pattern: fear of scarcity (not enough) results in accumulation (hoarding) that leads to monopolies (control) which ends in violence (slavery).[66]

McPherson opens her editorial by criticizing Joseph's social policies. When scarcity hit Egypt, she explained, and the food ran out, people came to him for help. Instead of giving them back their own corn, he sold it to them—first for money, next in exchange for their cattle, then for their lands, and finally for their very selves. She also compared the plutocracy of Egypt with America. Both hoarded wealth. People were slaves. They were overtaxed. They were overburdened. They were starved. "People became things—cogs in a great economic wheel." The U.S., she declared, was the new Egypt. "With ten percent of the people owning, or at least controlling, ninety percent of the wealth of the country; and the foreclosure of tens of thousands of mortgages on homes, farms and factories, the title to the wealth and real property of the nation is rapidly drifting into the hands of the bankers."[67]

McPherson, like Brueggemann, rejected scarcity ideology.[68] McPherson believed in a world of plenty, comparing the earth to an hourglass, she believed God placed enough resources down in the earth

---

women's rights), entrepreneurial, and patriotic. These are true qualities, but selective nonetheless. For example, while it is true Martin Luther King Jr. advocated civil rights, it is equally true that he criticized capitalism, war profiteering, corporate welfare, and promoted nonviolence and civil disobedience, something rarely highlighted in the official narrative.

65. Sutton, "Clutching to 'Christian' America," 321.

66. Brueggemann, "The Food Fight of Faith."

67. McPherson, "Joseph in Egypt," 2.

68. Brueggemann, "The Liturgy of Abundance, The Myth of Scarcity."

to supply the need of humanity until the day God returns.[69] God never meant for humanity to be poor spiritually, physically, or materially.[70]

Moreover, the early Foursquare Church's attitude toward natural resources was both utilitarian and hedonistic. Resources were not to be hoarded or exploited, but used for "our need and enjoyment."[71] If resources were scarce, she argued, the culprits were war, hoarding, and armament. "Famine, I repeat, always follows war." Why? Because "man-power and material are being invested in war implements instead of farming crops." She pointed to western Europe as an example. "Every present combatant country was on bread and meat cards within 90 days."[72] Armament, she said, contributed towards a tortured and half-starved world. She criticized nations for taxing people on the verge of starvation to build great military machines. "If nations would stop building warships and equipping armies we would be all but overwhelmed with prosperity."[73]

Capitalism

McPherson followed the capitalist storyline.[74] However, she did not take capitalism to its logical extreme of resource exploitation and wage labor. She was not anti-business. She was anti-exploitation. She did not advocate unfettered capitalism, nor did she overlook the abuses of capitalism. Admittedly, her context predates the dangers now faced from a linear economic system of extraction, production, consumption, and disposal—a system that externalizes costs through pollution, wage labor, and waste.[75] Nevertheless, she was disenchanted with her depression era world—a world where things were no longer weighed in the balance of equity or measured with the yardstick of kindness—but "weighted on the scales of penury, against weights of gold and greenbacks."[76]

69. McPherson, "The Hour Glass," 1; McPherson, "Sister Declares Road To God is Way Out of Depression," 6.

70. McPherson, "Jack and the Bean Stalk," 5.

71. "Missionary Services," 19; "News Flashes from Foursquare Mission Fields," 9; "The Opportunity of 1928," 4.

72. McPherson, "Hold Your Horses," 26.

73. McPherson, "The Way to Disarm is to DISARM," 3.

74. McPherson, "Free Love In Spain," 2.

75. Bakan, *The Corporation*, 60–84; Heinberg, *The End of Growth*, 252.

76. McPherson, "Fang and Claw," 2.

McPherson's welfare advocacy was as a kind of social protest to unregulated capitalism. First, her support for Roosevelt's New Deal reforms indicates she favored government regulations on behalf of nature and labor.[77] Second, she did not take an uncritical attitude toward corporations. She defended the rights of the working poor.[78] Third, she led her Temple Welfare Department into partnership with the state and advocated for the development of the U.S. welfare state.[79] Unlike conservative approaches to charity, her model incorporated political activism. She contributed to the progressive era tradition of moral reform by drawing on both social gospel ideals and the Pentecostal emphasis on personal regeneration.[80]

Although McPherson supported capitalism, she had moments of dissent. She rejected wealth concentration, criticized disparities of wealth, and believed capitalism, needed to be brought under the rule of Jesus for redemption. Capitalism, she declared, failed because it made no room for Jesus in its political program. Moreover, she believed all human institutions carried within themselves the seeds of their own destruction—"Greed, Avarice, and Lust for Gain."[81] Capitalism represented "godless consumerism" in which Americans bought "everything on credit" and paid with installments of "lost lives, broken bodies, and starving children."[82]

She also compared capitalists to Al Capone. "Capone's money, although obtained from unscrupulous methods, is no more unclean than the dollars of the man who amasses his millions from underpaid factory workers." She had a message for Capone-like capitalists within her congregation. "I do not excuse Al Capone. He and all his ilk should be shut away where they cannot prey upon society. Neither do I excuse the so-called decent children who sits with folded hands in his pew on Sunday and goes out to oppress his fellows on Monday. The Bible says, 'The oppressors are consumed out of the land.' There is no place for them in heaven."[83] McPherson's views were reiterated by Foursquare pacifist leader, Charles Walkem, who defined capitalism as the "quintessence of selfishness" in which riches were made by "defrauding laborers."[84]

77. Sutton, *Resurrection of Christian America*, 214.

78. Sutton, "Clutching to 'Christian' America," 314; McPherson, "A Bride Adorned," 25.

79. Marsh, "Religious Women in Modern American Social Reform," 117–18.

80. Sutton, *Resurrection of Christian America*, 187.

81. McPherson, "Behold He Cometh!," 30; McPherson, "The Seed of Destruction," 2.

82. McPherson, "Bill Collectors," 2–3.

83. "Gates To Hell May Be Crashed, Says Pastor," A8.

84. Walkem, "Capitalism versus Labor, Installment II," 8; Walkem, "Capitalism versus

Swords and plowshares

Drawing on one of her favorite anti-war themes, swords and plowshares, McPherson believed the pen (diplomacy) was mightier than the sword.[85] She chastised nations for beating plowshares into "implements of death" and believed swords were responsible for earth's destruction—"the burning of homes and forests [and] vapors of poisonous gas" as well as "diseases and pestilences attacking trees, fruit, and vegetables of our land." Factories, instead of producing instruments of agriculture "turns out guns and ammunition" and instruments of death to "destroy human life."[86]

Swords also jeopardized national security. McPherson criticized Woodrow Wilson's "making the world safe for democracy" propaganda. How, she wondered, can the U.S. make the world safe for democracy while arming the world with swords? The potential for blowback was certain, she believed. We sold battleships and iron only to "get it back in bullets."[87] Her message to America? Stop shipping "scrap-iron over to the Orient and Europe . . . those fire-arms might find lodging in your own heart."[88]

The worst kinds of politicians for McPherson were those who profited from the sword, and those who disguised greed as patriotism. She had names for them. They were cowards. They promoted "patriotic fervor" but never set foot on the battlefield. "As long as they can protect their own devoted hides and send the other fellow to the front, the clamour for war, especially when those manufacturing munitions and other war materials make it worth their while to promote the war spirit."[89] They were also called "salesmen of death" who saw within their "grasps millions of dollars won through the death of the innocent of the earth."[90] In Smedely Butler fashion, she noted, "At the beginning of the world war America boasted but 8,000 millionaires. At its close she had 30,000 millionaires and several billionaires."[91]

Labor," 4.

85. McPherson, "Fiddling While Rome Burns," 9; McPherson, "The Great Emancipator," 2; McPherson, "Swords and Plowshares."

86. McPherson, "Jesus is Coming Soon! Get Ready!," 1.

87. McPherson, "The First Peace Conference," 3.

88. McPherson, "Ships That Do Not Pass," 4.

89. McPherson, "War," 2.

90. "Signs of the Times," 8; Lee, "Demonstrated Gospel," 3.

91. McPherson, "Comes the Dawn," 7.

She also compared them to a "merry-go-round of national ruin" that goes "round and round" but never goes anywhere. They were "drunk with power and ambition" with the "blood of innocents" playing on their "little merry-go-round of their unholy reign of terror." She hoped their "little merry-go-round will break down and awaken them from their illusions of national greatness and personal power." Soon they will realize they were riding a "hobby horse—a wooden horse, with wooden hopes, on a wooden political machine, in a carnival of greed and slaughter, under the canopy of a fool's paradise."[92] She believed plowshares—a symbol of precious resources—were being melted by the gods of war and turned into swords for destroying humanity.[93] She anticipated the day when "implements of slaughter shall be devoted to the peaceful pursuits of agriculture."[94]

Prince of peace

Because swords were responsible for earth's destruction, McPherson sought to combat war with the promotion of peace. Her anti-war discourse was influenced by the peacetime pacifism of the 1930s.[95] She did not self-identify as a pacifist, but clearly sympathized with pacifist rhetoric. She also represented the neutralist position, or as she called it, the "stay in your own backyard" doctrine.[96] However, she was selective in her application of peace. For example, she believed it was wrong to kill unless you were defending the United States of America.[97] After Pearl Harbor, she abandoned peacetime convictions.[98] The fear of another war made Christian leaders neutralists and pacifists in the 1930s. The fear of totalitarianism and Hitler made them militarists and interventionists in the 1940s.[99] McPherson followed this trend. Nevertheless, the

92. McPherson, "Merry-Go-Rounds," 2.

93. McPherson, "Questionnaire from the N.Y.N.A."

94. McPherson, "Paths of Glory," 2.

95. Beaman and Pipkin, *Pentecostal and Holiness Statements on War and Peace*, 167–73.

96. McPherson, "Questionnaire from the N.Y.N.A."

97. Sutton, *Resurrection of Christian America*, 257.

98. McPherson, "Foursquaredom and Uncle Sam," 24; McPherson, "This is Worth Fighting For," 4.

99. Sittser, *A Cautious Patriotism*, 64.

interwar years provided her a socially acceptable context to criticize war and its destruction.[100]

McPherson's Prince of Peace theology was simple: If you want peace, follow the Prince of Peace. Peace failed, she believed, because nations do not make room for Jesus in their political programs of peace. She wondered, how can nations have peace conferences without the Prince of Peace? This led to her poking fun at people who run to and fro with "their little paper tablets of peace, wildly searching for peace," but looking everywhere except at the Prince of Peace.[101] When sword-wielding nations joined peace conferences, McPherson compared them to an "international Halloween party" being "held in the Haunted house of a world gone mad."[102] Equating the political establishment to a Halloween party is fitting given she believed peace conferences were full of moral hypocrites who cried peace while their "swords were red with blood."[103] McPherson's criticism of peace, therefore, was not a slam against nonviolence, but a critique of progressive hypocrites, who, much like today, "Cry peace, but prepare for war."[104]

Moreover, Matthew 24 moderated McPherson's Matthew 5 pacifist appeals.[105] Apart from the hypocritical demagogues of her day, she remained skeptical of peace because Jesus predicted the continuation of war.[106] However, the foretelling of an event in scripture did not prevent McPherson from trying to make positive social change. For example, she supported prohibition and disarmament although drinking and war were end-time predictions.[107] The same is true of conservation. She supported conservation although she believed the Bible predicted the destruction of the earth.[108] McPherson's life challenges the assumption that dispensational pre-millennialism is always inconsistent with peace and conservation.

---

100. Pipkin, "The Foursquare Church and Pacifism," 64–120.

101. McPherson, "The Coming Prince of Peace," 11–12.

102. "Temple Pastor Depicts War-Frenzied World," A3.

103. McPherson, "God in American History," 8.

104. McPherson, "The First Peace Conference," 3.

105. McPherson, "Questionnaire from the N.Y.N.A."

106. McPherson, "Wars and Rumors of War," 2; McPherson, "Behold He Cometh," 30; McPherson, "When is He Coming?," 6.

107. McPherson, "God in American History," 8; "The Way to Disarm is to DISARM," J3.

108. McPherson, "Shine as the Stars Forever," 20.

Conclusion

McPherson was a critic and apologist for war, labor, capitalism, and peace. Her life was full of moral ambiguity. She argued for lifeboat theology and was politically active. She fought racial inequality and opened segregated Foursquare churches.[109] She supported U.S. involvement in both World Wars, yet promoted nonviolence. She advocated gender equality, yet picked mostly men to lead her organization. She supported conservation, yet believed in earth's imminent demise. She talked right and walked left. She talked left and walked right. Her life provides something for everyone—for pacifists, warriors, patriots, for right wing and left wing.

It is unfair to judge her inconsistencies too harshly. Humans are complicated creatures, and McPherson embodies all the contradictions that make us human. As Aldous Huxley once said, the only completely consistent people are the dead.[110] Despite her inconsistencies, she took bold positions for progressive reform. She saw the need for regulations and laws to curb unjust capitalist behaviors. She rejected scarcity doctrine. She rejected concentrations of wealth. She protested war with the promotion of peace, and she believed conservation was patriotic.

McPherson believed the world should have a profound effect on Pentecostals. It should open our mouths and loosen our tongues "to protest against the sins of this generation."[111] However, we are a distracted culture. We are distracted by our careers. We are distracted by sports. We are distracted by celebrity gossip. We are distracted by fashionable consumption. This cult of distraction, warns Chris Rojek, is designed to mask the real disintegration of culture.[112] Everyday we are flooded with insignificant information and captivated by matters of no real importance.[113] Our attention is diverted toward the trivial, absurd, and spectacle.[114] Neil Postman called this "Amusing Ourselves to Death."[115] McPherson called this "Fiddling While Rome Burns." Both were arguing the same point. Amusements pacify discontent. We are diverted away from things that really matter. McPherson's advice? Stop fiddling your fingers. Civilization

---

109. Sutton, *Resurrection of Christian America*, 31–32.

110. Huxley, "Wordsworth in the Tropics."

111. McPherson, "Spiritual Unrest," 2.

112. Rojek, *Celebrity*, 90.

113. Chomsky, *Understanding Power*, 98–100.

114. Hedges, *Empire of Illusion*, 27, 182.

115. Postman, *Amusing Ourselves To Death*, xi.

is teetering on the brink oblivion while we continue fiddling with drink, dance, and sports.[116]

McPherson's world is not much different from today. Military budgets are overfunded. Families struggle with basic needs. Wealth remains concentrated. Politicians talk peace while they continue imperialist policies, and we still face the prospect of self-extermination through nuclear war and environmental destruction—both perpetuated by population growth, pollution, and the acceleration of technology.[117] As Wright warns, we are falling victim to our own success (e.g. nuclear weapons and greenhouse gases).[118] While McPherson's generation did not push the self-destruct button, our generation may be much closer.[119]

BIBLIOGRAPHY

Bakan, Joel. *The Corporation: The Pathological Pursuit of Profit and Power.* New York: Free, 2004.

Beaman, Jay, and Brian K. Pipkin. *Pentecostal and Holiness Statements on War and Peace.* Eugene, OR: Pickwick, 2013.

Blumhofer, Edith. *Aimee Semple McPherson: Everybody's Sister.* Grand Rapids: Eerdmans, 1993.

Brueggemann, Walter. "The Food Fight of Faith." Plenary speech at CEEP Episcopal Conference, March 8, 2012.

———. "The Liturgy of Abundance, The Myth of Scarcity." *Christian Century* (March 24, 1999). Republished by *Religion Online*, http://www.religion-online.org/showarticle.asp?title=533 (accessed September 28, 2013).

Challenger, Melanie. *On Extinction: How We Became Estranged From Nature.* Berkeley, CA: Counterpoint, 2012.

Chomsky, Noam. "Human Intelligence and the Environment." http://www.chomsky.info/talks/20100930.htm (accessed September 21, 2013).

———. *Understanding Power: The Indispensable Chomsky.* New York: New, 2002.

"Churches Faces World Chaos." *Foursquare Crusader* (March 31, 1937) 3.

"Commissary Need Growing." *Angelus Temple Bulletin* (August 2, 1942) 1.

"Debate between Aimee Semple McPherson and Charles Lee." n.d., 21. ICFG archives.

Epstein, Daniel Mark. *Sister Aimee: The Life of Aimee Semple McPherson.* San Diego: Harcourt Brace, 1993.

116. McPherson, "Fiddling While Rome Burns," 9.

117. Wright, *A Short History of Progress*, 128.

118. Ibid., 56.

119. Hennen, Miller, and McLaughlin, "U.N. Climate Change Report"; Tupper, "Evangelical Scientists Call for Climate Action."

"Forthcoming Convention to be Spiritual 'Call to Arms.'" *Foursquare Crusader* (May 3, 1943).

Foursquare Annual Convention Records, ICFC Corporate Documents, 1942, 5.

"Foursquare Program Proves Women Should Preach." *Foursquare Crusader* (April 11, 1934) 7.

Frost, David B. *John F. Kennedy in Quotations*. Jefferson, NC: McFarland, 2013.

"Gates To Hell May Be Crashed, Says Pastor." *Los Angeles Times*, July 29, 1935, A8.

Hedges, Chris. *Empire of Illusion: The End of Literacy and the Triumph of Spectacle*. New York: Nation, 2009.

Heinberg, Richard. *The End of Growth: Adapting to our New Economic Reality*. Gabriola Island, BC: New Society, 2011.

Hennen, Dave, and Brandon Miller and Ellott C. McLaughlin. "U.N. Climate Change Report Points Blame at Humans." CNN, http://www.cnn.com/2013/09/27/world/climate-change-5-things/?hpt=hp_t1 (accessed September 27, 2013).

Huxley, Aldous. *Do What You Will*. London: Chatto & Windus, 1949.

"Index to Register of Voters Precinct No. 1145." Los Angeles County, 1938, www.ancestry.com (accessed September 21, 2013).

Lee, Earl. "Demonstrated Gospel." *Foursquare Crusader* (November 18, 1936) 3.

Marsh, Sabrina. "Religious Women in Modern American Social Reform." PhD diss., University of Illinois, 2012.

McKinley, Rick. *Jesus in the Margins: Finding God in the Places We Ignore*. Colorado Springs, CO: Multnomah, 2005.

McPherson, Aimee Semple. "The Ancient Mariner." *Foursquare Crusader* (June 7, 1939) 3.

———. "Angelus Temple And It's Needy." *Foursquare Crusader* (May 5, 1937) 2.

———. "Behold He Cometh!" *Foursquare Crusader* (August 1931) 5.

———. "Bill Collectors." *Bridal Call Foursquare* (July 18, 1934) 2–3.

———. "The Blood Bank." *Foursquare Crusader* (September 1942) 6.

———. "Blue Beard Stalks Again." *Foursquare Crusader* (April 27, 1938) 1.

———. "The Boston Revival." *Bridal Call Foursquare* (November 1933) 11.

———. "A Bride Adorned." *Foursquare Crusader* (February 1940) 25.

———. "Comes the Dawn." *Foursquare Crusader* (February 11, 1931) 7.

———. "The Coming Prince of Peace." *Bridal Call* (January 1920) 11.

———. "Conformed or Transformed." *Foursquare Crusader* (November 10, 1937) 2.

———. "Distress of Nations." *Foursquare Crusader* (January 27, 1937) 2.

———. "Double Cure." *Bridal Call* (July 1921) 6–7.

———. "Fang and Claw." *Foursquare Crusader* (March 31, 1937) 2.

———. "Fiddling While Rome Burns." *Foursquare Crusader* (May 1940) 9.

———. "The First Peace Conference." *Foursquare Crusader* (December 28, 1938) 3.

———. "Flood Brings Death and Destruction." *Foursquare Crusader* (March 9, 1938) 1.

———. "Foursquaredom and Uncle Sam." *Foursquare Crusader* (February 1942) 24.

———. "Free Love in Spain." *Foursquare Crusader* (November 18, 1936) 2.

———. "God in American History in 1933." *Foursquare Crusader* (January 3, 1934) 8.

———. "God's Clock Strikes." *Foursquare Crusader* (May 3, 1939) 1.

———. "The Great Emancipator." *Foursquare Crusader* (February 10, 1937) 2.

———. "The Hidden Hand." *Foursquare Crusader* (January 13, 1937) 2.

———. "Hold Your Horses." *Foursquare Crusader* (September 1940) 24–25.

———. "The Hour Glass." *Bridal Call Foursquare* (January 1927) 1.

———. "The Hub of The Universe." *Bridal Call Foursquare* (September 1928, 23).

———. "Humpty Dumpty." *Foursquare Crusader* (May 3, 1939) 1–3.

———. "The Inter-World Bridge of Earth and Heaven." *Bridal Call Foursquare* (July 1943) 5.

———. "Jack and the Bean Stalk." *Foursquare Crusader* (April 20, 1938) 5.

———. "Jesus is Coming Soon! Get Ready!" *Bridal Call* (February 1918) 1.

———. "Joseph in Egypt." *Foursquare Crusader* (April 7, 1937) 2.

———. "Little Women." *Foursquare Crusader* (June 1934) 2.

———. "Los Angeles Marches On." *Foursquare Crusader* (August 25, 1937) 5.

———. "Merry-Go-Rounds." *Foursquare Crusader* (September 1, 1937) 2.

———. "The New Birth." *Bridal Call Foursquare* (January 1930) 6–7.

———. "Paths of Glory." *Foursquare Crusader* December 30, 1936) 2.

———. "Practical Christianity." *Foursquare Crusader* (February 19, 1936) 1.

———. "The Prodigal Son Called Sam." *Bridal Call-Crusader Foursquare* (July 3, 1935) 11–14.

———. "Pulpit and Politics." *Foursquare Crusader* (June 24, 1936) 4.

———. "Questionnaire from the N.Y.N.A." N.d. ICFG Corporate Documents.

———. "Roll Out The Barrel." *Foursquare Crusader* (September 13, 1939) 3.

———. "The Seed of Destruction." *Foursquare Crusader* (April 14, 1937) 2.

———. "Sherman Is Still Right." *Foursquare Crusader* (November 3, 1937) 2.

———. "Ship That Bore the Healer." *Foursquare Crusader* (May 25, 1938) 3.

———. "Ships That Do Not Pass In The Night." *Foursquare Crusader* (September 7, 1938) 4.

———. "Shine as the Stars Forever." *Bridal Call Foursquare* (June 1927) 20.

———. "Sister Declares Road To God is Way Out of Depression." *Bridal Call-Crusader Foursquare* (June 26, 1935) 6

———. "Spiritual Unrest." *Foursquare Crusader* (June 23, 1937) 2.

———. "Stunned Nation Prays as Drought Devastates." *Foursquare Crusader* (July 22, 1936) 1.

———. "Sunset Hour." *Foursquare Crusader* September 7 (1927) 3–4.

———. "Swords and Plowshares." Sermon. ICFG archives, May 30, 1940.

———. "This is Worth Fighting For." *Foursquare Crusader* (November 14, 1942) 4.

———. "Three Blind Mice." *Foursquare Crusader* (September 23, 1936) 1.

———. "Today in Prophecy." *Foursquare Crusader* (January 1943) 14.

———. "The Trojan Horse." *Foursquare Crusader* (February 17, 1937) 2.

———. "The Way to Disarm is to DISARM." *Los Angeles Times* (February 14, 1932) J3.

———. "War." *Foursquare Crusader* (March 3, 1937) 2.

———. "Wars and Rumors of War." *Foursquare Crusader* (November 17, 1937) 2.

———. "When is He Coming?" *Bridal Call* (December 1920) 6.

———. "The World Aflame." *Crusader Foursquare* (May 1941) 5–7.

"Missionary Services." *Foursquare Crusader* (November 1943) 19.

"News Flashes from Foursquare Mission Fields." *Foursquare Crusader* (September 1942) 9.

"The Opportunity of 1928." *Foursquare Crusader* (February 29, 1928) 4.

Pierson, Russ. "Mark Driscoll: Gas-Guzzlers a Mark of Masculinity." *God's Politics*, May 9, 2013. http://sojo.net/blogs/2013/05/09/mark-driscoll-gas-guzzlers-mark-masculinity (accessed September 16, 2013).

Pipkin, Brian K. "The Foursquare Church and Pacifism." In *Pentecostals and Nonviolence*, edited by Paul N. Alexander, 64–120. Eugene, OR: Pickwick, 2012.

Postman, Neil. *Amusing Ourselves To Death: Public Discourse in the Age of Show Business.* New York: Penguin, 1985.

Ray, Donna, E. "Aimee Semple McPherson and Her Seriously Exciting Gospel." *Journal of Pentecostal Theology* 19, no. 1 (1992) 155–69.

Robins, Roger G. *Pentecostalism in America.* Santa Barbara, CA: Praeger, 2010.

Rojek, Chris. *Celebrity.* London: Reaktion, 2001.

"Signs of the Times." *Bridal Call-Crusader Foursquare* (July 11, 1935) 8.

Sittser, Gerald L. *A Cautious Patriotism: The American Churches and the Second World War.* Chapel Hill: University of North Carolina Press, 1997.

"Sister in Great San Jose Meeting." *Foursquare Crusader* (July 1943) 20.

Sutton, Matthew Avery. *Aimee Semple McPherson and the Resurrection of Christian America.* Cambridge, MA: Harvard University Press, 2007.

———. "Clutching to 'Christian' America." *The Journal of Policy History* 17, no. 3 (2005) 308–38.

"Temple Pastor Depicts War-Frenzied World." *Los Angeles Times* (October 31, 1938) A3.

Todd, Anne Marie. *Communicating Environmental Patriotism: A Rhetorical History of the American Environmental Movement.* New York: Routledge, 2013.

"Toward World Peace." *Bridal Call-Crusader Foursquare* (May 22, 1935) 24.

Tupper, Janelle. "Evangelical Scientists Call for Climate Action." *God's Politics* (July 10, 2013). http://sojo.net/blogs/2013/07/10/evangelical-scientists-call-climate-action (accessed September 16, 2013).

Van Cleave, Nathaniel M. *The Vine and the Branches: A History of the International Church of the Foursquare Gospel.* Los Angeles: International Church of the Foursquare Gospel, 1992.

Wacker, Grant. *Heaven Below: Early Pentecostals and American Culture.* Cambridge, MA: Harvard University Press, 2001.

Walkem, Charles. "Capitalism versus Labor." *Foursquare Crusader* (August 3, 1938) 4.

———. "Capitalism versus Labor, Installment II." *Foursquare Crusader* (May 27, 1936) 8.

"What The Church Has Done For Our Nation." *Foursquare Crusader* (April 8, 1936) 3.

Wink, Walter. *Engaging the Powers: Discernment and Resistance in a World of Domination.* Minneapolis: Fortress, 1992.

Wright, Ronald. *A Short History of Progress.* New York: Carroll & Graf, 2004.

Yoder, John Howard. *Christian Attitudes to War, Peace, and Revolution.* Edited by Theodore J. Koontz and Andy Alexis. Grand Rapids: Brazos, 2009.

PART TWO

Theological Reflections

5

The Greening of the Spirit: Towards a Pneumatological Theology of the Flourishing of Nature

Veli-Matti Kärkkäinen

The role of sacred traditions in the preservation of nature: tentative clarifications

If, as seems clear to many in the beginning of the new millennium, "environmental pollution is considered to be our world's most dangerous, and constant, threat,"[1] this raises the question for the theologian of the role of religions in relation to the impending eco-catastrophe.[2] I am convinced, alongside Lawrence Sullivan, that not only "[h]uman beliefs about the nature of ecology are the distinctive contribution of our species to the ecology itself," but also that, importantly, "[r]eligious beliefs—especially those concerning the nature of powers that create and animate—become an effective part of ecological system."[3] Here we have a new challenge and opportunity for all religions and theologies to consider the threat

---

1. International Conference on Environmental Pollution and Remediation, July 15–17, 2013, Toronto, Canada, n.p., http://icepr2013.international-aset.com/index.htmlo.

2. In this essay, "pollution" is used as an inclusive umbrella term denoting all types of harm on environment by humans (whether directly or indirectly). The essay builds on and draws heavily from my forthcoming *Creation and Humanity: A Constructive Christian Theology for the Pluralistic World*, chap. 8.

3. Sullivan, "Preface," in *Hinduism and Ecology*, 11.

that only recently has become global in its force, namely, the state of the environment.[4]

It is noteworthy that, unlike the past, currently most religions make claims to being "green" and routinely appeal to their sacred Scriptures in support of the claim.[5] The theologian, however, should exercise proper caution. To begin with: is it really the case that we should assume that conservation of the environment be on the forefront of sacred traditions and can expect the ancient Scriptures to be ready resources for third-millennium needs for green thinking?[6] Indeed, it is not as much a matter of what the ancient scriptures of each tradition is saying about nature at face value, but rather, whether—in keeping with the deepest theological and spiritual teachings—an ecofriendly hermeneutics is feasible and available within that tradition.[7] Rightly the Muslim writer Craig Phillips concludes: "Though we tend to read our scriptures anthropocentrically, we must reflect on the fact that our scriptures are not anthropocentric, and nor are they ecocentric."[8]

Be that as it may, it is also noteworthy that while religions' voice is widely dismissed in public conversations concerning the care of environment, at the same time the sacred traditions are by default blamed for many environmental ills, at times even regarded as *the* reason for the rape of nature.[9] As flawed historically, hermeneutically, and analytically, as is the (in)famous essay by Lynn White, "The Historical Roots of Our Ecological Crisis," at least it has been able to fuel self-critical soul-searching and constructive responses among religious traditions. The issue of

4. Tucker and Grim, "Series Foreword," in *Hinduism and Ecology*, 15-32; Foltz, "Introduction," in *Islam and Ecology*, 38.

5. For an important current resource, see the theme issue edited by Thottakara, "Ecology and World Religions," 9–120. Continuously updated information, resources, and discussions can also be drawn from the official website of the Alliance of World Religions and Conservation, http://www.arcworld.org/. The organization claims to be "secular" but to be helping faith traditions cultivate a keen awareness of the habitat at large.

6. See further Hütterman, *The Ecological Message of the Torah*, 11. For a seasoned comment, see McFague, "An Ecological Christology," 35.

7. See Foltz, "Islamic Environmentalism," 249.

8. Phillips, "Green Creation," 6. He refers to Katz, "Faith, God, and Nature," 164.

9. White, "The Historical Roots of Our Ecological Crisis." For a rebuttal and response from an Islamic perspective, see Foltz, "Islamic Environmentalism," 249. From a Jewish perspective, see Lamm, "Ecology in Jewish Law and Theology," 162–85.

the role of Christianity and other religions in the suffering of nature will be discussed below.

Having clarified religions' role in relation to the environment, let us now delve into the theological work. The next section seeks to clarify the reasons the Judeo-Christian tradition, against its better knowledge, for too long tended to be either anti-environmentalist or at least failed to live up to its theological ideals. The rest of the essay, then, moves into constructive work and seeks to find theological resources from both pneumatology and eschatology to develop a theology in support of the greening of creation.

On the judeo-christian tradition not being inherently anti-environmentalist

A persistent myth when it comes to religion-environment conversation has to do with the alleged radical difference between Asiatic and Abrahamic traditions, namely, that whereas "Eastern religions promote a sense of harmony between human beings and nature. . . . the religions of the West . . . [are to be blamed for] promoting the separation of human beings and nature and encouraging acts of domination, exploitation, and control."[10] That charge, which appears in different forms in literature, however, is mistaken on two accounts. First of all, even a superficial knowledge of Buddhism and Hinduism, to name the most obvious Asiatic traditions, reveals that the attitude towards conservation of the environment is a highly complicated and difficult issue for Asiatic traditions. Rather than cosmo- or environment-centered, both traditions are deeply anthropocentric as their goal is the release from ignorance (differently conceived in each tradition). They are escapist rather than conservationist because of the "appearance" nature of reality (that is, what we see is not the "real" world, but rather, the real is beyond the seeming God-world dualities) and the cyclical worldview.[11] Secondly, without setting up any kind of contest between religions, let it suffice to remark that

10. Eckel, "Is There a Buddhist Philosophy of Nature?," 327. Eckel himself is not condoning the statement. A typical unfounded commendation of Asiatic-traditions' opinion, without any scriptural or theological support (and obviously without any knowledge of the traditions themselves), can be found at Snyder, *The Practice of the Wild*, 10.

11. A detailed discussion of the environmental resources and obstacles in Hinduism and Buddhism (along with Abrahamic traditions) can be found in *Creation and Humanity*, chap. 8.

the alleged anthropocentrism of the Judeo-Christian traditions[12] (which might lead to lack of efforts for caring for nature) is more than healed and corrected by weighty well-known theological resources such as God's charge to men and women to act as responsible vice-regents on behalf of other creatures and creation; the covenant spirituality of the Hebrews that binds human beings to God, other humans, and nature; the incarnational Christology of the Christian Scriptures in which Christ is the agent of creation and appears in created reality; the related sacramental theology in which God's grace is embodied; the expectation of the eschatological renewal of the heavens and earth; and so forth.[13]

That said, it is also important for contemporary Christian theology to acknowledge that the "ecological crisis of the modern world has its starting point in the modern industrial countries," which were shaped by Christian influence.[14] While this is not to put blame on Judeo-Christian religion per se because the most critical influence for dominating and exploiting nature comes from secular sources, particularly from the Enlightenment[15]—and as is well known, destruction of nature has been at least as rampant in atheistic lands[16]—it means that for too long a time Christian theology did not sufficiently clarify the ecological implications of its creation theology. As a result, it contributed passively, so to speak, to the abuse of God's creation.

Christian theology should have reminded itself more often that the mandate in Genesis 1:26–27 for humanity to act as God's faithful vice-regents does not justify abuse but rather is a call to responsible service on behalf of God's good creation.[17] Regretfully, the command to "subdue the earth" was too often taken in its literal sense in Christian tradition. Although there is the minor alternative "green" tradition in Christianity

---

12. Callicott and Ames, "Introduction: The Asian Traditions as Conceptual Resource for Environmental Philosophy," 3–4.

13. I was inspired by Tucker and Grim, "Series Foreword," xxv.

14. Moltmann, *The Spirit of Life*, 20.

15. It can also be shown historically that the domination of nature has its roots deeply in pre-Enlightenment Renaissance humanism and other related movements in which the human being rather than all creatures is put on a pedestal. See Bauckham, *Living with Other Creatures*, 47–58. See also chap. 3 in my *Creation and Humanity*.

16. Indeed, removing God from the center and the introduction of anti-Christian influences has caused much of the abuse and distancing from nature. See Kerr, *Immortal Longings*, 163; more widely in Borgmann, *Power Failure*.

17. See Welker, *Creation and Reality*, 60–73.

that includes mystics and saints to whom nature had intrinsic value and human dominion represented stewardship and care for creatures, in the main Christian tradition, greatly influenced by Greek philosophical movements (particularly Stoicism), nature was conceived to have been made for humans and their benefit. As a result, it was seen through a utilitarian lens; humanity's relation to nature was based on a hierarchical, dualist view emphasizing difference rather than solidarity.[18]

It is precisely as the image of God, reflecting the characteristic of Creator, that in Judeo-Christian tradition the human being is placed in the world as steward, accountable to God.[19] Rather than superiority, humanity should exhibit solidarity with creation to which it also belongs.[20] Indeed, says the Orthodox Zizioulas, humanity is called to exercise its priestly vocation on behalf of creation, and the "human being is not fulfilled until it becomes the 'summing up of nature,' as priest referring the world back to its Creator."[21] In the Christian vision, "ll creatures on this earth find their way to one another in the community of a common way, a common suffering and a common hope."[22] There is a continuity between the human and nature, and Christ died and was resurrected not merely for humans but for nature as well.[23]

Currently it is often suggested that in order to exploit these rich theological resources listed above in the service of environmental care, Christian theology should make a shift towards speaking of nature as divine. A growing number of ecologically minded religionists seem to believe that the virtual divinization of nature is necessary in order to foster an attitude of care. The ecofeminist Starhawk is a striking example. While her call to treat nature as "Goddess" does not mean envisioning "a being somewhere outside of this world," it still is an invitation to see nature as inherently divine.[24] Is that so? Although in particular the many mystical

---

18. For an excellent analysis, see Bauckham, *Living with Other Creatures*, chap. 2.

19. Pannenberg, *Anthropology in Theological Perspective*, 79; Fisher, *Human Significance in Theology and the Natural Sciences*, 40–42.

20. See Clifford, "When Being Human Becomes Truly Earthly," 173–89. See also, particularly, Ruether, *Gaia and God*, 19–22.

21. As paraphrased by Fisher, *Human Significance*, 152, with quotation from Zizioulas, "Preserving God's Creation," 2. Cf. Clark, *Biology and Christian Ethics*, 269.

22. Moltmann, *The Way of Jesus Christ*, 273.

23. Ibid.; italics original.

24. Starhawk, *Dreaming the Dark*, 11; see also her *The Spiral Dance*.

spiritual traditions of both the Christian East and West have approached creation with a deep reverence and sense of holiness,[25] theological tradition has refrained from speaking of nature as divine. Rightly so, because divinization blurs the boundary line between the Creator and creatures.[26] It is neither necessary nor useful, therefore, to divinize nature.

What about calling nature a sacrament?[27] While there are sacramental elements in nature, calling nature a sacrament extends the meaning of that technical spiritual/theological term in a way that is a categorical mistake. Rather than being a sacrament, the special conveyor of salvific grace, nature—including creatures embedded in nature's web—hopes for the final redemption according to the biblical promise (Rom 8:19–26).[28] Neither divine nor a sacrament, in theological perspective, "[n]ature remains sacred in the sense that it belongs to God, exists for the glory of God, even reflects the glory of God, as humans also do."[29] The de-divinizing of nature affirms creation as *creation*, finite and vulnerable, as well as valuable because of its goodness.[30]

Theological resources for healing and flourishing of creation

The task of an ecological constructive Christian theology is twofold: on the one hand, it has to clarify and help avoid ways of thinking and speaking of nature as creation that are detrimental to her survival and well-being. On the other hand, it also has to search for resources—theological insights, metaphors, approaches—that can help foster the flourishing and continuing *shalom* of God's creation.

Based on a trinitarian theology of creation, two interrelated themes will be brought into conversation here: the Spirit's work for continuous healing of creation and the eschatological hope for final redemption, culminating in God's Sabbath-rest of eternal delight and consummation. It is highly promising that a growing number of theologians and religious

---

25. For medieval mystical reverence of nature, see Dreyer, "An Advent of the Spirit," 123–62.

26. So Hall, *Imaging God*, 48; Fisher, *Human Significance*, 37–40.

27. Cf. Wallace, "Crum Creek Spirituality," 121–37.

28. Materially similarly, Pannenberg, *Systematic Theology*, 137–38.

29. Bauckham, *Living with Other Creatures*, 13.

30. See further, Bauckham, *Bible and Ecology*.

communities are engaging the task of both theological reflection and eco-logically sustaining activities in pursuit of a similar kind of vision.

An ecological pneumatology:
the vulnerability and healing of creation

Rich pneumatological resources in service of environmental care are hidden in various mystical traditions of the Christian church. The mysti-cal vision intuits the link between the Holy Spirit and the flourishing of nature,[31] going back even to biblical traditions.[32] Just recall the medieval saint Hildegard of Bingen's metaphor of the "Greening of the Spirit"—which occasioned the title for this essay—St. Bernard of Clairvaux's sym-bol of the Spirit as the "living water,"[33] or Thomas Aquinas's poems of "Warming Fire" and "Light."[34] Theology that is still done mostly in the Global North has much to learn in this regard from her counterparts in the Global South. The Korean Methodist J. Y. Lee's distinctive pictures of the Spirit as "cloth" or "weaver" invoke images of protection and care,[35] which also supplements the predominantly masculine God language with female images of the Spirit.[36]

Named in the creed as *vivificantem* (the "vivifier" or life-giver), the Holy Spirit is not only the divine energy-information-life-force that brings about and sustains life, the Spirit is also the source of flourishing, thriving, prospering, blooming, blossoming.[37] Theologically speaking, the "Spirit is the ecstasy that implements God's abundance and triggers

---

31. For the importance of nature-based metaphors applied to the Spirit, see Fatula, *The Holy Spirit*, 2–3, and passim; see also Moltmann, *Spirit of Life*, chap. 12, for an extensive discussion of various nature metaphors for the Spirit.

32. For the beauty of the earth described through the sensibilities of the Spirit's presence on the Day of Pentecost, see Fatula, *Holy Spirit*, 33–34.

33. See Dreyer, "Advent of the Spirit," 123–62.

34. In Donahoe, *Early Christian Hymns*, 156–59.

35. Lee, *The Trinity in Asian Perspective*, 104; for other metaphors, see Kim, *The Holy Spirit in the World*, 181.

36. Boff, *Holy Trinity*, 92; Comblín, *The Holy Spirit and Liberation*, 49; Müller-Fahrenholz, *God's Spirit*, 26.

37. Johnson, *Women, Earth and Creator Spirit*, 42.

the overflow of divine self-giving,"[38] a gift of endless divine hospitality encompassing the whole "fellowship" of creation.[39]

Instead of invoking pantheistic, semi-pagan resources, increasingly utilized in many ecological and "Green" pneumatologies of nature, the moderate Catholic Feminist E. Johnson's *Women, Earth, and Creator Spirit* resonates well with a responsible panentheistic[40] Christian way of envisioning the role of the Spirit in the healing of the ecosystem:

> [T]the Spirit's encircling indwelling weaves a genuine solidarity among all creatures and between God and the world. . . . When things get broken, which can happen so easily, this divine creative power assumes the shape of a rejuvenating energy that renews the face of the earth (Ps 104:30). The damaged earth, violent and unjust social structures, the lonely and broken heart—all cry out for a fresh start. In the midst of this suffering the Creator Spirit, through the mediation of created powers, comes, as the Pentecost sequence sings, to wash what is unclean; to pour water upon what is drought-stricken; to heal what is hurt; to loosen up what is rigid; to warm what is freezing; to straighten out what is crooked and bent.[41]

With the eco-pneumatologist M. I. Wallace, I wish to:

> . . . retrieve a central but neglected Christian theme—the idea of God as carnal Spirit who imbues all things—as the linchpin for forging a green spirituality responsive to the environmental needs of our time." This gives "hope for a renewed earth . . . founded on belief in God as Earth Spirit, the compassionate, all-encompassing divine force within the biosphere who inhabits earth community and continually works to maintain the integrity of all forms of life.[42]

While Wallace himself develops that idea in a troublingly robust panentheistic manner, at times flirting with soft forms of pantheism, that doesn't have to be the case. The statement can be aligned with the deepest

---

38. Pinnock, *Flame of Love*, 49–50.

39. Johnson, *Women, Earth*, 44.

40. In my *Trinity and Revelation*, part 2, I develop and argue for "Classical Panentheism," a middle way between Classical Theism and more radical contemporary panentheistic versions.

41. Johnson, *Women, Earth*, 43. See also Daneel, "African Independent Church Pneumatology and the Salvation of All Creation," 143–66.

42. Wallace, *Fragments of the Spirit*, 7.

intuitions of classical Christian tradition in which the omnipresence of the almighty, transcendent God, is so deeply imbued with the created reality that there is no place to hide from the divine presence (Ps. 139). Differently from typical misunderstandings, "spirit" (*ruach*, *pneuma*) in the biblical understanding is not something opposed to "earthly" or "bodily," but rather the divine life-energy penetrating and permeating all created reality.[43] Importantly, the Bible uses metaphors of the Spirit that are taken from nature, such as the "animating breath," "the healing wind," "the living water," and "cleansing fire."[44] To speak of the "earthen spirit"[45] is not to undermine the divine uniqueness of the Spirit, but rather to speak of the divine infinity in which finite and infinite are both transcended and embraced simultaneously.

In green theology, the Holy Spirit can also be depicted in terms of the "Wounded Spirit."[46] Wallace points out: "If Spirit and earth mutually indwell each other, then God as Spirit is vulnerable to loss and destruction insofar as the earth is abused and despoiled."[47] This is all good and useful. Where some eco-theologies take a dangerous and mistaken course is in speaking of the co-suffering of the Triune God in terms of deicide, the "death of god." Although the rhetoric warning that "the specter of ecocide raises the risk of deicide"[48] is just that—*rhetoric*—behind it are highly problematic theological and scientific assumptions. In light of current cosmological knowledge, it does not make sense at all to make any kind of link between what happens in one tiny, little planet in the margins of one of the galaxies among billions of other galaxies and Almighty Creator! For the Creator of this vast universe, the implications of even the most dramatic nucleocatastrophe are nil! Theologically, after even thousands of qualifications, to imply that the Creator's own creation could be a threat to the Creator, in any sense of the word, is simply absurd. In order to maintain the theologically pregnant meaning of Triune God's

---

43. Moltmann, *Spirit of Life*, 225–26; see also p. 40.

44. Wallace, *Fragments of the Spirit*, 8; for other nature metaphors from the Bible, see Wallace, *Finding God in the Singing River*, 6–9.

45. For this term I am indebted to Wallace, "Christian Animism, Green Spirit Theology, and the Global Crisis Today," 203–6.

46. Wallace, "The Green Face of God," 450–53.

47. Ibid., 451.

48. Ibid., 452.

deep imbuement of the cosmos through and in the Spirit, this kind of suspicious rhetoric should be exposed and corrected.

In biblical traditions, the Spirit of God is not only messianic but also eschatological. The Spirit's presence points to the arrival of God's future, the promised shalom and Sabbath. To that we turn next.

The eschatological sabbath-rest: the jewish-christian vision of shalom

In the biblical testimony, God "completed" creative work on the day of Sabbath (Gen 2:2), having first judged everything "very good" (Gen 1:31). In this light it is highly curious that Christian tradition speaks of six days of creation as if the seventh day, Sabbath, were meaningless. As a result, "[t]he resting God, the celebrating God, the God who rejoices over his creation, receded into the background." And yet, according to the biblical and Jewish intuition, "it is only the Sabbath which completes and crowns creation."[49]

Sabbath is not only looking back, it is also an eschatological feast as it "opens creation for its true future. On the Sabbath the redemption of the world is celebrated in anticipation." The institution of the year of Jubilee (Lev 25:8–55) continues and expands the Sabbath's rest and *shalom*.[50] The Sabbath is itself the presence of eternity in time, and a foretaste of the world to come.[51] As such it anticipates the arrival of the final *shalom*, "the beginning of that peace with nature which many people are seeking today, in the face of the growing destruction of the environment."[52]

Sometimes it is surmised that the Christian eschatological hope would lead to the dismissal of hope for the rest of creation. This is not the case. The Cambridge philosopher-theologian Janet M. Soskice rightly notes that if "there is no hope of the triumph of God's justice on earth, no point in praying that God's kingdom will come and will be done on

---

49. Moltmann, *God in Creation*, 6, 276. For important reflections from a First Nations perspective, see Woodley, *Shalom and the Community of Creation*, particularly ch. 1.

50. The Jubilee also reminds us of the need to give rest to the fields and ground. A corollary lesson is the need to keep in mind economic and social justice when thinking of Shalom: while the pollution of nature is not solely the function of economic considerations, much of it is. See further Bergmann, *Creation Set Free*, particularly chap. 5.

51. Moltmann, *God in Creation*, 276.

52. Ibid., 277.

earth as it is in heaven."[53] That is because we will be "redeemed *with* the world, not *from* it."[54] It is rather Platonic dualism that has served as the source of Gnosticism, escapism, and political irresponsibility.[55] Those dualities[56] should be eliminated and corrected in light of the expectation of the coming of God's universal rule in the new creation. Rightly, the American philosopher Kevin Corcoran writes that "we human beings have been made from the mud and dirt—God-blessed, God-loved, and God-embraced mud and dirt—and made for life in an equally earthy environment."[57] God's kingdom includes this whole world inasmuch as "God's reconciling, redemptive, and restorative activity takes place within the natural, material world. This is the theater of God's redemptive activity, the theater of God's kingdom."[58]

It is of utmost importance that contemporary Christian theology include in its eschatological vision not only humanity's *shalom* but also all other creatures' flourishing and rest from sufferings. Let it suffice to refer to biblical key passages such as Romans 8:23–26, among others. That said, it is also important to add that the inclusion of all creatures and all creation under the grand eschatological vision does not mean virtually eliminating the distinctive nature of humanity created in God's image and the unique religious ends for men and women—as is the stated goal in some new animal theologies. David Slough's systematic theology *On Animals* oddly argues that no more than the particularity of the incarnation (Jesus as Jewish male) can be interpreted as excluding Gentiles and females does it exclude nonhuman creatures, animals, from "salvation."[59] Although this deeply flawed (albeit obviously well-meant) reasoning,

---

53. Sockice, "Resurrection and the New Jerusalem," 57.

54. Moltmann, *Spirit of Life*, 89; italics original.

55. Moltmann, *The Trinity and the Kingdom of God*, 89–90.

56. The discussion of "dualism" is often hampered by philosophically and historically inaccurate and misleading statements. A major theological study would be needed for a comprehensive picture.

57. Corcoran, "Thy Kingdom Come," 67.

58. Ibid.

59. Clough, *On Animals*, chap. 3. Even worse, he opines Christ's humanity does not really mean humanity but rather "created reality" (Kindle# 316–82). Furthermore, distancing himself from all contours of theological tradition, he surmises that the need for redemption of animals is based on their moral responsibility (#3953–3965, 4105), even sinfulness (#4115, 4165), although differently from humans (# 4153), and so forth.

should be rejected, its basic plea for making the Christian eschatological vision include all creation should be robustly supported.

In lieu of conclusions: some theological tasks for the future

"Green" theology should not be an optional task for the like-minded and interested but rather, as Moltmann rightly states it, Christian theology of creation should be thoroughly "ecological."[60] Indeed, all theologies of creation are ecological in the sense that even without acknowledging it, they guide the attitudes of the faithful—similarly to what can be said of the "political" nature of each ecclesiology (church members do something "political" even if they claim to be a-political!). As discussed above, it took Christian theology a long time to become consciously ecological, and at times its silence or uncritical alliance with non-Christian viewpoints made it anti-ecological.

A continuing dialogue with natural sciences is a necessary task and asset in this pursuit. Although theology should never be merely the recipient of science's ever-new insights—the dialogue is rather a two-way process in which both parties speak to and challenge each other—no credible theology of creation and ecology can be constructed currently without deep investigation of scientific resources.

Similarly, the current pluralistic and globalized world calls for a continuing hospitable dialogue among religions. As discussed briefly in the first section, sacred traditions have an integral relation to the environment. Although they differ quite radically in their environmental resources, challenges, and potential, they have much to learn from each other.

Finally, as a systematic and constructive theologian, I look forward to a long-term interdisciplinary dialogue and collaboration with other theologians in pursuit of a coherent, dynamic, and sensitive theology of the "Greening of the Spirit."

60. This is consistent theme in Moltmann, *God in Creation*.

BIBLIOGRAPHY

Bauckham, Richard. *Bible and Ecology: Rediscovering the Community of Creation*. Waco, TX: Baylor University Press, 2010.

———. *Living with Other Creatures: Green Exegesis and Theology*. Waco, TX: Baylor University Press, 2011.

Bergmann, Sigurd. *Creation Set Free: The Spirit as Liberator of Nature*. Grand Rapids: Eerdmans, 2005.

Boff, Leonardo. *Holy Trinity: Perfect Community*. Maryknoll, NY: Orbis, 2000.

Borgmann, Albert. *Power Failure: Christianity in the Culture of Technology*. London: SPCK, 1997.

Callicott, J. Baird, and Roger T. Ames, "Introduction: The Asian Traditions as Conceptual Resource for Environmental Philosophy." In *Nature in Asian Traditions of Thought: Essays in Environmental Philosophy*, edited by J. Baird Callicott and Roger T. Ames, 1–24. Albany: State University of New York Press, 1989.

Clark, Stephen R. L. *Biology and Christian Ethics*. Cambridge: Cambridge University Press, 2000.

Clifford, Anne M. "When Being Human Becomes Truly Earthly: An Ecofeminist Proposal for Solidarity." In *In the Embrace of God: Feminist Approaches to Theological Anthropology*, edited by Ann O'Hara Graff, 173–89. Maryknoll, NY: Orbis, 1995.

Clough, David L. *On Animals: Systematic Theology*. Vol. 1. Kindle edition, London: T. & T. Clark, 2012.

Comblín, José. *The Holy Spirit and Liberation*. Translated by Paul Burns. Maryknoll, NY: Orbis, 1989.

Corcoran, Kevin. "Thy Kingdom Come (On Earth): An Emerging Eschatology." In *Church in the Present Tense: A Candid Look at What's Emerging: Emergent Village Resources for Communities of Faith*, edited by Scot McKnight et al., 59–74. Grand Rapids: Brazos, 2011.

Daecke, S. M. "Profane and Sacramental Views of Nature." In *The Sciences and Theology in the Twentieth Century*, edited by A. R. Peacocke, 127–40. Notre Dame, IN: University of Notre Dame Press, 1981.

Daneel, M. L. "African Independent Church Pneumatology and the Salvation of All Creation." *International Review of Mission* 82, no. 326 (1993) 143–66.

Donahoe, Daniel Joseph. *Early Christian Hymns*. Series 2. Middletown, CT: Donahoe, 1911.

Dreyer, Elizabeth A. "An Advent of the Spirit: Medieval Mystics and Saints." In *Advents of the Spirit: An Introduction to the Current Study of Pneumatology*, edited by Bradford Hinze and Lyle Dabney, 123–65. Marquette, WI: Marquette University Press, 2001.

Eckel, Malcolm David. "Is There a Buddhist Philosophy of Nature?" In *Buddhism and Ecology: The Interconnection of Dharma and Deeds*, edited by Mary Evelyn Tucker and Duncan Ryūken Williams, 327–49. Cambridge, MA: Harvard University Press, 1997.

Fatula, Ann. *The Holy Spirit: Unbounded Gift of Joy*. Collegeville, MN: Liturgical, 1998.

Fisher, Christopher L. *Human Significance in Theology and the Natural Sciences: An Ecumenical Perspective with Reference to Pannenberg, Rahner, and Zizioulas*. Eugene, OR: Pickwick, 2010.

Foltz, Richard C. "Islamic Environmentalism: A Matter of Interpretation." In *Islam and Ecology: A Bestowed Trust*, edited by Richard C. Foltz, Frederick M. Denny, and Azizan Baharuddin, 249–79. Cambridge, MA: Harvard University Press, 2003.

Hall, Douglas John. *Imaging God: Dominion as Stewardship*. Grand Rapids: Eerdmans, 1986.

Hütterman, Aloys. *The Ecological Message of the Torah*. Atlanta: University of Southern Florida, 1999.

International Conference on Environmental Pollution and Remediation, July 15–17, 2013, Toronto, Canada, n.p., http://icepr2013.international-aset.com/index.html0.

Johnson, Elizabeth. *Women, Earth and Creator Spirit*. Mahwah, NJ: Paulist, 1993.

Katz, Eric. "Faith, God, and Nature: Judaism and Deep Ecology." In *Deep Ecology and World Religions*, edited by David Barnhill and Roger Gottlieb, 153–67. Albany: State University of New York Press, 2001.

Kerr, Fergus. *Immortal Longings: Versions of Transcending Humanity*. London: SPCK, 1997.

Kim, Kirsteen. *The Holy Spirit in the World: A Global Conversation*. Maryknoll, NY: Orbis, 2007.

Kärkkäinen, Veli-Matti. *Creation and Humanity: A Constructive Christian Theology for the Pluralistic World*. Vol. 3. Grand Rapids, Eerdmans, forthcoming.

———. *Trinity and Revelation: A Constructive Christian Theology for the Pluralistic World*. Grand Rapids: Eerdmans, 2014.

Lamm, Norman. "Ecology in Jewish Law and Theology." In *Faith and Doubt: Studies in Traditional Jewish Thought*, 160–83. New York: Krav, 1972.

Lee, Jung Young. *The Trinity in Asian Perspective*. Nashville: Abingdon, 1996.

McFague, Sallie. "An Ecological Christology: Does Christianity Have It?" In *Christianity and Ecology*, edited by Dieter Hessel and Rosemary Ruether, 29–45. Cambridge, MA: Harvard University Press, 2000.

Moltmann, Jürgen. *God in Creation: A New Theology of Creation and the Spirit of God*. Translated by Margaret Kohl. Minneapolis: Fortress, 1993.

———. *The Spirit of Life: A Universal Affirmation*. Translated by Margaret Kohl. Minneapolis: Fortress, 1992.

———. *The Trinity and the Kingdom of God: The Doctrine of God*. Translated by Margaret Kohl. San Francisco: Harper & Row, 1981.

———. *The Way of Jesus Christ: Christology in Messianic Dimensions*. Translated by Margaret Kohl. Minneapolis: Fortress, 1993.

Müller-Fahrenholz, Geiko. *God's Spirit: Transforming a World in Crisis*. New York: Continuum: WCC, 1995.

Pannenberg, Wolfhart. *Anthropology in Theological Perspective*. Translated by Matthew J. O'Connell. Philadelphia: Westminster, 1985.

———. *Systematic Theology*. Vol. 2. Translated by Geoffrey W. Bromiley. Grand Rapids: Eerdmans, 1994.

Pinnock, Clark H. *Flame of Love: A Theology of the Holy Spirit*. Downers Grove, IL: InterVarsity, 1996.

Phillips, Craig. "Green Creation: Comparative Ecological Theology in the Bible and Qur'ān." *Journal of Comparative Theology* 2, no. 1 (2011) 4–20.

Ruether, Rosemary Radford. *Gaia and God: An Ecofeminist Theology of Earth Healing* San Francisco: HarperCollins, 1992.

Snyder, Gary. *The Practice of the Wild*. San Francisco: North Point, 1990.

Sockice, Janet Martin. "Resurrection and the New Jerusalem." In *The Resurrection*, edited by Stephen T. Davis, Daniel Kendall, and Gerald O'Collins, 41–58. Oxford: Oxford University Press, 1997.

Starhawk. *Dreaming the Dark: Magix, Sex, and Politics*. Boston: Beacon, 1982.

———. *The Spiral Dance: A Rebirth of the Ancient Religion of the Great Goddess*. San Francisco: Harper & Row, 1979.

Sullivan, Lawrence E. "Preface." In *Hinduism and Ecology: The Intersection of Earth, Sky, and Water*, edited by Christopher Key Chapple and Mary Evelyn Tucker, 11–14. Cambridge, MA: Harvard University Press, 2000.

Thottakara, Augustine. "Ecology and World Religions." *Journal of Dharma* 26, no. 1 (2001) 9–120.

Tucker, Mary Evelyn, and John Grim. "Series Foreword." In *Hinduism and Ecology: The Intersection of Earth, Sky, and Water*, edited by Christopher Key Chapple and Mary Evelyn Tucker, 15–32. Cambridge, MA: Harvard University Press, 2000.

Wallace, Mark I. "Christian Animism, Green Spirit Theology, and the Global Crisis Today." In *Interdisciplinary and Religio-Cultural Discourses on a Spirit-Filled World: Loosing the Spirits*, edited by Veli-Matti Kärkkäinen, Kirsteen Kim, and Amos Yong, 197–212. New York: Palgrave Macmillan, 2013.

———. "Crum Creek Spirituality: Earth as a Living Sacrament." In *Theology That Matters: Ecology, Economy, and God*, edited by Darby Kathleen Ray, 121–37. Minneapolis: Fortress, 2006.

———. *Finding God in the Singing River*. Minneapolis: Fortress, 2005.

———. *Fragments of the Spirit: Nature, Violence, and the Renewal of Creation*. New York: Continuum, 1996.

———. "The Green Face of God: Recovering the Spirit in an Ecocidal Era." In *Advents of the Spirit: An Introduction to the Current Study of Pneumatology*, edited by Bradford Hinze and Lyle Dabney, 444–64. Marquette, WI: Marquette University Press, 2001.

Welker, Michael. *Creation and Reality*. Translated by John F. Hoffmeyer. Minneapolis: Fortress, 1999.

White, Lynn, Jr. "The Historical Roots of Our Ecological Crisis." *Science* 155, no. 3767 (1967) 1203–7. http://www.drexel.edu/~/media/Files/greatworks/pdf_fall09/HistoricalRoots_of_EcologicalCrisis.ashx.

Woodley, Randy S. *Shalom and the Community of Creation: An Indigenous Vision*. Grand Rapids: Eerdmans, 2012.

Zizioulas, John. "Preserving God's Creation: Three Lectures on Theology and Ecology: Lecture One." *King's Theological Review* 12, no. 1 (1989) 1–5.

6

Maximus the Confessor and a Deeper Actualization of the Apostolic Dimensions of Pentecostal Movements

Steve Overman

In his now famous and controversial 1967 lecture, "The Historical Roots of Our Ecologic Crisis," medieval historian and Presbyterian layman Lynn White, Jr. suggested that many of the unhealthy and unsustainable attitudes toward and treatment of nature found in modern times were to a great extent made possible by the dogmas of especially medieval and modern western Christianity. In contrast to older pagan systems, which viewed humankind as one part of a much larger and animated whole, from the perspective of these dogmas human beings could be seen as separate from and superior to nature and free to objectify and exploit it for their own ends.

In light of this, White challenged the churches to "rethink" how their faith might lead them to view their relationship with nature, calling them to move beyond exploitation, and even notions of "stewardship," to a deeper mutuality he termed "a spiritual democracy of all God's crea-tures." As possible alternative Christian resources for this reform, White called attention especially to St. Francis of Assisi, but also the more an-cient eastern Christian traditions.[1]

Meanwhile, in a recent contribution towards the construction of a distinctly Pentecostal ecotheology, A.J. Swoboda has argued that in order to recapture its original vitality, to discover within itself its latent vision for enriched relationship with the creation, and to in general more faithfully fulfill its calling in our time, Pentecostalism must enlarge and extend some of its rich core concepts such as Spirit-baptism, Charismatic Community, Holistic Spirit, and Eschatological Mission. He goes on to suggest that Pentecostals will be aided in this important task of enlarge-ment and extension by engaging with other, non-Pentecostal communi-ties, including the witness of the early eastern churches.[2]

Taking up these cues, I propose to explore one expression of this more ancient and eastern tradition, as found in the cosmic vision of Maximus the Confessor. After a brief sketch of his life and times and his relationship to the larger orthodox tradition I will attempt to lay out some of the chief features of both his theological and cosmological framework and his ascetic way of practice in community. I will conclude by sug-gesting that both this framework and way of practice can indeed help resource healing of humankind's relationship with one another and the other realms of the creation and that an appropriation of aspects of this stream of the Christian tradition in the coming decades can help global Pentecostal movements influence societies toward greater social and eco-logical health.[3]

1. White, "Historical Roots." See also Riley, "A Spiritual Democracy of All God's Creatures," who interprets White's thesis from within the context of his larger body of writings.

2. Swoboda, *Tongues and Trees*. Others have likewise encouraged Pentecostal engagement with the eastern traditions, notably E. Rybarczyk and C. M. Robeck in Rybarczyk, *Beyond Salvation*.

3. As many have pointed out, since the eco-crisis is an extension of the general relational and social crisis, the former cannot be addressed apart from the latter. See for example Brown, *Ethos of the Cosmos*, 25–27.

Life, times and tradition

Maximus the Confessor (580–662 C.E.) was apparently born in Constantinople, where he received a classical education. At the age of thirty he became the proto-secretary of the Emperor Heraclius but after three years resigned his post to enter monastic life, which he pursued first in the nearby monastery of Chrysopolis, then later for a short time in Cyzicus and finally in Carthage (modern day Tunis) where he stayed for fifteen years.

With an empire threatened by Persian and later Islamic Arab incursions from without, and weakened within by still remaining divisions among the Christian churches over whether to speak about Christ as having one or two natures, various emperors proposed compromise formulas, attempting to unite the churches. The last one of these compromise formulas proposed that the churches speak of Christ as having two natures, but operative in only one energy (Monergenism) and one will (Monothelytism).[4] But in Maximus' mind, and in the minds of others, including the bishop of Rome, the principles of the Council of Chalcedon (451), with its characteristic affirmation of a hypostatic consubstantiality "without confusion (*asynchytos*), without change (*atreptos*), without division (*adiaretos*), and without separation (*achoristos*)," and the teachings of the Fathers sought to establish two distinct and actual natures in an ineffable union. And since natures have energies and wills, to say there was only one energy or will in Christ was to destroy the integrity of the natures.

The enforced imperial assertion temporarily had its way. Unable to assent either to the doctrine or to the right of the emperor to impose it on the churches, ultimately the elder monk had his tongue cut out and his right hand cut off. He died soon thereafter in exile at the age of 82. A mere twenty years later the doctrine that Christ had two wills—a divine will and a human will, in an ineffable, hypostatic union—was affirmed at the Sixth Ecumenical Council of Constantinople of 680. Widely considered to be the father of Byzantine Christianity, the Confessor is one of a small group of saints who belong equally to the spirituality of both the Eastern and Western traditions.[5]

Andrew Louth rightly states that for Maximus the orthodox tradition could be summarized as Scripture (absolutely primary), Fathers,

4. The *Ecthesis* of 638.
5. Jaroslav Pelikan, in Berthold, *Maximus*, 1.

Councils, Saints, and Sacraments.[6] In addition to the work of the Ecumenical Councils, some of the more prominent streams of the tradition feeding into Maximus' synthesis include: The monastic tradition, especially Evagrius, but also the Desert Fathers, the Macarian Homilies and Diodochus of Photike; Origen; the Cappadocian fathers, especially Gregory of Nazianzus, "The Theologian"; The Alexandrian Christological tradition of Athanasius and Cyril; Pseudo Dionysius; and the post Chalcedonian Christology of Leontius and Justinian.[7]

Maximus has left a large body of writings, including works on monastic spirituality such as *The Ascetic Life* (AL), the four *Centuries on Love* (CC), and the two *Centuries on Theology and the Incarnate Dispensation of the Son of God* (CT), treatments of difficult interpretations of theology, including the *Ambigua* (Ambig.), commentaries on *The Lord's Prayer* (LP) and the *Mystagogia* of the church (Myst.), and of course, epistles (Ep.)

Since these writings are for the most part in response to specific occasional requests or issues and even more because his entire thought-world is so beautifully and co-inherently interwoven and *symphonic*, it is difficult to excise pieces of it. In addition, the dense richness and complex distinctions in the material makes for quite a bit of important detail. Nevertheless, for our purposes we can attempt to highlight a few of its main features.

Theological and cosmological framework

Union and distinction

Historically Maximus has been most well known for developing from the tradition a rich and mature Christology which is at once breathtakingly cosmic in scope and minutely coherent in detail. But as Hans Urs von Balthasar and others since him have observed, in addition to articulating the characteristic details of his Cyrilline Chalcedonianism he also takes those characteristics and turns them into metaphysical and ontological principles which he sees operative in all dimensions

---

6. Louth, *Maximus*, 22.

7. Maximus also utilizes certain philosophic tools, listed in Toronen, *Union and Distinction*, 17–34. Tollefsen, *Christocentric Cosmology*, 10–13 clarifies that Maximus probably knows these concepts in their original contexts, but utilizes them as they are employed in their "Christianized" form in the Fathers.

of creation and redemption, something Balthasar has called Maximus'
"Chalcedonian logic."[8]

To illustrate how Maximus takes this "Chalcedonian logic" and expands it into a "fundamental law of metaphysics," "which discovers the formal structure of all created being," Balthasar quotes two stunningly panoramic passages from the *Mystagogia*, where Maximus is showing how the Church reflects the mysterious structure of the universe. Here is the first:

> God created all things with his limitless power, brought them into being, holds them there and gathers them together and sets boundaries to them; in his providence, he links them all- intellectual beings as well as sensible- to each other as he does to himself. In his might, God draws up all things that are naturally distinct from each other and binds them to himself as their cause, their origin and goal; and through the power of this relationship to him as source, he lets them also be drawn toward each other. This is the power through which every being is brought to its own indestructible, unconfused identity, both in activity and in being. No being can permanently isolate itself through its own particularity or through the drive of its nature toward some other end; rather, everything remains, in its very being, bound and without confusion to everything else through the single, enduring relationship of all to their one and only source. This supreme power overshadows the individual relationships that are to be seen in every individual nature, not in a way that corrupts or eradicates or terminates them, but in order to dominate and illuminate them as the whole does its parts –or, better, in order to reveal itself also as the cause of whole things, thanks to which both the whole and the parts of the whole are revealed and come to be, while the power itself remains the radi- ant cause of them all. Just as the sun outshines the reality and the luminous activity of the stars, so the ultimate ground of being conceals the being of creatures: for as the parts come to be from the whole, so created beings come to be from their cause and are recognized in its light, and if they are totally possessed by their movement toward this cause, through the power of the relation- ship itself, then they tend to cease from their own individual being. For God, who is 'all in all' and infinitely exalted over all, is recognized by the pure of heart as the sole ultimate One, at

---

8. Balthasar, *Cosmic Liturgy*, 65–70. Cf. Louth, *Maximus*, 50–51.

the moment when their minds gather the intelligible meanings (*logoi*) of all things together in contemplation, and grow quiet before God as the beginning and cause and end of the world's being, the undivided root and ground that embraces all things. In this same way, the holy Church of God, made in God's image, reveals the same mystery to us and brings it to reality.[9]

Melchisedec Toronen has rightly pointed out that this extended "logic," found in so many passages throughout the Maximian corpus, rests not only on the Chalcedonian Definition, but finds its grounding also in the broader and earlier tradition of a more general simultaneous union and distinction. As a result we indeed find this principle or "rule" of simultaneous and extreme and radical union without confusion and distinction without separation running through virtually every area of Maximus' thought, including his conception of Trinity, Incarnation, Creation, Scripture and Church and the rich, mutual, dynamic coinherence of the elements of the ascetic practice.[10]

It is important to note that while Maximus will use concepts and terms such as "union without confusion" or "distinction without separation" in speaking about God and Christ, he also emphasized as much as any other eastern father that while we can use such terms or concepts, at the same time we must insist God is also utterly beyond any thought, conception, or human category, i.e. an apophatic principle.[11]

The doctrine of the logoi

In keeping with the tradition, Maximus is careful to maintain a distinction between the nature of the uncreated and the created. At the same time, through the presence of the Divine Logos in the *logoi* of each created entity the Divine beautifully and powerfully interpenetrates all of creation.[12] Pre-existing as potentialities of divine intentions in God but

---

9. *Myst.* I, PG 91:664D–665C (trans. Balthasar, *Cosmic Liturgy*, 68–69).

10. Toronen, *Union and Distinction*, 47–52. Similarly Thunberg, *Microcosm*, 427 finds "unity in differentiation" to be "the working idea of this thought."

11. In relation to the Divine, Maximus will use these kinds of terms "in a manner of speaking." See Toronen, *Union and Distinction*, 51. See also Balthasar, *Cosmic Liturgy*, 81–97.

12. Maximus's most striking development of the doctrine of the logoi appears in *Ambig.* 7, 1077C–80D, found in Blowers and Wilken, *Cosmic Mystery*, 54–58. On the doctrine of the logoi in Maximus see Tollefsen, *Christocentric Cosmology*. For a concise tracing of the evolution of the doctrine from Plato to Maximus see Bradshaw, "The

brought into being at the appropriate time by the Creator, the *logoi* then are particular expressions of the Divine Logos variously embodied within each entity of the creation. Every creature has its particular *logos* of being, its fundamental character and purpose. Creatures of all kinds, human beings, animals, insects, plants, minerals and so forth, even entities such as the commandments, the Scriptures or the virtues, have not only a presenting surface but also an underlying *logoi* of being which comprises its true nature, principle and meaning.[13]

Subsisting as the parts of the whole, the *logoi* are not only held together in God but are also oriented toward God, so that when we perceive and encounter not just the presenting surface of another entity but its true *logoi*, we are drawn toward God, in whom we find ourselves and experience more deeply our true unity with one another.

The role of humankind

Drawing especially on the writings of Gregory of Nyssa and Pseudo-Dionysius, and employing one of his characteristic phrases alluding to the tradition, in *Ambigua 41* Maximus asserts that, "they say the substance of everything is divided into five (natural) divisions," which he articulates as created and uncreated, rational and sensible, heaven and earth, paradise and the inhabited world (*oikoumene*) and male and female.[14] The human being, as a sort of microcosm, has a touch or place in each of the sides in each division: It is both male and female; it experiences the spiritual paradise but lives in the society of the inhabited world; it has a touch with and is destined for heaven while living on the earth; it is a composite of both rational and sensible; and though it is a creature, it is created in the image and likeness of the uncreated and through grace and participation may become completely whatever God is, save at the level of being.[15]

Logoi of Beings," 9–17.

13. Tollefsen, *Christocentric Cosmology*, 228.

14. *Ambig.* 41, 1304D–5A; Louth, *Maximus*, 156–57.

15. The God-given task of mediation by various means works its way back through the divisions until, "finally, beyond all these, the human person unites the created nature with the uncreated through love (O the wonder of God's love for us human beings!) showing them to be one and the same through the possession of grace, the whole wholly interpenetrated (perichoresas) by God, and become completely whatever God is save at the level of being and acquire as a kind of prize for its ascent to God the most unique God himself, as the end of movement of everything that moves toward it, and the firm unmoved rest of everything that is carried towards it, being the undetermined

God did this, Maximus suggests, so that humankind could work as an integrator or unifier. From this "middle place" humankind could use its natural powers to work to prevent natural distinctions from becoming separations. And when unnatural separations occur, it could work to bridge, reconcile, and heal them. [16]

The fall

But humankind was deceived into thinking that it could find fulfillment in sensory experiences alone. Instead of moving toward God, to whom it is naturally oriented and upon whom it is dependent, humankind moved unnaturally toward lower things, things less stable than itself, and crossed natural boundaries or limitations.

As a result humankind's perception became distorted and its natural drives disintegrated and it was not able to effectively play its God given part. Instead of unifying things that have become separated, humanity misuses its natural powers to separate that which is united. And because of humankind's intimate relationship with all the other realms of the creation they are affected as well. [17]

In Epistle 2 Maximus explains that in moving away from God and crossing natural boundaries, humankind "has brought into being from itself the three greatest, primordial evils, and (to speak simply) the begetters of all vice": "Ignorance", which means primarily ignorance of the Cause of all things; "Self-love" (*philautia*); and "tyranny", by which he means sometimes the tyranny now exercised over the minds and emotions of human beings by our own disordered desires, fragmented thoughts (*logismoi*) or disordered demonic forces and other times the tyranny we then impose on our sisters and brothers, our "kin". "For by the misuse of our own powers –reason, desire and incensive power – these evils are established."[18]

---

and infinite limit and definition of every definition and law and ordinance, of reason and mind and nature." *Ambig.* 41, 1308B; Louth, *Maximus*, 158.

16. As Maximus describes them, each one of the mediations or integrations is complex but extremely important for the healthy functioning of the interpenetrated and co-creative cosmos. For a fuller explication of the means of these mediations, beginning with the mediation of male and female in its true logoi of "bare" humanity, see Thunberg, *Microcosm*, 373–426.

17. At least since Athanasius, the east has understood the Fall and the redemption not only as anthropological but also cosmic events. See Louth, "Man and Cosmos," 68.

18. *Ep.* 2 PG 91:396D–97A (trans. Louth, *Maximus*, 87).

Of these three, which depend upon and sustain one another, the most central is *philautia*. In contrast to a healthy love of self, which Maximus calls a "spiritual" (*noera*) love, a love of the mind when it is attached to the divine, as "the mother of all (disordered) passions" and "the mother of all vices", *philautia* is a disintegrated, overly self-focused and ultimately destructive orientation, the general attitude which spawns all other disordered expressions. Because of this fundamental preoccupation we are unable to perceive the universe and other entities as they truly are, seeing things mostly or even only from our own individual perspective. In addition, this fundamental, disintegrating overly inward turn catalyzes a disordering of the soul, shattering our natural passion into divisive and destructive forces.

For Maximus the Fall does not directly affect the inviolate *logos* of humankind or any other realms of the creation, but their particular *tropos*, their mode of existence, or how we express that true nature. As Louth explains, it is "not that the natures are distorted in themselves, but rather that the natures are misused . . . In a fallen world the *logoi* of everything natural remains inviolate, but natures may act in a way (or mode, *tropos*) that runs counter to their fundamental *logoi*" [19] Nevertheless, as a result of this unnatural downward movement humankind became distorted in its perception and tyrannized by its now disordered desires. Unable to recognize the universe as it really is, and less able to govern its own integrated body-soul composite, it is unfulfilled and unable to perform its unifying role in the universe.[20] Additionally, because as a created being it is not self-moved, it is unable to achieve its reorientation on its own.

The incarnation

It is important to understand and remember that for Maximus, ascetic practice is never an entirely self-generated or self-empowered pursuit but an ongoing graced response to and partnership with God's love, manifest through the creation, through the revelation in the Scriptures and preeminently in the Incarnation of the Divine Logos, and experienced through the liturgy and sacraments of the community. Far from being a mere reaction to the fissure produced by humankind's downward move-

19. Louth, *Maximus*, 57–58.

20. One of the things Maximus will say about evil is that it is what results when natural human capacities are either unfulfilled or misused. See Thunberg, *Microcosm*, 155.

ment in the Garden, the Incarnation has existed before the foundations of the world as an expression of the Mystery of the universe. Nevertheless through its manifestation, the unmoved Logos has accomplished for humanity and the creation what it could not accomplish for itself. By taking humanity and all of creation into himself, and divinely living a truly human life, Christ recapitulated or "reinstituted" the natures and performed the initial mediations of the divisions humankind was unable to perform:

> Through himself he has, in accordance with nature, united the fragments of the universal nature of the all, manifesting the universal *logoi* that have come forth for the particulars, by which the union of the divided naturally comes about, and thus he fulfills the great purpose of God the Father, to 'recapitulate everything both in heaven and earth in himself' (Eph.1:10) . . . Thus he divinely recapitulates the universe in himself, showing that the whole creation exists as one, like another human being, completed by the gathering together of its parts one with another in itself and inclined towards itself by the whole of its existence . . ."[21]

As a result humankind can now be reconciled to its true nature and return from creating separation and division to working to complete and preserve the unity of created things. The free gift of "adoption by grace" is received through the foundation of baptism.[22] But in order to fully participate in that true nature and purpose the soul must journey out of its distortion, into clarity, and its ultimate fulfillment of transfigured deification in God.

Ascetic practice in community

If human beings were able to clearly perceive not only the presenting surface of Scripture, the virtues, other human beings and entities, but more importantly their true essence and meaning, and were able to understand and manage themselves, they would be better able to see their own true role in the larger whole, to enjoy its beauty and goodness and to relate to and partner with the other entities to preserve and heal the co-creativity of the unified cosmos. As it is, given the state of the planet, there is a manifest need to recover some of the ancient ascetic understandings and practices.

21. *Ambig.* 41, PG 91:1308D; 1312AB (trans. Louth, *Maximus*, 159,160).
22. *CT* 1.87.

Maximus was, after all, a monk, and the monastic ascetical and liturgical tradition he inherited, which was developed over many years, took seriously the limitations and maladies which hinder people from reforming their *tropos,* and the means through which this reform can take place.[23]

Three-stage spiritual development

Maximus received, further developed and utilized a three stage model with which to conceive of the journey to spiritual recovery.[24] In the first stage, typically referred to as *praktike or praxis,* the goal is to overcome the tyranny of the passions and reintegrate them until the soul achieves a state of detachment from disordered drivenness, a stability or equilibrium known as *apatheia.*[25] This is achieved through following the commandments and practicing the virtues, including faith, fear of God, humility, considered to be a foundation, meekness, self-mastery, hope, gentleness, mercy, longsuffering, joy, peacefulness, and above all, love, which is also more than a virtue. This enables the soul to move into the second stage of contemplation of nature (*physike theoria*) and finally that of *theologike mystike,* a mystical knowledge beyond knowing, where the soul is deified in love.[26]

As a person becomes purified and freed from the passions they begin to become able to perceive not just the surface presentation of other people, beings and things but their true essence and meaning (*logoi*). Since these *logoi* are not only held together in God but also oriented toward God, the person is through these deep seated realizations and encounters drawn up toward and finally into God, in whom all of creation experiences the true unity of our being, and a deified transfiguration which restores a radiant transparency to personal and cosmic life. But the movement is not only upward, because once the movement toward the center of the radii has occurred and ineffable union is realized, there then

23. "His whole system," remarks Polycarp Sherwood, "is ascetical and mystical." *The Ascetic Life,* 28.

24. This description follows Thunberg, *Microcosm,* 335–37.

25. Maximus characterizes apatheia as "a peaceful state of the soul in which it becomes resistant to vice." *CC* I.35 Though often understood only in its negative sense of "detachment," it also then has the positive sense of serenity, stability, or even integrated passion, apropos of which Louth quotes Diodochus's striking phrase "the fire of apatheia." Louth, *Maximus,* 42.

26. For examples, see in Berthold, trans., Maximus, *CC* I.86; *CT* II.8; 1.37–39; I.51–56.

can also occur outward or downward movement which can serve in other places to heal and preserve the dynamic, life giving and co-creating unity.

Predictably for Maximus these three stages are not traveled upon strictly one after the other in a purely linear fashion. Rather they are to be conceived of not only as movement toward a destination but also as an ongoing spiraling dynamic.[27]

Liturgical and sacramental community

Notwithstanding the role of solitude in healthy human life, or extreme callings on particular people, the reintegration of human and extra human life is worked out not in individual isolation but also within the rhythms and rituals of the community. The "agents of deification" then, to use Sherwood's phrase, include not only the virtues and commandments and intentional disciplines such as prayer, fasting, watches, Scripture reading, meditation, "sleeping on the ground," and so forth, but also (experiential) participation in the liturgy and sacraments.

It is not surprising that the two texts where Maximus discusses at length his understanding of Monad and Triad, in *On the Lord's Prayer* and in *Mystagogia* 23, both occur in the context of liturgical worship, for it is in worship that we experience a mystical knowing-beyond-knowledge of God, and therefore a fundamental (re)orientation to reality and our place in it. For example, Maximus says that when we confess the Trinitarian symbol or express worship toward the Triune God, because the symbol of union and distinction is the mysterious key to the universe, this intuited reality is communicated to us, imprinting itself in us, and we are shaped by it into its likeness.[28] And because of humanity's intimate connection with the other realms of the creation our personal and communal journey of purification unto transfigured deification affects the entire cosmos, causing our worship to become a "cosmic liturgy." This is not only because the rhythms and rituals present to us, draw us into, and create within us the very fabric of the universe but also because in participating in them we somehow, through our connection with it, help restore the fragmented cosmos. Humanity gathers up, says Maximus, the spiritual *logoi* of things as creation's gifts to honor God, intimating a

---

27. Thunberg, *Microcosm*, 432.

28. *Myst.* 23 (trans. Berthold, *Maximus*, 204–6); cf. *Ambig.* 10 PG 91:1193D, 1196AB (trans. Louth, *Maximus*, 145–46).

deeply discerning and prayerful posture Andre Louf has termed a kind of "ecological priesthood."[29]

Deification in love

Reading through *The Ascetic Life*, the *Centuries on Love* or the *Centuries on Knowledge*, one is struck by the complex and nuanced interweaving of an understanding of the human soul, the relationships between the various vices and how particular virtues combat and overcome them, and the generally nuanced and personalized nature of the monastic ascetical wisdom. The material is not naïve, but cuts deeply into the subtle hypocrisy which can, unbeknownst to them, lodge within monks, bishops, emperors, and lay people alike, though perhaps sometimes in different ways. There is material on holy relationship with and use of money ("The one who loves God surely loves his neighbor as well. Such a person cannot hold on to money but rather gives it out in God's fashion to each who has need." CC 1.23).[30] We find in these collections of monastic wisdom encouragements to eat and live simply, to not "misuse God's creatures for the service of your own passions," to take only what you need and to not abuse others but to treat them as a friend, loving as God does all others equally.[31]

And this is a particular, even crowning emphasis in Maximus. For whereas Evagrius conceives of the last stage of spiritual development as finally moving beyond the material into a state of mystical "pure mind," for Maximus deification is synonymous with love, even as God is love (1 Jn. 4:7-8).[32] As the fulfillment of the commandments and sum of the virtues and all good things, true love is one love, God's, and an equal love which "does not know 'mine and thine.'"[33] Toronen concludes, "Love, finally, draws everything into unity without violating the integrity of the particular. This is love which deifies, love which unites us one with an-

29. Louf, "Prayer and Ecology," 126.

30. Berthold, *Maximus*, 37.

31. CT 2.41 (trans. ibid., 136).

32. "In fact, the most perfect work of charity and the end of its activity is to allow, through reciprocal attribution (i.e. communicatio), the individual characteristics (idiomata) of those who are bound together by it, as well their names, to become mutually useful, so that man is made god and God is called and appears as man." *Ep.* 2 PG 91:401B (trans. Thunberg, *Microcosm*, 432).

33. *Ep.* 2 PG 91:404D–5A, trans. Louth, *Maximus*, 91–92.

other, love which unites us with God, which *is* God and makes us gods, or better said: it is God who is love which unites us with himself without confusion, and which through us unites us one with another and with the whole world in a simultaneous union and distinction."[34]

But would Maximus extend this vision of love in union and distinction to our thoughts about and treatment of extra human being and ecosystems? Of course we don't know. But his most immediate heirs, the Orthodox churches, certainly see the intentions of this vision naturally trajecting to address aspects of our present ecological crisis.[35] Torstein Tollefsen, for example, suggests that given the tradition as explicated by Maximus and others, from the Orthodox point of view, "man should live in accordance with his *logos*, and actualize friendship, harmony and love among natural beings."[36]

Evaluation

The system is not perfect. But it seems to me, as White had suspected, this more ancient and eastern expression of the Christian tradition does offer significant resources for an alternative perspective to the objectification and exploitation about which he was concerned, in some ways even pointing towards the deeper mutuality for which he called.

Its radically relational theological and cosmological framework has the capacity to remind us of and possibly reorient us toward our profound interconnection and interdependence, first of all with God, but then also with one another and the other realms of the creation. The conception of the universe as comprised of entities in simultaneous union without confusion and distinction without separation calls for a protection of the integrity of beings and systems, including for example biodiversity. The re-enchantment or even re-sacralization of matter and nature through the doctrine of the *logoi* with its call to see beneath mere utilitarian objectification has the potential to redeem and enrich human and extra human relationships, restoring an appropriate humility, respect, and care.

---

34. Toronen, *Union and Distinction*, 198.

35. For examples of Orthodox Ecotheology, see Chryssavgis and Foltz, *Toward an Ecology of Transfiguration*; Chrysavvgis, in his *Cosmic Grace, Humble Prayer*, asserts, "The truth is that we respond to nature with the same delicacy, the same sensitivity, the same tenderness with which we respond to a human person in a relationship" (25).

36. Tollefsen, "Ethical Consequences," 399.

And the tradition's insistence on an apophatic dimension is not only consistent with our ongoing exploration and discovery of the universe but also works to rightfully restrain presumptuous tendencies and the temptation to overreach.

Likewise it seems to me the ancient grace-empowered ascetic practice in community, with its fundamental orientation toward repentance, purification and restoration, contains rich resources for the healing of social and ecological relationships, and in a great many specific ways. For example, the monastic and liturgical vision as understood and practiced by Maximus possesses and develops an acute sense of the global, even cosmic power of personal, local acts. Could it be that our intuition to make personal, local acts which affect global systems, which seems to be corroborated by an analysis of global economic systems, also be supported by the tradition? Since the practical systems for discernment, deliverance, and restoration of the soul exhibit nuance and make great allowance for the difference in particular people, and since Maximus himself, especially in his later writings, uses the categories of the "science" of his day,[37] the ancient paradigm would not discourage further discovery of creation through natural science or the use of insights from social science for our recovery.

Conclusion

As a philosopher of the ancient east who arguably carries within himself much of the mature fruit of the early eastern Christian tradition and of classical Hellenistic culture, as a truly global, ecumenical person on so many levels, who lived in a time of tectonic global transition, it seems the vision of Maximus the Confessor can serve in general as a resource for societal recovery from some of the excesses and weaknesses of modernism.

But what about Pentecostals? Does this brief and initial exploration of one example of the earlier, eastern way show promise as an aid to an appropriate enlargement and extension of Pentecostal core concepts to serve the development of a Pentecostal ecotheology? While a detailed look at how facets of this eastern tradition might be able to inform each of Swoboda's four proposed enlarged categories—"Spirit Baptized Creation," "Charismatic Community of Creation," "Holistic Spirit of Creation," and

37. "Maximus, like the other Fathers of the Church, took for granted the scientific wisdom of his day and readily made use of it." Louth, "Man and Cosmos," 59.

"Spirit of Eschatological Ecological Mission"—is not possible in this space, I think we can provisionally answer in the affirmative. It seems for example Swoboda's claim that, "Spirit baptized people are aware of a deeper presence in all entities," can be buttressed, enlarged, and enriched through the eastern witness to the presence of the *logoi* in all entities of the creation.[38]

In addition, with respect to the general Pentecostal contribution to a healing of our social and ecological crises, we can imagine that the Pentecostal intuition of a more holistic or "full" gospel can likewise be buttressed and enlarged through the eastern witness to the fall and re-demption as not just personal but cosmic realities, which would include the creation. Pentecostal efforts to help humanity recover from its lostness and brokenness through finding an experiential knowledge of the Lord and personal transformation can also expand through the rich resources of the eastern tradition's witness to mystical knowledge of God unto dei-fication. And Pentecostal spiritual practices, such as prayer and fasting, and work with spirit deliverance and healing of the soul can be further enriched by the accumulated wisdom of the eastern monastic practice.

It's true that original Pentecostal visions of a restoration of "Apostolic" unity had decidedly primitivistic connotations. And through their history Pentecostals have exhibited ambivalence toward tradition.[39] But recently Pentecostals have begun to intentionally engage with the more historic and "apostolic" traditions, including those of the east.[40]

In his groundbreaking comparison of Pentecostal and early Orthodox approaches to becoming like Christ, Ed Rybarczyk helpfully points out that many of what appear to be great differences between the two traditions are a result of their very different "meta-contexts."[41] But especially when taking these different contexts into account, with their more holistic gospels, emphasis on experience and the power of worship, embrace of supra-rational and mystical dimensions, and concern with transformation unto holiness, the Pentecostal churches exhibit significant

---

38. Swoboda, *Tongues and Trees*, 201.

39. On this, see Friesen, "Pentecostal Antitraditionalism."

40. As examples of recent Pentecostal engagement with the eastern traditions, see Rybarczyk, *Beyond Salvation*; and Kärkkäinen, "Ecumenical Potential." For a Pentecostal ecumenical engagement with the early church Fathers, see *On Becoming a Christian: Final Report of the Fifth Phase of the International Catholic–Pentecostal Dialogue*.

41. Rybarczyk, *Beyond Salvation*, 324–26.

affinities with the ancient churches of the east. Rybarczyk notes that many of these shared visions came into Pentecostalism via the holiness movements, through the "sieve" of John Wesley, who according to Rybarczyk not only knew, but preferred the eastern Fathers to those of the west.[42]

As one of the fastest growing religious movements in the world, and especially the majority world, Pentecostalism is in a position over the next several decades to help influence the way societies think about and relate to one another and the natural world. Perhaps these more ancient and eastern traditions, as expressed here in the cosmic vision of Maximus the Confessor, in this increasingly global era, could serve as an additional resource for a more faithful fulfillment of that role. As such, it might represent a timely, deeper actualization of the "Apostolic" dimensions of Pentecostal movements.

BIBLIOGRAPHY

Balthasar, Hans Urs von. *Cosmic Liturgy: The Universe According to Maximus the Confessor.* Translated by Brian E. Daley. San Francisco: Ignatius, 2003.

Berthold, George C., trans. *Maximus Confessor: Selected Writings.* New York: Paulist, 1985.

Blowers, Paul M., and R. M. Wilken, trans. *On the Cosmic Mystery of St. Maximus the Confessor: Selected Writings.* Crestwood, NY: St. Vladimir's Seminary Press, 2003.

Bordeianu, Radu. "Maximus and Ecology: The Relevance of Maximus the Confessor's Theology of Creation for the Present Ecological Crisis." *Downside Review* 127, no. 447 (2009) 103–26.

Bradshaw, David. "The Logos of Being in Greek Patristic Thought." In *Toward An Ecology of Transfiguration: Orthodox Christian Perspectives on Environment, Nature, and Creation,* edited by John Chryssavgis and Bruce V. Foltz, 9–22. New York: Fordham University Press, 2013.

Brown, William P. *The Ethos of the Cosmos: The Genesis of Moral Imagination in the Bible.* Grand Rapids: Eerdmans, 1999.

Chryssavgis, John. *Cosmic Grace and Humble Prayer: The Ecological Vision of the Green Patriarch Bartholomew.* Rev. ed. Grand Rapids: Eerdmans, 2009.

Friesen, Aaron. "Pentecostal Antitraditionalism and the Pursuit of Holiness: The Neglected Role of Tradition in Pentecostal Theological Reflection." Paper Presented at the 42nd Annual Meeting of the Society for Pentecostal Studies.

Kärkkäinen, Veli-Matti. "The Ecumenical Potential of Theosis: Emerging Convergence Between Eastern Orthodox, Protestant, and Pentecostal Soteriologies." *Sobornost/ Easter Churches Review* 23, no. 2 (2002) 45–77.

42. Ibid., 10.

Louf, Andre. "Prayer and Ecology." *The Way* 45, no. 4 (2006) 119–36.

Louth, Andrew. "Man and Cosmos in Maximus the Confessor." In *Toward An Ecology of Transfiguration: Orthodox Christian Perspectives on Environment, Nature, and Creation*, edited by J. Chryssavgis and B. Foltz, 59–74. New York: Fordham University Press, 2013.

———. *Maximus the Confessor*. London: Routledge, 1996.

On Becoming a Christian: Insights from Scripture and the Patristic Writings with Some Contemporary Reflection. Report of the Fifth Phase of the International Dialogue Between Some Classical Pentecostal Churches and Leaders and the Catholic Church (1998–2006). 2009, *Information Service* 127 (III): 164–215. The report may be viewed online at www.prounione.urbe.it/dia-int/pe-rc/doc/e_pe-rc5-contents.html.

Riley, Matthew T. "A Spiritual Democracy of All God's Creatures: Eco-theology and Lynn White's Animals." In *Divinanimality: Animal Theory, Creaturely Theology*, edited by Stephen D. Moore. New York: Fordham University Press, forthcoming.

Rybarczyk, E. J. *Beyond Salvation: Eastern Orthodoxy and Classical Pentecostalism on Becoming Like Christ*. Waynesboro, GA: Paternoster, 2004.

Sherwood, Polycarp, trans. *Maximus the Confessor: The Ascetic Life, The Four Centuries on Charity*. Ancient Christian Writers 21. New York: Newman, 1955.

Swoboda, A. J. *Tongues and Trees: Toward a Pentecostal Ecological Theology*. Journal of Pentecostal Theology Supplement 40. Blandford Forum, UK: Deo, 2013.

Thunberg, Lars. *Microcosm and Mediator: The Theological Anthropology of Maximus The Confessor*. 2nd ed. Chicago: Open Court, 1995.

Tollefsen, Torstein. *The Christocentric Cosmology of Maximus the Confessor*. Oxford: Oxford University Press, 2008.

———. "The Ethical Consequences of the Christian Conception of Nature As Created By God." *St. Vladimir's Theological Quarterly* 454 (2001) 395–408.

Toronen, Melchisedec. *Union and Distinction in the Thought of Maximus the Confessor*. New York: Oxford University Press, 2007.

White, Lynn, Jr. "The Historical Roots of Our Ecologic Crisis." *Science* 155, no. 3767 (1967) 1203–12.

7

Pentecostal Eco-Transformation: Possibilities for a Pentecostal Ecotheology in Light of Moltmann's Green Theology

Peter Althouse

Introduction

The litany of ecological catastrophes continues whether they are natural in origin, the result of human activity, or a combination of both. The 2011 Fukushima Daiich nuclear disaster in Japan is second in radioactive contamination only to the Chernobyl nuclear disaster in the Ukraine twenty-five years earlier. Although the Fukushima disaster was precipitated by a devastating tsunami, regulators determined that the meltdown was preventable. The 2010 BP oil spill in the Gulf of Mexico was due to human negligence, safety violations, and an endless global thirst for gasoline. For eighty-seven days, a total of 4.9 million barrels of crude oil spewed into the gulf resulting in ecological disaster for marine life in the area. The long-term effects of the oil spill are unknown. Global warming, which is the result of human manipulation and industrialization of nature, continues to be a significant threat to human civilization and the planet as a whole. According to the United Nations, the last two decades have witnessed the hottest years on record. Glacial melt is significant with 160 square miles of ice breaking away from Antarctica in 2008.[1] These are just some of the incidents and developments that have occurred in recent years illustrating the ecological problems now faced by the human race.

Although individual Pentecostals may rightly be concerned about these ecological crises and their impact of the future of the human species, Pentecostalism as a whole has remained reticent on issues related to nature and ecology.[2] To date, a Pentecostal ecological theology is underdeveloped. A number of chapters in *The Spirit Renews the Face of the Earth* edited by Amos Yong addresses issues of creation-care and ecojustice from a Pentecostal perspective directly, though the primary purpose of the volume is to form a dialogue between science and religion.[3] One can see latent concerns for ecological issues in a number of Pentecostal theologians, even if they do not directly engage the topic. For instance, Frank Macchia's work in *Spirituality and Social Liberation* draws on the pietistic theology of Johann and Christoph Blumhardt in order to develop a framework of social justice. Johann's concern for bodily healing and Christoph's concern for dying trees can be extrapolated into a Pentecostal theology of creation and its care.[4] In *The Spirit Poured out on All Flesh*, Amos Yong offers a brief comment on the potential for a pneumatological theology of the environment in order to extend love of neighbor to the creation that God calls good.[5] Likewise, Veli-Matti Kärkkäinen suggests

---

1. https://www.un.org/en/globalissues/climatechange/ (accessed January 3, 2014).

2. Pentecostalism here includes all branches within the family resemblance of classical Pentecostal, charismatic, and neo-charismatic varieties.

3. Yong, *The Spirit Renews the Face of the Earth*. A number of chapters addressing ecological issues include Boone, "Created for Shalom," 17–29; Waddell, "Revelation and the (New Creation)," 30–50; Clifton, "Preaching the 'Full Gospel' in the Context of Global Environmental Crises," 117–54, Tallman, "Pentecostal Ecology," 135–54; Althouse, "Implications of the Kenosis of the Spirit for a Creational Eschatology," 155–72.

4. Macchia, *Spirituality and Social Liberation*.

5. Yong, *The Spirit Poured Out on All Flesh*, 299–301.

the development of an ecological pneumatology as part of the overall work of the Spirit.[6] My own work in *Spirit of the Last Days* was an attempt to construct a Pentecostal eschatology that was congenial to social ethics and ecological issues. A.J. Swoboda proposes that Pentecostal/ Charismatic scholars take three broad approaches in addressing ecological issues: social justice theology, Spirit/Creation theology and ecotheology.[7] Swoboda's book *Tongues and Trees: Toward a Pentecostal Ecological Theology* is the most extensive treatment, and a full-blown Pentecostal ecotheology.[8]

Ecotheology is therefore a lacuna in Pentecostalism and Pentecostal theology. In order to address this, I hope to appropriate a number of salient themes in Moltmann's ecotheology in order to place them in dialogue with Pentecostal theology.

To accomplish this I will first discuss Moltmann's transformational eschatology as foundational for constructing an ecotheology and suggest ways in which Pentecostals could appropriate Moltmann's work for the construction of their own ecotheology. Secondly, while one could construct an ecotheology protologically based in a theology of the stewardship of creation, I will work from a cosmic eschatological perspective of the new creation in which the kenotic ("self-emptying") self-limitation of God to create is the basis for an ecotheological ethic. The Spirit's presence in creation coincides with charismatic notions of the Spirit in Pentecostalism, though I will argue for a shift from individualistic approaches to a more cosmic understanding. Finally, I hope to take up Moltmann's understanding of a simple and moderate lifestyle as congenial to the sanctification of creation in order to construct a Pentecostal theology of eco-holiness. Pentecostalism as a whole has been concerned about God's sanctification, and its personal as well as social implications; however I will make an argument that a Pentecostal eco-holiness needs to be cosmic in scope in order to include creation.

Eschatological existence and ecotheology

Eschatology became a central focus of twentieth century theology. The most prominent Protestant theologian to revitalize the place of escha-

6. Kärkkäinen, *Pneumatology*, 159–64.

7. Swoboda, "Eco-Glossolalia," 101–16.

8. Swoboda, *Tongues and Trees*.

tology in all theological discussions is Jürgen Moltmann. Beginning with *Theology of Hope* (1967) and through his entire career, eschatology is prominent.[9] Yet his eschatology is not limited to internal ecclesial debates, but has become a driving impulse for his ecotheology taking shape initially with *God in Creation* (1985) and traced through subsequent writings, and has influenced numerous theological trajectories in the last several decades.[10] Moltmann's latest publication, *Ethics of Hope* (2012) takes up the relationship between eschatology and ecotheology anew, and will be prominent in my current appropriation of Moltmann's transformational eschatology for the purpose of constructing a Pentecostal ecotheology.

In order to ground his ecological ethics, Moltmann first outlines four eschatological positions that contribute to various approaches to ecotheology: apocalyptic eschatology, Christological eschatology, separatist eschatology, and transformational eschatology.

1) *Apocalyptic eschatology* comes from Martin Luther's two kingdom theology, which articulates a bifurcation between the city or kingdom of God and the city or kingdom of the devil. These two kingdoms are engaged in an apocalyptic struggle that will continue until the end of time. In it, the future is not yet decided and therefore the apocalyptic struggle persists. A secondary distinction is made in the kingdom of God between the "rule" of the spiritual kingdom of Christ Jesus and the life-sustaining kingdom of the world. The kingdom of the world seeks justice through law, reason, and armed enforcement in order to provide for the social well-being of its citizens. The spiritual kingdom seeks justice through Word and Spirit, grace, and faith. It provides eternal salvation. These two kingdoms are separate and not permitted to interfere in the matters of the other, except when it becomes necessary for the spiritual kingdom to resist the state's power to compel its citizens to engage in sin.[11] Moltmann critiques the passivity of this type of eschatology, especially in reaction to Carl Schmitt's political theology, stating that the problem is that apocalyptic alarmism paralyzes the state to act in its efforts to thwart chaos and evil thereby preventing it from dealing with historical and ecological crises in an appropriate manner. In the twenty-first century, humanity is now faced with international terrorism and suicide regimes that care little

9. Moltmann, *Theology of Hope*. The German edition was published in 1965.

10. Moltmann, *God in Creation*.

11. Moltmann, *Ethics of Hope*, 9–11.

for the survival of the human species. How does a state negotiate with terrorists who are willing to rain death on all of humanity? Moreover, the theologies of Armageddon and Christian Zionism that are popular in some Evangelical and Pentecostal end-time communities, place the present in a continuous state of war religiously by separating believers from unbelievers, or politically by establishing "friend-enemy" binaries. In the Cold War, countries such as Russia or Eastern Europe were defined as enemies to be overcome. Today, Middle Eastern countries such as Iran or Iraq, or Far Eastern countries such as North Korea, have become symbols for the apocalyptic struggle.[12]

These criticisms notwithstanding, the openness to creation and God's future found in Moltmann's theology suggest at least a partial intersection with apocalyptic struggle as an ongoing impulse in the transformative energies of the eschaton. Moltmann has clearly advocated for the openness of God to and in creation that implies two possible futures: one in favor of the coming kingdom of God, and the other a collapse of creation into chaos. Moltmann writes, "But if creation is subject to change and is open to time from the beginning, then it cannot be a closed system; it must be an open one."[13] Nevertheless, he is unwilling to allow an apocalyptic passivity to interfere with a theological engagement with nature and its future.

2) *Christological eschatology* is a type that emerges from the theology of John Calvin and made explicit in Karl Barth's Christology. The Christological descriptor is somewhat misleading though, because it suggests that the other three eschatologies are somehow non-Christological, or at least less Christological. Nevertheless, the Reformers did not see an antithesis between the law and the gospel, but viewed the two as simultaneously under the inclusive rule of Christ. The two were distinguishable, but the state was viewed theologically as existing under the rule of the kingdom of God. Moltmann focuses primarily on Barth's theology and sums up his Christological eschatology as follows: first, objectively, the world is already in Christ and subject to his rule. Christ has been given the power to rule because God raised him from the dead and exalted him to the right hand of the Father. Second, because Christ is already Lord and all power has been given him, then the power of the state ultimately belongs to Christ. The dignity, function, and purpose of the state's power

12. Moltmann, *Ethics of Hope*, 15–17.
13. Moltmann, *The Future of Creation*, 118.

serve Christ in the justification of the sinner. Third, the eschatological symbols of kingdom of God and new creation as depicted in the New Testament are political descriptors. Christ's liberating rule is now manifest in the world and therefore Christianity is responsible in all sectors of life. Moltmann concludes that Barth's eschatology is realized or presentative in that little is left for the future except for the universal unveiling of what God has done in Christ.[14]

3) *Separatist eschatology* draws on the theology of the Anabaptist tradition and takes up the political theology of Stanley Hauerwas. In this rendition, Christians are called to the ethic and discipleship of Jesus to live in accordance to his New Testament life and teachings. Discipleship is the way of Jesus, who in utter obedience gave his life in the cross and brings hope in his resurrection and exaltation. The Anabaptists were committed to non-resistance and a violence-free life as examples of the way of the cross, even in the face of persecution and violence. The kingdom of God then was found in the heavenly Christ rather than on this earth. The Anabaptists, according to Moltmann, while diverse agreed on one aspect: that this corrupt world would be completely annihilated and replaced by a new creation. They inserted an ontological dualism between heaven and earth for Luther's apocalyptic dualism. As a result, the church was to have nothing to do with this world, resulting in its denial of and attachment from worldly affairs. The Anabaptists formed voluntary communities of believers in order to counter the violence of society that could rule only through law and restraint. Believers were to admonish, forgive, and love, whereas society coerces, judges, and retaliates. In other words, they lived a life of peace, vulnerability, and were readily prepared to suffer like Jesus.[15]

In the context of America's social experiment that merged Christianity and democracy into a "civil religion," Hauerwas takes up the Anabaptist cause in order to espouse a retreat from society and to produce an antagonistic counter-voice between the voluntary fellowship of believers and the corruption of society. The church then does not produce a social ethic per se, but an alternative social reality that demonstrates the way of Christ in fellowship and peace in contradistinction to the world of sin and violence. The "Constantinianization" of the church in America stands condemned by the holiness of God in the church that

14. Moltmann, *Ethics of Hope*, 19–23.

15. Ibid., 28–30.

leaves social change to God solely. However, Moltmann is critical of this type of eschatology because it is sectarian and fails to confront the world with the gospel.[16]

4) *Transformational eschatology*, Moltmann's position, is, he believes, well placed for the construction of an ethics of creation. Inspired by the civil rights movement led by Martin Luther King, who sought to liberate oppressed African-Americans from white racism in the US, King placed democracy and liberation in the context of the forward looking messianic hope of the coming kingdom. In *Theology of Hope*, Moltmann proclaims that Christian eschatology is forward looking hope that transforms the present. As such, it undergirds all Christian proclamation in the promise of the crucified and resurrected Christ.[17] According to Moltmann, "Because the kingdom of God is the future of all history, it transcends the historical future and all anticipations within history. But in this very way, the kingdom will become the power of hope in history and the source these anticipations within which we prepare for the coming of God."[18] As such, salvation is multidimensional and includes economic justice, human dignity, solidarity against alienation, and hope against despair.

In contrast to Barth's Christological eschatology, Moltmann presents an eschatological Christology that is messianic in that "the beginning of the coming consummation of salvation has already taken place in the coming of Christ, and with Christ the eschatological future has already begun."[19] This messianic Christology leads to a messianic ethic whereby the present has already been gripped by the eschatological future that becomes present while remaining future. This eschatological Christology opens up to the outpouring of the Spirit as the powers of the Spirit for the world to come and the beginning of Christ's *parousia*. Consequently, the discipleship of Christ is an ethic that anticipates his future that begins in the Spirit and is completed in kingdom glory. An ethics of hope is anchored in Christ's resurrection and looks to the future new creation in anticipation for active change in the transformation of the present.[20]

Moltmann's eschatological theology is helpful for constructing a Pentecostal ecotheology. He offers an eschatological framework that

16. Ibid., 30–33.
17. Moltmann, *Theology of Hope*, 16.
18. Moltmann, *Ethics of Hope*, 36–37.
19. Ibid., 37–38.
20. Ibid., 35–41.

places ecological concerns in the context of the propleptic anticipation of the eschatological new creation that has transformative power to change the present. I have dealt extensively with this theme elsewhere and will therefore only highlight a few salient points. In *Spirit of the Last Days* I employed Moltmann's transformational eschatology in order to revision Pentecostal eschatology in a fashion that would open up Pentecostals to theological concerns for social justice and the environment. Although my concern for an ecotheology was latent in the background of the text, one of the underlying problems, as I saw it, was the cognitive dissonance between the looming potential catastrophes such as nuclear holocaust or global warming and a Pentecostal eschatology that took the proverbial "ostrich head in the sand" approach in the form of fundamental dispensationalism in which the faithful would be raptured before world destruction.[21]

Pentecostal eschatology from the mid-twentieth century on has aligned itself to fundamentalist dispensationalism at the expense of its own logic of the charismatic outpouring of the Spirit in the world. The cessationism of dispensationalism does not allow for the charismatic gifts to operate in the church and the world, but this notion is antithetical to Pentecostal faith and practice. Dispensational eschatology is similar to apocalyptic eschatology as described by Moltmann (above) in that the faithful took a passive stance in relation to the world in the hope that God would take them into glory before the world deteriorated. The concept of the secret rapture captures this abdication of responsibility and leaves the world to the devices of chaos and evil and eventual annihilation. However, by tapping into an earlier Pentecostal eschatology of the "latter rain," which hoped in anticipation for the immediacy of the coming of the Lord and the coinciding fervency of the church in preparing for Christ's return, I was able to construct a transformational Pentecostal eschatology that looked for the kingdom of the new creation that also enlivened the faithful to work as co-laborers in anticipation of God's coming kingdom. The implication for ecotheology is that Christians who claim to live under the reign of Christ in hope for the new creation—which is nothing less than the renewal of creation separated from the powers of sin and death (what Moltmann terms the negation of the negative)—are responsible for and commissioned to participate in the care of creation. Creation-care

---

21. Althouse, *Spirit of the Last Days*.

under a transformational eschatological ethic includes personal, social and global responsibilities.

Cosmic ecoeschatology and the spirit of pentecost

As outlined in *The Coming of God*, Moltmann's transformational eschatology has a fourfold structure that includes personal, socio-historical, cosmic, and divine elements. Personal eschatology probes the question of life after death for the individual that is addressed by the resurrection of the body. Socio-historical eschatology probes the question of the future end of history in relation the dawning of the kingdom of God and the energies of its dawning for the cause of justice and peace. Cosmic eschatology probes the ecological implications of the transformation of this creation into the new creation. And, finally, divine eschatology argues that God will be glorified in the culmination and realization of divine purposes when God will be all in all.[22] Moltmann's eschatology includes all four eschatological goals and sets the framework for engaging an eco-theology of transformation. However, I will deal specifically here with cosmic eschatology as it pertains to the double movement of the kenosis and presence of the creating Spirit.

Moltmann places cosmic eschatology in critical dialogue with evolutionary and emergent theories. He proposes a panentheistic theology of creation that is tripartite with creation consisting of its original in the beginning, its continuation through history (cosmic and planetary), and its consummation in the new creation.[23] For Moltmann, creation comes into existence through a sovereign and free act of God to withdraw into the divine self in order to make time and space for creation.[24] Divine withdrawal as a kenotic act of triune self-limitation and self-emptying is an expression of divine love that opens God up to the vulnerabilities and suffering of creation.[25] Kenosis of Spirit as an act of self-limitation

22. Moltmann, *The Coming of God*, 131–32, 323–25.

23. Whereas pantheism envisions the world as a mode of God's being, panentheism sees God and the world as mutually dependent. See Migliore, *Faith Seeking Understanding*, 110. Moltmann's panentheism is different than process theology in that he articulates a Trinitarian indwelling in relation to the world in the dialectic between transcendence and immanence. See Moltmann, *God in Creation*, 103; Moltmann, *Trinity and the Kingdom*, 106–8; also Chester, *Mission and the Coming of God*, 35–36.

24. Moltmann, *Science and Wisdom*, 38–47; Moltmann, *God in Creation*, 87–88.

25. Moltmann, *Science and Wisdom*, 57.

coincides with her indwelling presence in creation, sustaining it and giving it life.[26] In other words, the Spirit is present in creation as God's Shekinah through the prior act of self-limitation as the manifestation of love. The double movements of self-limitation and presence are the basis through which the Spirit draws creation into its consummate glory into the new creation.

Darwin's evolutionary theory is compatible with Moltmann's tripartite understanding of creation, but with qualifications of the theory's interpretations and outcomes. Nevertheless, what evolution reveals is that humans are not "godlike" and set apart from the rest of creation, but one species among the whole community of biodiversity on the planet. "Since we have come to realize that it is the religious-scientific anthropomorphism of modern times which has brought us to the present ecological crisis of nature and human civilization," declares Moltmann, "we no longer see Darwin's evolutionary theory as an attack on Christian anthropology, but begin to understand that the human belongs to the same family as other living things on this fruitful earth." [27] The problem with evolutionary theory, however, is that while it tells us how things came into existence and how past arrangements lead to present conditions, it does not tell us the future. Thus Moltmann supplements evolutionary theory with emergence theory that reveals how the "new" emerges in unexpected ways that cannot be explained by past configurations. There are qualitative leaps—neutrons emerge from protons, molecules from atoms, living organisms from cellular organism, etc.,—that are simply inexplicable from its constituent parts. However, in distinction from nontheistic funded science, Moltmann insists that emergent developments are indicators of the Spirit's presence and work in all life, directing it to its future constellations.[28]

My initial reflection on Moltmann's pneumatology was an attempt to appropriate his theology of Spirit kenosis and creational eschatology in order to construct a theology of missional service in which the Pentecostal doctrine of Spirit-baptism epitomized self-giving in a suffer-

26. In keeping with the different gender designations of *ruach* (fem.) and *pneuma* (masc. and neut.), I shift gender designations of Spirit but without identifying the Spirit as gendered.

27. Moltmann, *Ethics of Hope*, 124–25.

28. Moltmann, *Ethics of Hope*, 126. Cf. Moltmann, *God in Creation*, 203–4.

ing and vulnerable world.[29] Just as the Spirit descends and self-empties in the work of creation and the event of the cross, so the Spirit-baptized are called to live a life of self-giving and service. Seen in this light, the event of Pentecost coincides with the event of the cross in that just as the kenosis of Jesus led him to take the way of the cross, so too the Spirit self-limits and makes herself vulnerable to a suffering creation in order to bring forth the new cosmic reign. The cross of Jesus and the Pentecost of the Spirit anticipates and guarantees the eschatological coming. The presence of the self-emptying Spirit in creation as the breath and energies of life has implications for eco-pneumatology. The kenosis of Spirit does not mean that the Spirit is pantheistically diffused in the orders of creation, but the Spirit makes itself vulnerable for the sake of a vulnerable creation and its ecological well-being in order to overcome the destructive forces of chaos. The violence that the human species unleashes on creation through national and global wars, economic privilege, and technological prowess, oppresses the ecological order of nature and must be labeled as sin. The Spirit's presence vitiates the world in order to overcome the violence rained down on what God has pronounced "good." This theology takes a Pentecostal pneumatological focus, but shifts it from an individualistic and anthropocentric orientation that views salvation as solely for humans, to provide a cosmic orientation that sees the whole of creation and the universe writ large as the locus of God's redeeming purposes wrought through the activity of the Spirit.

The Pentecostal theology of Spirit-baptism offers inroads into the renewal of creation by way of its focus on the narrative of Acts 2. Pentecostals take Luke's narrative as authoritative regarding the work of God in the world through the life-giving power of the Spirit. Sometimes overlooked in their reading of Acts 2 is the imagery of God's renewal of creation as a fundamental meaning for the descent of the Spirit at Pentecost. The Spirit is depicted as a "rushing mighty wind" (Acts 2:2) descending on the disciples in the upper room who then begin to speak in other tongues. This image alludes to the creation hymn where the "Spirit (*ruach*) of God moved upon the face of the waters" (Gen 1:2). The implication is that the infilling of the Spirit accompanied by speaking in tongues depicts nothing less than the renewal of creation. In other words, embedded in the Pentecostal doctrine of Spirit-baptism is a cos-

---

29. Althouse, "The Implications of the Kenosis of Spirit for a Creational Eschatology," 155–72.

mic reading of eco-pneumatology. Macchia, who views the Pentecost event as divine theophany,[30] argues that the tension between creation's inherent goodness placed in tension with the bondage of sin and death "groans" for its liberation, a groaning that is expressed in the tongues of Spirit-baptism.[31] The groaning of creation is also suggestive as a birthing metaphor experiencing the pangs of the coming new creation. While discussing Moltmann's creational eschatology, Macchia says that the kingdom is both present and coming, and that the kingdom will not annihilate present creation but transform it through God's indwelling. The outpouring of the Spirit in history is directed toward the advent of divine indwelling in creation.[32]

The infilling of the Spirit is a kenotic act that makes the Spirit present in the world and in creation. It harkens back to the kenosis of creation when the Spirit's presence fills the earth with life. The Spirit is poured out on all flesh.[33] Moreover, the kenosis of Spirit that manifests the Spirit's presence in creation also anticipates the cosmic realities of the new creation where the goal of Spirit kenosis is the de-limitation of God who will be fully present with and in the renewed creation. Because Pentecostals view Spirit-baptism as empowerment for mission (however limiting empowerment is for a full understanding of the doctrine), by implication the baptism of the Spirit also empowers for the care of creation. Those who have been baptized in the Spirit are representatives of the renewal of creation as God's mission in the world and are therefore called to care for creation. The Spirit's presence is made real through a prior act of kenosis so that we might participate with God as co-laborers in the ongoing development of creation.

Eco-holiness and the sanctification of creation

According to Moltmann, the overproduction of carbon dioxide and methane gases, the overuse of chemical fertilizers and pesticides, the

30. Macchia, "Tongues as Sign," 61–76.

31. Macchia, *Baptized in the Spirit*, 96, 119.

32. Macchia, *Baptized in the Spirit*, 96–97.

33. This expression is a favorite among Pentecostals that links Joel 2:28 to Acts 2:17. It is seen as the empowerment of all people through the baptism in the Spirit without respect to class, race, or gender. Moltmann takes it up but also links the Spirit's outpouring to Gen 9:10 to claim that all life includes the biodiversity of life found on the planet. Moltmann, *The Source of Life*, 12.

depletion of rain forests and expanding deserts through human intrusion and as a result of rapid population growths contribute to the ecological crisis. Unlike past catastrophes that were natural in origin,[34] the ecological crisis facing the world today is created by human advancements and subjugation of nature. While the biodiversity of life recovered in the natural catastrophes of the past, it is uncertain whether or not the human species will survive the ecological crisis today that is developing as a consequence of human attempts at control over nature, or even whether the biodiversity of life itself will survive.[35] Moltmann's response is one of ecojustice in which human dignity and rights are based on the dignity and rights of all created life. He shifts the discussion from an anthropocentric view of ecotheology to a biocentric view.[36]

Moltmann argues that the assault on nature for the sake of human privilege calls for nothing less than a theology of the sanctification of nature. Sanctification accents life's sacredness and the mystery of God's creation. Consequently, sanctification resists the manipulation, secularization, and destruction of nature. Creation is loved by God as God's beloved and must be respected and protected.[37] For Moltmann, the eternal sabbath represents the time for God's cosmic sanctification of creation and while we are invited to participate in it, the eternal sabbath is celebrated by all creaturely being. He writes: "God 'hallowed' the sabbath . . . To hallow or sanctify means, roughly speaking, choosing or electing, separating off for oneself, declaring something to be one's own property and inviolable . . . [S]anctification of the sabbath benefits all created things on the seventh day, that is to say, it is universal."[38] Sanctification means to be free from striving, performance, and achievement in order to be present with and in God. It is both a remembrance of the sabbath of creation and a promise for the eternal sabbath of cosmic rest.[39] The ecological implication is that the promise of the new creation presupposes ecological rest of creation, without the crisis of environmental pollution.[40] In *Coming*

---

34. There have been five life extinction events in the history of the planet with the most popularized being the extinction of the dinosaurs.

35. Moltmann, *Ethics of Hope*, 133.

36. Ibid., 145.

37. Moltmann, *Spirit of Life*, 31.

38. Moltmann, *God in Creation*, 283

39. Ibid., 286.

40. Ibid., 296.

of God, Moltmann connects holiness and rest to the indwelling of cosmic Shekinah. The eschatological indwelling when God is fully present in creation is characterized by holiness and glory. Because God is holy, everything that is made by God will be made holy as a vessel for God's indwelling. The holiness and glory of the cosmic indwelling is the goal of creation and all living creatures.[41]

However, this cosmic understanding of sanctification presupposes personal responsibility. In *Ethics of Hope*, Moltmann calls for individual responses. The accumulation of personal choices has global ecological consequences. Moltmann therefore proposes the adoption of a simple lifestyle of moderation and cultural solidarity. Living an ecological lifestyle means a return to embodied existence and a global ecological consciousness with local lifestyle choices.[42]

At this point I would like to take up Moltmann's ecotheology proposal for cosmic sanctification in order to construct a Pentecostal eco-holiness. As a rule, Pentecostals have historically been concerned about holiness. On the one hand, those Pentecostals aligned with the Wesleyan holiness movement adopted sanctification as a theological locus of the full gospel. Following later developments in Wesleyan holiness theology, sanctification was believed to be a second blessing experience of "abiding love" and a precursor to baptism in the Spirit. One the other hand, those Pentecostals influenced by Reformed circles,[43] while rejecting the second blessing understanding, placed an equally strong accent on holiness as the daily abiding of the Spirit in the formation of spiritual identity. Despite problems where holiness degenerated into legalistic codes, where dress, behaviors, and norms were defined as prohibitions, abiding love (inward) was believed to bring about a personal transformation that was expressed in the love of God and love of neighbor (outward). In the end, the difference between the fivefold (Wesleyan) and fourfold (Reformed) gospel in Pentecostalism was a matter of accent rather than substance.[44]

The difficulty within Pentecostalism is that holiness was interpreted through an individualistic lens. Just as sin was viewed as a personal affront to God, holiness was viewed as one's personal inward transforma-

41. Moltmann, *Coming of God*, 317–18.

42. Moltmann, *Ethics of Hope*, 151–56.

43. Included under the Reformed rubric are baptistic, revivalist, and Keswick views that were all mediated through evangelical networks.

44. See Dayton, *Theological Roots of Pentecostalism*, 21–25.

tion that followed personal conversion. Occasionally, personal holiness was translated into social action as was the case when Pentecostals engaged in mission work (e.g., establishing orphanages, medical centers, schools, etc.), but the social implications of their theology of holiness was left underdeveloped. Terry Johns, however, notes that the intersection of eschatology and holiness and its implications for society. Taking my proposal of "proleptic anticipation" in the working of justice and peacemaking in history,[45] he argues that the full eschatological trajectory from creation to eschaton calls people to the life of holiness and peaceable existence that implies "commitment to preservation of life as expression of an eschatological kingdom ethic."[46] Cast in a cosmic eschatological framework, one begins to understand the ecological implication of holiness. Eco-holiness cuts to the heart of the Pentecostal desire for the Spirit's presence, which is nothing less than the indwelling cosmic Shekinah calling creation and all living beings to the time of God's eternal rest. Human striving and ambitions that have a destructive impact of the natural order is antithetical to eco-holiness. A simple and moderate ecological lifestyle is an expression of abiding love that allows people to be at peace with the inter-connectedness of life that reflects the cosmic sanctification of creation as the time of God's indwelling Shekinah.

Conclusion

Pentecostal theology has resources for constructing an ecotheology, even if that theology is currently embryonic and needs time and space to flourish. I have proposed (in dialogue with Moltmann's ecotheology) that a transformational eschatology is easily taken up by a Pentecostal eschatology that is situated in proleptic anticipation of the already but not yet of the reign of God. I specifically engage Moltmann's cosmic eschatology of the new creation in which the kenosis of Spirit who is poured out on all flesh is also the Shekinah or the presence of God in creation anticipating the eternal Sabbath. The Pentecostal accent on the Spirit's presence would be nourished by engaging Moltmann's pneumatology and helps in the construction of a Pentecostal ecoeschatology and eco-pneumatology. Finally, I have argued that Moltmann's understand of the sanctification of creation that calls for a lifestyle of holiness helps Pentecostals expand

45. See Althouse, "'Left Behind'—Fact or Fiction."
46. Johns, "The Practice of Holiness," 310.

their own understanding of holiness in a more cosmic orientation in order to construct an eco-holiness. By shifting Pentecostal theology from its more individualistic sense of the redeeming purposes of God to a social and cosmic sense provides for them an ecotheology that establishes engagement of ecological issues as part of the ongoing work of the Spirit.

BIBLIOGRAPHY

Althouse, Peter. "Implications of the Kenosis of the Spirit for a Creational Eschatology." In *The Spirit Renews the Face of the Earth: Pentecostal Forays in Science and Theology of Creation*, edited by Amos Yong, 155–72. Eugene, OR: Pickwick, 2009.

———. "'Left Behind'—Fact or Fiction: Ecumenical Dilemmas of the Fundamentalist Millenarian Tensions within Pentecostalism." *Journal of Pentecostal Theology* 13, no. 2 (2005) 187–207.

———. *Spirit of the Last Days: Pentecostal Eschatology in Conversation with Jürgen Moltmann*. London: T. & T. Clark, 2003.

Boone, R. Jerome. "Created for Shalom: Human Agency and Responsibility in the World." In *The Spirit Renews the Face of the Earth: Pentecostal Forays in Science and Theology of Creation*, edited by Amos Yong, 17–29. Eugene, OR: Pickwick, 2009.

Chester, Tim. *Mission and the Coming of God: Eschatology, the Trinity and Mission in the Theology of Jürgen Moltmann and Contemporary Evangelicalism*. Eugene, OR: Wipf & Stock, 2006.

Clifton, Shane. "Preaching the 'Full Gospel' in the Context of Global Environmental Crises." In *The Spirit Renews the Face of the Earth: Pentecostal Forays in Science and Theology of Creation*, edited by Amos Yong, 117–54. Eugene, OR: Pickwick, 2009.

Dayton, Donald W. *Theological Roots of Pentecostalism*. Grand Rapids: Baker Academic, 1987.

Johns, Terry. "The Practice of Holiness: Implications for a Moral Theology." In *A Future for Holiness: Pentecostal Explorations*, edited by Lee Roy Martin, 297–311. Cleveland, TN: CPT, 2013.

Kärkkäinen, Veli-Matti. *Pneumatology: The Holy Spirit in Ecumenical, International, and Contextual Perspective*. Grand Rapids: Baker Academic, 2002.

Macchia, Frank D. *Baptized in the Spirit: A Global Pentecostal Theology*. Grand Rapids: Zondervan, 2006.

———. *Spirituality and Social Liberation: The Message of the Blumhardts in the Light of Wuerttemberg Pietism*. Metuchen, NJ: Scarecrow, 1993.

———. "Tongues as Sign: Towards a Sacramental Understanding of Pentecostal Experience." *Pneuma* 15, no. 1 (1993) 61–76.

Migliore, Daniel E. Faith *Seeking Understanding: An Introduction to Christian Theology*. 2nd ed. Grand Rapids: Eerdmans, 2004.

Moltmann, Jürgen. *The Coming of God: Christian Eschatology*. Translated by Margaret Kohl. Minneapolis: Fortress, 1996.

———. *Ethics of Hope*. Translated by Margaret Kohl. Minneapolis: Fortress, 2012.

————. *The Future of Creation: Collected Essays.* Translated by Margaret Kohl. 1979. Minneapolis: Fortress, 2007.

————. *God in Creation: A New Theology of Creation and the Spirit of God.* Translated by Margaret Kohl. London: SCM, 1985.

————. *Science and Wisdom.* Translated by Margaret Kohl. Minneapolis: Fortress, 2003.

————. *The Source of Life: The Holy Spirit and the Theology of Life.* Translated by Margaret Kohl. Minneapolis: Fortress, 1997.

————. *Theology of Hope: On the Ground and the Implications of a Christian Eschatology.* Translated by James W. Leitch. London: SCM, 1967.

————. *Trinity and the Kingdom: The Doctrine of God.* Translated by Margaret Kohl. Minneapolis: Fortress, 1993.

Swoboda, A. J. "Eco-Glossolalia: Emerging Twenty-First Century Pentecostal and Charismatic Ecotheology." *Rural Theology* 9, no. 2 (2011) 101–16.

————. *Tongues and Trees: Toward a Pentecostal Ecological Theology.* Journal of Pentecostal Theology Supplement 40. Blandford Forum, UK: Deo, 2013.

Tallman, Matthew. "Pentecostal Ecology: A Theological Paradigm for Pentecostal Environmentalism." In *The Spirit Renews the Face of the Earth: Pentecostal Forays in Science and Theology of Creation*, edited by Amos Yong, 135–54. Eugene, OR: Pickwick, 2009.

Waddell, Robby. "Revelation and the (New Creation): A Prolegomena on the Apocalypse, Science, and Creation." In *The Spirit Renews the Face of the Earth: Pentecostal Forays in Science and Theology of Creation*, edited by Amos Yong, 30–50. Eugene. OR: Pickwick, 2009.

Yong, Amos. *The Spirit Poured Out on All Flesh: Pentecostalism and the Possibility of Global Theology.* Grand Rapids: Baker Academic, 2005.

Yong, Amos, ed. *The Spirit Renews the Face of the Earth: Pentecostal Forays in Science and Theology of Creation.* Eugene, OR: Pickwick, 2009.

8

A Green Apocalypse: Comparing Secular and Religious Eschatological Visions of Earth

Robby Waddell

Introduction

Post-apocalyptic dystopias have captured the attention and imagination of our present culture—dominating at the box office and populating the bestseller lists. Packed with religious overtones, the secular eschatologies undergirding these stories combine a mixture of both hope and despair. One part fantasy and one part science fiction, post-apocalyptic dystopias may contain zombies, vampires, aliens, or artificial intelligence, for example *World War Z*, *District 9*, or the *Matrix* trilogy. Perhaps even more haunting are movies like *The Hunger Games*, *V for Vendetta*, or *The Manchurian Candidate*, which present a more realistic, albeit equally disturbing, vision of the future.

What these stories share is a popular, pessimistic outlook, rooted in the assumption that if humanity stays on its present trajectory then a collapse of the status quo—societal and ecological—is unavoidable. A cataclysmic event, often spelling disaster for the environment, is therefore an essential element to the backstory of any post-apocalyptic tale.[1] Various causes of the catastrophe include global pandemic, overpopulation, climate change, nuclear holocaust, and so on. Hence, it is not uncommon

---

1. Some apocalyptic stories only contain the threat of a disaster. In the end, a hero comes to save the day, and the tragedy is avoided, though normally not without great cost, e.g., *Armageddon*.

for the setting of a post-apocalyptic story to be depicted as a veritable wasteland, for example *The Book of Eli*.[2] In some stories, however, Earth has become practically uninhabitable, causing humans to seek refuge in outer space as interstellar immigrants pursuing a heavenly utopia.

One such story is the science-fiction thriller *Elysium*. Set in the year 2154, the poor (and the robots that police them) are the only inhabitants of a desolate and overpopulated Earth. The wealthy, on the other hand, dwell on a luxurious space station called Elysium, where advanced technology is available that functions like a tree of life, preventing diseases and providing healing for anyone who is injured. Disregarding immigration laws that would prevent citizens of Earth from visiting Elysium, the protagonists of the story invade the heavenly city and download software into its operating system that in effect makes everyone living on Earth legal citizens of Elysium. In order to complete the download the messianic hero has to sacrifice his life. As a result, the healing technology that had been reserved for the space station is now dispatched to the people who are living on Earth.

The not-so-subtle political critiques of the story notwithstanding, the shape of the film's hope-filled conclusion begs comparison with a popular Christian eschatological view. Not unlike *Elysium*, dispensational eschatology predicts a future time—post-rapture yet pre-millennium—when the elect will inhabit a heavenly paradise while the rest of humanity suffers on a desolated Earth, a time known as the Great Tribulation. The end game in this story is a complete and utter annihilation of Earth and an eternal bliss for the select few in heaven. *Elysium* inverts this storyline in an important way. The escape from Earth is penultimate. The ultimate goal is not so much to get up to paradise but rather to bring paradise down to Earth.

Somewhat anthropocentric, *Elysium* focuses on providing justice for humanity but stops short of ecological renewal. Be that as it may, the secular hope for a future life *on Earth* stands in stark contrast to the otherworldly orientation of dispensationalism.[3] A variation of this plotline, though not as common, includes an explicit hope for the restoration of

2. *Waterworld* offers a unique variation of the post-apocalyptic wasteland—a global deluge, which contradicts the promise in Genesis that the world will never again be destroyed by a flood.

3. Unlike *Elysium*, where the story ends back on Earth, a minority of post-apocalyptic science fiction films conclude with humanity having to escape in dispensational fashion to an intergalactic final destination, such as *Cloud Atlas* or *After Earth*.

Earth as part of the eschatological vision.[4] In these *post*-apocalyptic stories, the presupposed ecological tragedy may have severely altered the environment, but it has not annihilated it. In fact, what has happened is that the apocalyptic catastrophe has neutralized the ecological threats that were the original catalysts for the devastation in the first place. The environment receives an opportunity to rebound once its abusers have faced judgment. In other words, Earth may get beaten black-and-blue, yet the final effect is a green apocalypse—an event that rids Earth of its destructive inhabitants or at least counterbalances their negative effects, giving the global ecosystem a chance to renew.

One example of this sort of green apocalypse may be found in the whimsical, though thought-provoking, Walt Disney film *Wall-E*. In this story, Earth's ecosystem has collapsed and can no longer sustain organic life forms. Humanity has abandoned the planet and is now living on a giant spaceship where technological advances have automated every aspect of life. Earth's sole inhabitants are the story's unlikely hero Wall-E, a robotic trash compactor, and his lone companion—a cockroach. Wall-E is busy working on his appointed task of cleaning up Earth one small block of trash at a time, when his life is interrupted by an investigative probe named Eva, who had been sent from the spaceship to search for possible signs of life on Earth. Eva, who becomes Wall-E's love interest, does indeed find a single small plant, suggesting that the ecosystem is recovering and that humanity can return to Earth. Through a variety of twists and turns and by overcoming a number of challenges that threatened to prevent their cause, Wall-E and Eva succeed in the end and lead humanity back to its earthly home. As Peter Gabriel's song *Down to Earth* plays in the background, the people determine to help renew Earth and keep it from future harm.[5] This ecofriendly post-apocalyptic tale is instructive, though its portrayal of a green apocalypse is by no means a novel idea. In fact, the renewal of creation rather than its annihilation is a characteristic

---

4. Examples of films that exhibit an explicit ecological hope would include *The Day After Tomorrow*, *Oblivion*, and *2012*, which is a retelling of the global flood story.

5. For a critique of *Wall-E's* plotline see Anderson, "Post-Apocalyptic Nostalgia." Anderson offers this insightful critique: "Embedded within its lament over large-scale environmental destruction is a nostalgic fondness for consumer goods, a sentiment that complicates the film's powerful if heavy-handed warnings about consumerism and environmental pollution" (267). *Wall-E* is an anthropocentric version of this sort of post-apocalyptic story. Other versions of the green apocalypse, such as *The Planet of the Apes*, displace humanity as the ruling species of the planet.

of apocalyptic texts that are as old as the genre itself. In theological terms, a green apocalypse is an essential element of transformational eschatology, which was the leading view of both early and medieval Christian theologians.[6]

The alternative outlook, which envisages an annihilation of the world, continues to be widespread in both secular and religious circles, especially within certain sectors of conservative Christianity. Several factors contribute to this ongoing popularity, including the late-modern fear of a nuclear holocaust, the increased public awareness of our ecological crisis, and last but not least the interpretation of the apocalyptic language used in religious texts. Viewed from an ecological perspective, the doctrine of global annihilation raises serious ethical concerns. If all of creation is going to be burned then what value is there in environmental conservation? Of course, there is a case to be made: care of the environment is not illogical, even with the expectation of obliteration, if conservation is framed as stewardship of the natural resources which are necessary for the future of humanity. However, if the expectation of the total destruction of Earth is coupled with a belief in the imminent end of space-and-time—as it is with the dispensational eschatology that is so prevalent within Pentecostalism—then all reasonable support for creation-care is lost.[7]

In order to respond to this conundrum, new scholarship is desperately needed, not unlike what can be found in this volume, which contributes to a robust Pentecostal ecotheology.[8] With this goal in mind, I offer the following ecological readings of two apocalyptic stories, both of which contain a green eschatology—one is Jewish (*1 Enoch*) and the other is Christian (Revelation). My approach to these texts utilizes elements from a method of ecological hermeneutics that has been developed by Norman Habel and others from the Earth Bible team.[9] While

6. Moltmann, *The Coming of God*, 268.

7. Volf, "Loving with Hope," 28–31. Another theological challenge to the doctrine of annihilation of Earth is the divine pronouncement in Genesis that the creation is good. Contrary to the divine decree, the doctrine of annihilation presumes that Earth "must be either so bad that it is not possible to redeem it," writes Volf, "or so insignificant that it is not worth being redeemed" (30).

8. The first monograph length study on the development of a Pentecostal ecological theology is presented in the recent work by A. J. Swoboda in his *Tongues and Trees*.

9. For a historical overview of the development of the method, see Habel, "The Origins and Challenges of an Ecojustice Hermeneutic," 141–59.

ecotheology and ecohermeneutics may overlap with one another, they are nevertheless quite distinct. It is my hope that these ecological readings with their attention to the concept of a green apocalypse may be useful in the further development of a Pentecostal ecotheology.

Ecological hermeneutics

The most central feature of ecological hermeneutics is that Earth is recognized as a subject who can be known and who has a significant role to play in the biblical narrative rather than merely acting as the backdrop or the setting for an otherwise anthropocentric story. This concept draws heavily on the work of ecological theorists who are challenging the mechanistic views of nature that have dominated Western thought.[10] Although he is not cited by the Earth Bible Team, Martin Buber's word combination *I-Thou* is quite instructive for this discussion.[11] Buber suggests that a person either relates to another person or thing as one subject to another subject (I-Thou) or as a subject to an object (I-It). In the subject-object relationship, the objectified person or thing is reduced to a utility or experience. In Western culture, the relationship of humanity to Earth has predominately been one of I-It, often resulting in the maltreatment of Earth and its resources.

Anthropocentric dualism has often been indicted as a major catalyst for the ecological crisis. This debate is beyond the scope of this chapter, though I would recommend Richard Bauckham's analysis (which counterbalances Lynn White's famous thesis) that the blame for this dualism can be traced to the so-called *cultural mandate* in Gen 1:26–28. Instead, Bauckham indicts the humanism of the Renaissance, placing the lion's share of the blame on Francis Bacon's interpretation of Genesis 3: "Man by the fall fell at the same time from his state of innocency (sic) and from his dominion over creation. Both of these losses can in this life be in some part repaired; the former by religion and faith, the latter by arts and sciences."[12] In ecological hermeneutics the relationship between Earth and the interpreter is I-Thou.

10. For example, Birch, *On Purpose*; and Goodenough, *The Sacred Depths of Nature*.

11. Buber, *I and Thou*.

12. *Novum Organon* 12:52m, in Bacon, *The Works of Francis Bacon*, 247–8; cited in Bauckham, *Living with Other Creatures*, 48. Also see White, "The Historical Roots of Our Ecological Crisis."

This represents a radical departure from ecological theology or the doctrine of creation, in which Earth is merely a topic or theme to be analyzed. Therefore, in this chapter "Earth" is used as a proper name, which is why it is always capitalized and never receives the definite article. Earth is described by Norman Habel as: "the total ecosystem, that is, the web of life—the domain of nature with which we are familiar, of which we are an integral part, and in which we face the future."[13] Once Earth has been identified as a character in the story, an ecological interpreter must proceed with caution. If Earth is going to be respected as a true fellow subject, then the rules for engagement with Earth will be different than they are in other more anthropocentric methodologies. Ecological hermeneutics—as it has been recently practiced in biblical studies—presupposes six such ecojustice principles that guide the interpretation:

1. The principle of *intrinsic worth*: The universe, Earth and all its components have intrinsic worth/value.

2. The principle of *interconnectedness*: Earth is a community of interconnected living things that are mutually dependent on each other for life and survival.

3. The principle of voice: Earth is a subject capable of raising its voice in celebration and against injustice.

4. The principle of *purpose*: The universe, Earth and all its components are part of a dynamic cosmic design within which each piece has a place in the overall goal of that design.

5. The principle of *mutual custodianship*: Earth is a balanced and diverse domain where responsible custodians can function as partners with, rather than rulers over, Earth to sustain its balance and a diverse Earth community.

6. The principle of *resistance*: Earth and its components do not only suffer from human injustices but also actively resist them in the struggle for justice.[14]

Within the parameters of these ethical guidelines, ecological hermeneutics utilizes three primary strategies: suspicion, identification, and retrieval.[15] Foundational to academic biblical studies, a hermeneutic

13. Habel, "Introduction to Ecological Hermeneutics," 3.

14. Ibid., 2.

15. For examples of all three hermeneutical strategies, see Lamp, *The Greening of*

of suspicion is, of course, not unique to ecohermeneutics, though this facet of the method takes on a unique ecological perspective. Not unlike feminist and postcolonial readings, ecohermeneutics is first and foremost suspicious of hierarchical power structures used to marginalize and mute Earth.[16] This critique of the anthropocentrism of the text and/or its traditional interpretation is a corollary to the subject-subject relationship already discussed. Many ecological theologies would recast Gen 1:26–28 as a story about stewardship rather than domination. Contrary to this approach, an ecological hermeneutic of suspicion would interrogate the theology of stewardship being as anthropocentric, leaving intact the vertical dualism that exalts humans over the rest of creation.[17]

The hermeneutic of identification, the second aspect of ecohermeneutics, requires the interpreter to acknowledge solidarity between humanity and Earth. According to Gen 2:7, the first human was not created *ex nihilo* but rather out of Earth. Put bluntly, humans simply cannot have God as their Father unless they also have Earth as their mother. The hermeneutic of identification correlates with the principle of interconnectedness. In other words, not only are humans from Earth but they are also dependent on it. Earth existed long before there was a human audience, but humans have never existed without Earth. If its intrinsic value is accepted, then stewardship of every square inch of Earth is not required other than preserving its right to exist by establishing natural reserves that prevent human encroachment. The ecological question is, "Will Earth survive its human inhabitants?" The theological answer is that humans—as the sole sinful members of Earth's community—have not only brought judgment on themselves but have fatally marred all of creation. This is why the biblical story of redemption is inclusive of all creation and not reserved for humanity alone (cf. Rom 8). According to Jürgen Moltmann, "Christian eschatology cannot be reduced to human eschatology, and human eschatology cannot be brought down to the salvation of the soul in heaven beyond. There are no human souls without human bodies, and no human existence without the life

---

Hebrews. Lamp has written the most extensive ecological reading to date of the book of Hebrews.

16. See McFague, *Super, Natural Christians.*

17. Consider the words of Aldo Leopold: "God . . . likes to hear birds sing and see flowers grow." Cited in Meine, *Aldo Leopold,* 215. For a critique of the idea of stewardship, see Northcott, *The Environment and Christian Ethics,* 129.

system of the earth, and no earth without the universe."[18] Another way of saying this is that in order for there to be a bodily resurrection for humans there must also be some form of a green apocalypse—a resurrection so to speak of Earth.[19]

The final facet of an ecological hermeneutic is the process of retrieval such as identifying ecofriendly aspects of the text that have been previously overlooked. Once Earth is identified as a fellow creature, then the ecological interpreter is compelled to listen to what Earth has to say. By assigning consciousness to Earth, this method is admittedly somewhat anthropomorphic and as such is vulnerable to its own critique. Not unlike relationships to other human subjects, this method runs the risk of being little more than a self-projection of the interpreter, though Freud and Derrida might say the same thing about any interpretation. Birch refers to this possible error as the *pathetic fallacy*.[20] Nonetheless, my intent here and the intent of the Earth Bible Team is not to deform Earth into the image of a human but rather to relate to Earth as an I-Thou.

Enoch's green apocalypse

First Enoch, a compilation of five identifiable works, contains some of the earliest representations of the apocalyptic genre, dating back to the late third and early second century B.C.E.[21] Utilized by numerous later Jewish texts such as *Jubilees*, the *Testament of the Twelve Patriarchs*, the *Assumption of Moses*, *2 Baruch*, and *4 Ezra*, *1 Enoch* is paradigmatic for both apocalyptic literature and other related genres. For students of New Testament theology it is also significant for its depiction of the Messiah, called the Son of Man, as a pre-existent heavenly being who will pass judgment on both heavenly and earthly beings. While Jude is the only

---

18. Moltmann, *Science and Wisdom*, 71. Cf. Bauckham echoes a similar sentiment, "We recognize that, in continuity with the Old Testament [the New Testament] assumes that humans live in mutuality with the rest of God's creation, that salvation history and eschatology do not lift humans out of nature but heal precisely their distinctive relationship with the rest of nature." Bauckham, "Jesus and the Wild Animals (Mark 1:13)," 4.

19. Reid, "Setting aside the Latter to Heaven," 241–45. Also see Middleton, "A New Heaven and a New Earth," 73–97.

20. Birch, *On Purpose*, 243.

21. *1 Enoch* undoubtedly went through numerous editorial stages. Although a redactional analysis may be able to distinguish one tradition from another, for the present interpretation I am going to focus on the final form of the text, which is the version that would have most likely been available to the New Testament authors.

New Testament text to explicitly cite *1 Enoch*, its influence can be seen throughout the New Testament and within other early Christian literature. The most prominent theme in *1 Enoch* is its eschatological outlook which consists of a description of the final judgment, the destruction of the wicked—comprised of both fallen angels and apostate Jews—and the resurrection of the righteous, including converted gentiles. It may come as a surprise to many readers of the New Testament who are unfamiliar with second temple literature that themes such as the inclusion of the gentiles—a major topic of debate in the New Testament—is not an issue that was unique to early Christianity. The ecological outlook found in the eschatology of *1 Enoch* also begs comparison with the eschatology of the New Testament, especially with its sole apocalypse: the book of Revelation.

Given that Jewish apocalyptic literature is somewhat esoteric, a few preliminary comments should be helpful. John Collins offers a concise and useful definition of an apocalypse: "a genre of revelatory literature with a narrative framework, in which a revelation is mediated by an otherworldly being to a human recipient, disclosing a transcendent reality which is both temporal, insofar as it envisages eschatological salvation (and judgment), and spatial insofar as it involves another, supernatural world."[22] Another noteworthy feature is that all Jewish apocalyptic literature is pseudonymous. Functioning as an implied author, the human recipient of the revelation is portrayed as a prominent historical figure from the distant past. By using a pseudonym, the actual author, who is living during the intertestamental period, is able to appeal to the authority of a revered forefather.[23] Though valuable as a literary device, the use of a pseudonym presents one significant challenge for the interpreter. Given that the historical setting of the narrative predates the time period of the author, identifying any historical referent in the story is difficult and can only be made by way of analogy. However, this also has the side benefit of making the apocalyptic story applicable to a variety of times and settings. In *1 Enoch*, the seer is none other than the prediluvian character from Genesis—the father of Methuselah and the great-grandfather of Noah. Genesis provides little detail about Enoch other than the rather enigmatic

22. Collins, *The Apocalyptic Imagination*, 5.

23. Casting the fictional author as a character from the ancient past also enables the actual author to depict historical events as if they are fulfillment of prophecy—a literary device known as *vaticinium ex eventu*.

comment that "Enoch walked with God; then he was no more, because God took him" (5:24, NRSV). Apparently this was enough to fuel the speculation that he experienced an otherworldly journey, which is the premise of the book that bears his name.

Known as the Book of the Watchers, *1 Enoch* 1–36 elaborates on an opaque story found in Gen 6—the story of the "sons of God" having sex with human women, who then give birth to giants. The canonical account is vague and provides few details. It opens with a reference to a spike in population growth—an often disregarded point that may be more consequential once the story is viewed from Earth's perspective. Overpopulation disrupts the delicate balance an ecosystem, depleting the natural resources, and—if left unchecked—threatens to destroy the land and its various inhabitants. In the biblical account, God responds to this bizarre event by sending the flood. The central section of the Book of Watchers (6–16) fills in the gaps of this story and more. The heavenly culprits, referred to as "Watchers" (think "Peeping Toms"), are clearly identified as angels, who took human women as their wives. In a vision, Enoch witnesses the Watchers being arrested and jailed, where they must await the final judgment: "The Lord said to Raphael, 'Bind Azaz'el hand and foot and throw him into darkness . . . in order that he may be sent to the fire on the great day of judgment" (10:4–6).[24] Interestingly, the imprisonment of the Watchers is accompanied by a renewal of Earth: "And give life to the earth which the angels have corrupted" (10:7). This promise of eventual renewal parallels the green apocalypse of modern day post-apocalyptic stories.

It is important to note that *1 Enoch* draws a direct corollary between the sins of the Watchers and the exploitation of Earth. Their transgressions were twofold. First, they were guilty of sexual sins as indicated in the canonical account, which resulted in the birth of a race of giants—the Nephilim. The Genesis account speaks highly of the giants, describing them as "the heroes that were of old, warriors of renown" (6:4). On the contrary, *1 Enoch* accuses the giants of consuming all of the available food. Once the food was gone, they began to devour the people and even resorted to cannibalizing one another (7:4–6).

In addition to their sexual sins, which produced the all-consuming giants, the Watchers were also guilty of providing inappropriate revela-

24. All translations of *1 Enoch* are from Isaac, "The Book of Enoch," in ed. James Charlesworth, *The Old Testament Pseudepigrapha*, 13–89.

tions to their human wives.[25] This provision of forbidden knowledge is similar to and yet distinct from the canonical story of the origin of evil found in Genesis 3. In the Garden of Eden, Eve received forbidden revelation when she ate from the tree of the knowledge of good and evil, though the Genesis account is ambiguous regarding the details of her education. According to *1 Enoch* and contrary to Genesis, the knowledge of good and evil was revealed by the Watchers and included information on how to manufacture weapons, medicine, jewelry, and cosmetics as well as how to interpret the stars. Had *1 Enoch* been canonized then I suspect that early Pentecostals would have quoted it—alongside 1 Pet 3:3–4—as a proof-text against wearing jewelry and cosmetics. In seriousness, the historical referent behind the criticism of the angelic revelations may very well be the Hellenization that was taking place during the time of the actual author. The Greek generals, who succeeded Alexander the Great, would have appeared as powerful as giants with their advanced weaponry and sheer size of their armies. They wreaked havoc in the Jewish world. Not only had they conquered the land and enslaved the people, but they were threatening to transform or—from the perspective of certain apocalyptic sects—deform the culture.[26]

The first character in *1 Enoch* to protest the injustices caused by the sins of the angels is none other than Earth (7:6). Once Earth has broken the silence, other members of the global community speak out as well: "And the people cried and their voice reached unto heaven" (8:4). After this, Earth's complaint starts to gain traction as it becomes a topic of discussion among the archangels. Finally, as if making it through the last court of appeals, Earth brings its indictment to the very gates of heaven, saying, "And now, O holy ones of heaven, the souls of the people are putting their case before you pleading, 'Bring our judgment before the Most High'" (9:3).[27] So the imprisonment of the Watchers mentioned

25. In stark contrast to the improper revelations of the Watchers, Enoch is shown the truth about the universe through his otherworldly journey, which constitutes the majority of the second half of the book. The point that is being made is that God is in control and is going to make all things right—eventually.

26. Nicklesburg, "Apocalyptic and Myth in 1 Enoch 6–11." Given that the text was used by the Qumran community it is also very possible that the historical referent may have been the perceived corruption of the priestly system in Jerusalem. Collins, *The Prophetic Imagination*, 50.

27. This lament of the people resembles very closely the prayer of the martyrs in Rev 6:9–10.

above actually takes place as a result of Earth coming to voice. This section of *1 Enoch* concludes with the following pronouncement from God: "Cleanse the earth from all injustice, and from all defilement, and from all oppression, and from all sin, and from all iniquity which is being done on earth; remove them from the earth . . . it shall not happen again that I shall send these upon the earth from generation to generation and forever" (10:20–22).

By foregrounding ecojustice principles number three (voice) and number six (resistance), this ecological reading highlights the role of Earth in ways that traditional interpretations of this text would have overlooked. The theme of justice for both people and Earth continues throughout later sections of *1 Enoch*, including warnings against exploiting the poor (96:5), references to a bodily resurrection (92:3), and to a new creation (72:1). This theme of justice for the entire Earth community can also be found in Revelation, which I will turn to after one more comment on the stronger apocalyptic language in *1 Enoch* that I have bracketed out of the discussion thus far.

I have been working within a hermeneutics of identification that presupposes that human beings are intricately interconnected with Earth—the global ecosystem. Motivated by this premise, my reading of *1 Enoch* has sought to highlight the concept of a green apocalypse that is analogous to the secular eschatologies of some late modern post-apocalyptic stories. However, I would be remiss not to acknowledge that *1 Enoch* is not devoid of typical apocalyptic language. For example, the opening chapter announces the coming judgment on the Watchers in terms that seem like certain doom for everyone and everything: "Mountains . . . will fall down . . . high hills . . . shall melt like a honeycomb . . . the earth shall be rent asunder; and all that is upon the earth shall perish" (1:6–7). This type of language, which can also be found in the New Testament (see 2 Pet 3:1–13), has contributed to eschatological views that—if I were to extend my color metaphor—could be classified as a black apocalypse, i.e. the expectation of an annihilation of Earth and an escape to an other-worldly utopia.

Horrible things have been done both to Earth and on Earth that have been justified based on a belief that our space-time-matter reality, including Earth and those who dwell on her, is transient, and therefore can be used and abused. This dark history of effects notwithstanding, I would like to offer, with Tom Wright's help, one final act of retrieval.

Apocalyptic language was employed by ancient authors primarily as a way of "*describing* what we would call space-time events and *investing* them with their theological or cosmic *significance*."[28] To illustrate this point, Wright offers the following example:

> Instead of saying "Babylon is going to fall, and this will be like a cosmic collapse," Isaiah said, "The sun will be darkened, the moon will not give its light, and the stars will be falling from heaven" (Isa 13:10). The Jewish Bible is full of such language . . . and we would be quite wrong to imagine that it was all meant to be taken literally . . . Jews of Jesus's day did not, by and large, expect that the space-time universe was going to come to a stop. They did expect that God was going to act so dramatically within the space-time universe, as he had done before at key moments like the Exodus, that the only appropriate language would be the language of the world taken apart and reborn.[29]

The most famous piece of apocalyptic literature is arguably the last book found in the New Testament canon, the Revelation. The title of the genre actually derives from this book, owing to the fact that it was the first piece of apocalyptic literature to use the word *apocalypse*. In its history of interpretation, Revelation has often been understood as a black apocalypse, though that is largely due to an excessively literal reading. When Revelation is reread from an ecological perspective, another vision of the future for Earth comes into focus.

John's green apocalypse

According to the final vision in Revelation, there is a restoration of both Earth and its creational counterpart—Heaven. Although ecological theology often uses the term creation as shorthand for Earth, this is technically as misnomer.[30] John, on the other hand, is very precise with his language. When he wants to talk about heaven, he uses the common word *ouranos*. When he makes comments about Earth—or Earth's ecosystem—he uses *ge* (along with a variety of other words that represent the different aspects

28. Wright, *The Challenge of Jesus*, 38; emphasis original.

29. Ibid.

30. This misnomer has unfortunately contributed to a dualism that sees heaven as eternal and perfect and earth as transient and marred. The *Earth Bible* team refers to this concept as heavenism. Habel and Balabanski, "Ecojustice Hermeneutics: Reflections and Challenges," 3.

of Earth's ecosystem such as words for sea, rivers, trees, stars, sun and so on). However, when John refers to creation he uses the word *cosmos*. Although usually translated as world, it should not be understood as a synonym for Earth alone but rather Heaven-and-Earth. John only uses *cosmos* a total of three times, twice in the phrase "the foundation of the world" (13:8 and 17:8). In both instances, John is referencing the original creation in such a way that highlights the sovereignty of God. From the perspective of Earth, it is John's other use of *cosmos* that is most consequential. It occurs in the account of the final trumpet in Rev 11:15–18. Although he is only halfway through his story, John reveals a brief picture of the final scene.

> The seventh angel sounded his trumpet, and they were loud voices in heaven, which said: "The kingdom of world (*cosmos*) has become the kingdom of our Lord and his Messiah, and he will reign forever and ever." And the twenty-four elders, who were seated on the thrones before God, fell on their faces and worshiped God, saying: "We give thanks to you, Lord God Almighty, the one who is and who was, because you have taken your great power and have begun to reign. The nations were angry, and your wrath has come. The time has come for judging the dead, and for rewarding your servants the prophets and your people who revere your name, both great and small—and for destroying those who destroy the earth" (NIV).[31]

This final phrase is paradigmatic for an ecological reading of Revelation, though before exploring its meaning more fully there are several other items in this key text that require attention—first, is John's use of *cosmos*. In my opinion, this use of *cosmos* is unique from the other two. As opposed to looking back to the first creation—before the foundation of the world—John is looking forward to the new creation—the coming kingdom of our Lord and his Messiah, described later as the descent of the New Jerusalem. John shows us a glimpse of the end in what is essentially the answer to a portion of the Lord's Prayer: "your kingdom come and your will be done on earth as it is in heaven." A number of details in the text support this interpretation.

Look again at the passage and pay careful attention to the temporal description of God in Rev 11:17—"the one who is and who was." This is

---

31. John's description of judgment echoes *1 Enoch* 10:26, "Destroy (lit. 'disappear') injustice from the face of the earth."

the fourth time in Revelation that John has used this phrase to describe God. In the previous occurrences the expression contained three references to time: present, past, and future: "the one who is and who was and who is to come" (1:4, 8; 4:8).32. Grammatically speaking, the reference to the present and the past are statements of being. The final comment—technically a present participle (*ho erchomenos*) though used here as an idiom for the future—is a statement of action. God is not the one who is, and who was, and who will be but rather the one who is, and who was, and who is to come.[33] In Rev 11:17, the reference to the future is omitted. God is no longer the one who is to come because in this part of the story God comes and establishes the promised eschatological kingdom. In other words, this is a story of the end. It mirrors the final story of the book—the descent of the New Jerusalem (Rev 21–22).

In addition to foreshadowing the end, Rev 11:15–18 also evokes memories of another worship service that was described earlier in the book. In 11:17, the twenty-four elders herald the arrival of the kingdom of God with their worshipful response: "We give thanks to you, Lord God Almighty, the one who is and who was, because you have taken your great power and have begun to reign." This is not the first time the elders have sung this song, although the lyrics have been modified for this special occasion *ad libitum*. Previously they had been led in worship by the four living creatures, who were singing their own version of the qedushah from Isa 6: "Holy, Holy, Holy is the Lord God Almighty; the whole earth is full of your glory." Numerous "covers" were made of Isaiah's original version—by both Jewish and early Christian artists—almost all of which made some modification to the lyrics. Richard Bauckham has ingeniously detected that except for Rev 4:8 all subsequent versions of the qedushah contain a comparable second line: "the whole earth is full of your glory."[34] John substitutes this line with the phrase: "the one who was and who is and who is to come." As Bauckham points out, the implication of this variance is that for John the whole Earth is not yet full of God's glory be-

32. The third occurrence in 4:8 is the only time that the present and past tenses are inverted. This may reflect a subtle emphasis in the literary context. Normally the emphasis is on the presence of God; hence the present tense comes first. In Rev 4, God is being worshipped for creating all things; and therefore, the past tense is placed first, emphasizing God as Creator.

33. Bauckham, *Theology*, 29.

34. Bauckham, *Living with Other Creatures*, 179.

cause it presently being subjugated by those who would destroy it.[35] This is not a statement of ecological despair on John's part. Far from it, it is a declaration of hope. The living creatures are worshipping a God who is still to come and who will bring judgment and salvation. Then the whole Earth will be filled with the glory of God—but not yet.

Signs of the destruction of Earth fill John's vision with vivid imagery. The four horsemen of the apocalypse bring in turn conquest, war, economic disaster, and famine and disease. Trumpets are blown resulting in the burning of the grass and trees. Volcanoes erupt and a giant asteroid falls from the sky. These disasters are repeated as bowls filled with plagues are poured out all over the ground, the sea, the rivers, and the sky. The devastation is so severe that it's no wonder these images have inspired fictional end-of-the-world scenarios. However, the vision of the final judgment in Rev 11:18 suggests that it is not Earth that gets destroyed but rather the destroyers of Earth. If the apocalyptic judgments are not meant for Earth but for its destroyers, then the question that needs to be answered is: "Who are the destroyers of Earth?" One way to find the answer to this question is to flip to the end of the book and see which characters in the story are thrown into the lake of fire and utterly destroyed. The answer comes in John's most detailed telling of the final judgment in Rev 20:7–15. It is here that we learn that destruction comes to the Devil, the Beast, the False Prophet, and those who had sided with them.

At the final judgment, even Death and Hades will be thrown into the lake fire (20:14). It is significant that neither Earth nor Heaven are thrown into the lake, rather John sees them flee from the great white throne, as though they had been dismissed from the court proceedings altogether (20:11). It would be a mistake to interpret their dismissal as their destruction because the very next story tells of their renewal. In John's depiction of the new Heaven and the new Earth, it is important to note that John did not say that God is making all new things but making all things new. The coming of the kingdom of our Lord and his Christ does not result in the annihilation of Earth but in the annihilation of the destroyers of Earth (Rev 11:18). This is a transformation story rather than an annihilation story. As Moltmann writes, "What will be annihilated is Nothingness, what will be

---

35. Ibid. Although he does not explicitly discuss them, Bauckham's perspective correlates nicely with the six ecojustice principles of the Earth Bible Team.

slain is death, what will be dissolved is the power of evil, what will be separated from all created beings is separation from God, sin."[36]

The revelation of a green apocalypse

The historical setting of an apocalyptic narrative—either in the distant past of a famous pseudonym or the distant future of science fiction—creates a certain temporal ambiguity, giving the false impression to the uninitiated that this story is about some other time. Although the stories have a future orientation and envisage an eschatological judgment and salvation, it is crucial to note that the target audience of any apocalypse is not reducible to some eschatological group. The authors of apocalyptic stories—both past and present—write for their own contemporaries as much as for future readers. The stories serve as both warnings of things to come and encouragements to persevere in the resistance of evil.

In the religious versions of these stories, the revelation of a final divine judgment of evil serves as an apocalyptic vaccine against present despair. For the Christian, the revelation of John's green apocalypse is twofold. First, we are called to join with Earth and the rest of the Earth community in worshiping our Creator. Bauckham makes an important point that: "A living sense of participation with other creatures in the worship that all creatures owe and give to God is the strongest antidote to Christian anthropomorphism."[37]

Second, it is our responsibility to resist along with Earth the evil that will eventually be judged. According to Rev 12, those who keep the commandments of God and bear the testimony of Jesus are able to conqueror the Devil "by the blood of the Lamb and by the word of their testimony, for they loved their lives even unto death" (12:11). Later in this same chapter, Earth joins the resistance movement by coming to the aid of the woman clothed in the sun by stepping in to take the destructive punishment that the Devil had intended for her (12:16). Practically speaking from an ecological perspective, the resistance may take several forms but it includes recycling, minimizing our own carbon footprints, and raising the awareness of the ecological crisis. "Resolving the ecological crisis of our planet," writes Desmond Tutu, " . . . is no longer a problem we can leave to the scientists. Just as we are all part of the problem, so

---

36. Moltmann, *In the End–The Beginning*, 145.
37. Bauckham, *Living with Other Creatures*, 163.

we are all also part of the solution."[38] It may look like giants or beasts have conquered our homeland and are destroying our environment, but in the end the God who created all things (Rev 4:11) will make all things new (Rev 21:5).

Juxtaposing the secular eschatology of post-apocalyptic dystopias with ancient apocalyptic texts has highlighted the similarities of these genres, especially in regard to the aspect of a green apocalypse. It is my hope that ecological readings of apocalyptic texts—both secular/religious and present/past—may be useful in the formation of a more developed Pentecostal ecotheology and may also offset the unfortunate popularity of Christian fiction that purports a black apocalypse rather than a green one.[39]

BIBLIOGRAPHY

Althouse, Peter. "'Left Behind'—Fact or Fiction: Ecumenical Dilemmas of the Fundamentalist Millenarian Tensions within Pentecostalism." *Journal of Pentecostal Theology* 13, no. 2 (2005) 187–207.

Anderson, Christopher Todd. "Post-Apocalyptic Nostalgia: WALL-E, Garbage, and American Ambivalence toward Manufactured Goods." *Literature Interpretation Theory* 23, no. 3 (2012) 267–82.

Bauckham, Richard. "Jesus and the Wild Animals (Mark 1:13): A Christological Image for an Ecological Age." In *Jesus of Nazareth: Essays on the Historical Jesus and the New Testament Christology,* edited by Joel B. Green and Max Turner, 3–21. Grand Rapids: Eerdmans, 1994.

———. *Living with Other Creatures: Green Exegesis and Theology.* Waco: Baylor University Press, 2011.

———. *The Theology of the Book of Revelation.* Cambridge: Cambridge University Press, 1993.

Birch, Charles. *On Purpose.* Kensington: University of New South Wales Press, 1990.

Buber, Martin. *I and Thou.* Translated by Walter Kaufmann. New York: Scribner's Sons, 1970.

Collins, John J. *The Apocalyptic Imagination: An Introduction to Jewish Apocalyptic Literature.* Grand Rapids: Eerdmans, 1998.

Coulter, Dale M. "Pentecostal Visions of The End: Eschatology, Ecclesiology and the Fascination of the Left Behind Series." *Journal of Pentecostal Theology* 14, no. 1 (2005) 81–98.

38. Tutu, "Foreword," vii.

39. For a critical assessments of the *Left Behind* series and its effects on Pentecostalism, see Althouse, "'Left Behind'—Fact or Fiction"; Coulter, "Pentecostal Visions of The End"; and van der Laan, "What is left behind?"

Earth Bible Team, "Ecojustice Hermeneutics: Reflections and Challenges." In *The Earth Story in the New Testament*, edited by Norman C. Habel and Vicky Balabanski. Sheffield: Sheffield Academic, 2002.

Goodenough, Ursula. *The Sacred Depths of Nature*. Oxford: Oxford University Press, 1998.

Habel, Norman C. "Introducing Ecological Hermeneutics." In *Exploring Ecological Hermeneutics*, edited by Norman C. Habel and Peter Trudinger, 1–8. SBL Symposium 46. Atlanta: SBL, 2008.

———. "The Origins and Challenges of an Ecojustice Hermeneutic." In *Relating to the Text: Interdisciplinary and Form-Critical Insights on the Bible*, edited by Timothy Sandoval and Carleen Mandolfo, 4–59. London: T. & T. Clark, 2003.

Isaac, E. "The Book of Enoch." In *The Old Testament Pseudepigrapha*, edited by James Charlesworth, 1:5–89. Peabody, MA: Hendrickson, 1983.

Lamp, Jeffery S. *The Greening of Hebrews? Ecological Readings in the Letter to the Hebrews*. Eugene, OR: Pickwick, 2012.

McFague, Sallie. *Super, Natural Christians: How We Should Love Nature*. Minneapolis: Fortress, 1997.

Meine, Curt D. *Aldo Leopold: His Life and Work*. Madison, WI: University of Wisconsin Press, 2010.

Middleton, J. Richard. "A New Heaven and a New Earth: The Case for a Holistic Reading of the Biblical Story of Redemption." *Journal for Christian Theological Research* 11 (2006) 73–97.

Moltmann, Jürgen. *In the End—The Beginning: The Life of Hope*. Translated by Margaret Kohl. Minneapolis: Fortress, 2004.

———. *The Coming of God: Christian Eschatology*. Translated by Margaret Kohl. Minneapolis: Fortress, 1996.

———. *Science and Wisdom*. Minneapolis: Fortress, 2003.

Nicklesburg, G. W. E. "Apocalyptic and Myth in 1 Enoch 6–11." *Journal of Biblical Literature* 96 (1977) 383–405.

Northcott, Michael S. *The Environment and Christian Ethics*. Cambridge: Cambridge University Press, 1996.

Reid, Duncan. "Setting aside the Ladder to Heaven: Revelation 21:1—22:5 from the Perspective of the Earth." In *Readings from the Perspective of Earth*, edited by Norman C. Habel, 232–45. Sheffield: Sheffield Academic, 2000.

Swoboda, A. J. *Tongues and Trees: Toward a Pentecostal Ecological Theology*. Journal of Pentecostal Theology Supplement 40, Blandford Forum, UK: Deo, 2013.

Tutu, Desmond. "Foreword." In *The Earth Story in the New Testament*, edited by Norman C. Habel and Vicky Balabanski, vii–viii. London: Sheffield Academic, 2001.

van der Laan, Paul N. "What is Left Behind? A Pentecostal Response to Eschatological Fiction." *Journal of the European Pentecostal Theological Association* 24 (2004) 49–70.

Volf, Miroslav. "Loving with Hope: Eschatology and Social Responsibility." *Transformation* 7 (1990) 28–31.

White, Lynn. "The Historical Roots of Our Ecological Crisis." *Science* 155 (1967) 1203–7.

Wright, N. T., *The Challenge of Jesus: Rediscovering Who Jesus Was & Is*. Downers Grove, IL: InterVarsity, 1999.

9

Jesus as Sanctifier:
Creation Care and the Fivefold Gospel

Jeffrey S. Lamp

Introduction

At the 2012 annual meeting of the Society for Pentecostal Studies (SPS), I presented a paper surveying early Pentecostal periodical literature. I demonstrated that current interest among Pentecostals in the care of creation is not merely a fad, but rather is rooted in some early Pentecostal soteriological affirmations that the whole of the created order is the object of God's saving action in Christ.[1] Part of my study cited select examples of current Pentecostal rationales for the care of creation, including an essay by Matthew Tallman, "Pentecostal Ecology: A Theological Paradigm."[2]

Tallman adopts a traditional Pentecostal paradigm that describes Jesus as Savior, Spirit-baptizer, Healer, and Coming King, to outline a Pentecostal approach to creation-care. In the question-answer period following the presentation of the paper, Chris Thomas questioned what it would look like for Pentecostals to consider creation-care in light of the fifth plank of the fivefold gospel: Jesus as Sanctifier.

This essay will explore what the theological construct of Jesus as Sanctifier would add to a Pentecostal approach to creation-care (acknowledging that Tallman's formulation is adequate in terms of his fourfold presentation). The essay will briefly survey the role of the fivefold gospel

1. Lamp, "New Heavens," forthcoming.
2. Tallman, "Pentecostal Ecology," 135–54.

in Pentecostal theological reflection. Following this survey, the essay will present Tallman's model for a Pentecostal ecology. From there, it will suggest that the view of Jesus as Sanctifier contributes to a Pentecostal approach to creation-care in terms of three biblical motifs: (1) creation as sacred space in which the human vocation to serve and care for creation is priestly, (2) the biblical image of the created order as co-worshipers of God alongside human beings, and (3) the fitting of creation to be the eschatological dwelling place of God. The essay will conclude with a statement of how this fivefold gospel approach to creation-care advances that presented by Tallman.

The fivefold gospel in pentecostal theological reflection

There is growing interest among Pentecostal thinkers regarding what precisely delineates a theology as "Pentecostal." Much of this attention simply seeks to identify Pentecostalism's distinctives. Walter J. Hollenweger argues that narrativity (rather than any given doctrinal formulation) is the distinctive element uniting Pentecostals.[3] As we find, Pentecostals draw heavily upon the narrative of Acts for self-identification, pointing to their experience of the Spirit as continuance of the Acts narrative in God's redemptive program. Frank Macchia, though acknowledging the importance of narrative in Pentecostal identity, finally sees narrative as insufficient in terms of distinctiveness, and opts instead for the distinctive traditional doctrine of the baptism of the Holy Spirit as a unifier for Pentecostals.[4] Macchia then reworks the metaphor of Spirit-baptism into a more comprehensive theological construct for Pentecostals.[5]

Another recent focus is the utilization of the "full gospel" as a paradigm for Pentecostal theological formulation. Prominent Pentecostal thinkers give credit to Donald Dayton's study of early Pentecostalism for stimulating this recent line of reflection.[6] Dayton argues that from the earliest stages of the Pentecostal movement, the "full gospel" understanding of Jesus as Savior, Healer, Spirit-baptizer, Sanctifier, and Coming King

3. Hollenweger, "After Twenty Years of Research," 6.

4. Macchia, *Baptized in the Spirit*, 49–57.

5. This is the focus of Macchia's *Baptized in the Spirit*, and also his subsequent volume, *Justified in the Spirit*.

6. Dayton, *Theological Roots*, chap. 1.

served as that which rendered Pentecostals distinctive and that which shaped their theological reflection. Several recent studies have sought to utilize this construct to conceptualize various theological tenets. For instance, Steve Land employed the fivefold gospel as paradigmatic in his portrayal of Pentecostal spirituality.[7] Similarly, Chris Thomas used the construct to provide the contours for a Pentecostal consideration of ecclesiology in hope of stimulating further application of the fivefold gospel model in Pentecostal theological reflection.[8] Ken Archer took up the challenge, providing further rationale for the model and an expansion on Thomas's ecclesiological application.[9] Though not central to his thesis, Chris Green employed the fivefold gospel in his study urging Pentecostals to rediscover a robust theology and practice of the Eucharist.[10] Amos Yong argues for the use of the construct in his formulation of a Pentecostal political theology.[11]

In the minds of many, this fivefold gospel offers promise for constructing a distinctively Pentecostal theology. In some respects, it provides for Pentecostals what the so-called Wesleyan Quadrilateral provides for Wesleyans, a methodological paradigm for addressing theological issues. In one key respect, it advances on what the Quadrilateral provides for Wesleyans—it not only provides methodological direction, but it also provides the substantial center around which to formulate theology. Pentecostal theological identity draws on its understanding of Jesus in terms of the categories Savior, Healer, Spirit-baptizer, Coming King, and to many, Sanctifier. Theological reflection from this orientation provides an opportunity to develop distinctively Pentecostal contributions not only in its own communities, but also in the larger Christian community.

One significant issue (giving rise to the present discussion) is that within Pentecostalism, there remain two strands of divergent views on the extent of the "full gospel." In general, those from the Finished Work strand adopt the fourfold model of Jesus as Savior, Healer, Spirit-baptizer, and Coming King, while those from the Wesleyan strand add Jesus as Sanctifier. While acknowledging that the earliest phases of Pentecostalism, represented by the Wesleyan strand, held to the fivefold model, Dayton

7. Land, *Pentecostal Spirituality*.
8. Thomas, *Spirit of the New Testament*, 19–22.
9. Archer, "Fivefold Gospel," 7–45.
10. Green, *Lord's Supper*, 272–80.
11. Yong, *Days of Caesar*, 95–98.

argues that the fourfold model that emerged later more clearly reflects the logic of Pentecostal theology.[12]

Several Pentecostals, however, argue that the focus on Jesus as Sanctifier is essential to Pentecostal theological identity. Archer argues that the earliest Pentecostal community is one in which the fivefold gospel served as the central narrative conviction, functioning as a narrative web with Jesus at the center.[13] The fivefold gospel functioned as the story that made sense of the early community's experiences of the Spirit in their worship and communal life. Sanctification as the ontological transformative reality is crucial to the soteriology at the core of this narrative, as it helps to define the community. As pertains to the focus of the present discussion, we will show that inclusion of Jesus as Sanctifier helps to bind together the other four components of the "full gospel." First, however, we will survey Tallman's presentation of a Pentecostal ecology based on the fourfold model.

Tallman's fourfold gospel approach to creation-care

Tallman's appropriation of the fourfold gospel is not an exhaustive presentation of a Pentecostal ecology or ecotheology. Rather, it offers suggestions for the types of considerations that would go into the construction of a full-orbed Pentecostal ecological theology. He does not stick rigidly to traditional language concerning the four planks of the model.

Tallman begins by examining creation-care in terms of Jesus as Savior, which he labels "soteriological ecology."[14] Tallman notes a common caricature of Pentecostals—that they are somewhat dualistic in outlook and thus limit salvation to the redemption of human beings from sin, ignoring the more cosmic dimensions of salvation. As such, Pentecostals often succumb to an anthropocentric creation theology that emphasizes hierarchical or dominating expressions. Interestingly, Tallman also makes a connection between dualistic and anthropocentric tendencies toward the environment and racism and sexism. Tallman suggests that the historic foundation of Pentecostalism at Azusa Street (that transcended racial and gender distinctions) has within its soteriology the resources to combat environmental degradation. He offers the

12. Dayton, *Theological Roots*, 17–23.

13. Archer, "Fivefold Gospel," 55–56.

14. Tallman, "Pentecostal Ecology," 138–42.

Roman Catholic focus on the cruciform aspects of Christology, Jürgen Moltmann's emphasis on the crucified God, and Lyle Dabney's proposal of a *pneumatologia crucis*, as counterbalances to the overly triumphalistic Christology of many Pentecostals. Such correctives are necessary for the development of a robust Pentecostal soteriological ecology.

Next Tallman discusses Jesus as Healer under the heading "ecological healing."[15] He finds irony in the fact that despite Pentecostalism's insistence upon Jesus meeting the practical, physical needs of his people through bodily healing, there is little attention paid to unhealthy lifestyles and specific ecological sins that lead to disease and death. But Tallman finds reason for encouragement with regard to Pentecostal involvement in creation-care through the image of Jesus the Healer. If Pentecostals were to extend the scope of healing beyond human beings alone to all of creation, the image of healing would prove a powerful impetus for Pentecostals to care for creation. Again, anthropocentrism limits a Pentecostal participation in the practice of creation-care. But the early Pentecostal focus on both natural and supernatural healing should provide current Pentecostals the framework to "begin preaching and living out the lifestyle necessary to begin the process of global ecological healing."[16]

The lengthiest segment of Tallman's discussion centers on Jesus the Spirit-baptizer, treated under the heading "pneumatological ecology."[17] In Tallman's mind, this plank of the model offers the most viable grounds for a Pentecostal ecology. Pneumatological experience and praxis are perhaps the most noticeable distinctives of Pentecostals and clearly ground pneumatology at the foreground of their theological reflection. The focus on pneumatology among non-Pentecostal groups in care for creation makes pneumatology a fruitful avenue through which to pursue a Pentecostal ecology. This outside focus on pneumatology and ecology provides Pentecostals common ground from which to enter into fruitful dialogue as to how Pentecostals might expand the scope of their pneumatology to include the Spirit's work in all of creation as well as among human beings. Moltmann and Clark Pinnock are cited as especially noteworthy conversation partners. Current Pentecostals and Charismatics

15. Ibid., 142–45.

16. Ibid., 145.

17. Ibid., 145–50.

already are doing exciting work in this area,[18] but Tallman suggests that such dialogue would help Pentecostals develop a prophetic voice to address pressing environmental problems.

Tallman concludes with a brief examination of how Jesus as Coming King would inform a Pentecostal ecology.[19] Under the heading "eschatological ecology," Tallman notes that the focus of many Pentecostals on Christ's imminent *parousia* has led them to disregard any prospect for a future hope for the other-than-human created order. God is going to destroy creation in the end, so why work toward its betterment in the present, especially if such an emphasis would detract from the priority of evangelism in the mission of Pentecostal Christians? Tallman suggests that if Pentecostals might be convinced to expand their vision in terms of soteriology, healing, and pneumatology, as noted above, then perhaps they might be persuaded to entertain the possibility of alternative eschatologies and how a vision for the future might inform present ecological praxis in the world. Here again, Moltmann, particularly in his theology of hope, is a fruitful conversation partner to encourage Pentecostals to see the future transformation of the entire cosmos as an impetus to see present ecological praxis as a holy act that contributes to the future glorification of the cosmos.

The common thread in Tallman's discussion is the necessity for Pentecostals to expand the scope of what they mean when speaking in terms of the fourfold gospel. A Pentecostal ecology requires Pentecostals to see the beneficiaries of Jesus' work as extending beyond human beings alone. That work is underway among Pentecostals, and Tallman's configuration of Pentecostal creation-care under the rubric of the fourfold gospel is a meaningful paradigm for Pentecostal engagement in ecological praxis. The remainder of this discussion will seek to delineate how viewing Jesus as Sanctifier might enhance the model proffered by Tallman.

Jesus as sanctifier: "doxological ecology"

In the spirit of Tallman's discussion, we will assign a heading for the fifth plank in our fivefold gospel model, opting for the label "doxological ecology." Three biblical motifs will be noted in justification of this label: creation as sacred space in which the human vocation to serve and care

18. See discussion in Lamp, "New Heavens," forthcoming.

19. Tallman, "Pentecostal Ecology," 150–52.

for creation is understood as a priestly vocation; the biblical image of the created order as co-worshipers of God alongside human beings; and the fitting of creation to be the eschatological dwelling place of God. At the outset we also note Tallman's refrain that Pentecostals will need to expand the scope of their understanding of the extent of the efficacy of sanctification beyond human beings alone to include all of the created order.

Priests in the temple of creation

Scholars often argue that a key motif in the Old Testament redemption narrative is that the world is to be transformed into the temple of God.[20] William P. Brown suggests that the Gen 1 creation narratives mirrors the creation of the tabernacle in Exod 25—40.[21] God in the creation narratives embodies the roles of Moses as instruction giver, Aaron as priest, and Bezalel as artisan. Moreover, Bezalel is described as endowed with the *ruach* to perform this work, suggesting that the *ruach* in Gen 1:2 signifies the creative presence of God. The parallels between these narratives suggest that in the construction of the tabernacle is seen the destiny for the whole created order: transformation of the world into the dwelling place of God.

If creation is to be transformed into the dwelling place of God, then humans are the priests who tend this sanctuary. Foundational to this motif is the pair of creation stories in Gen 1—2. In chapter 1, human beings are created "in the image of God." Richard Middleton's insightful study on the image of God shows that in its Ancient Near Eastern context, an image is established in a location to represent the presence of a king in a distant land.[22] The image mediates the presence of the monarch where the monarch is physically absent. Human beings as the image of God, as depicted in Gen 1:26-28, are to go forth as mediators of the divine presence in the world to reflect the nature and character of God, to subdue the earth and have dominion, to function as God's viceroys for the management of the world. This mandate has been variously evaluated and criticized, ranging from positions that it provides the rationale for

20. Beale, *Temple*, 29–167; Laansma, "Hidden Stories," 9–18; Walton, *Ancient Near Eastern Thought*, 113–34.

21. Brown, *Seven Pillars*, 47.

22. Middleton, *Liberating Image*, chap. 3.

human exploitation of creation[23] to positions that at least in a "pre-fall" world it serves as a call to extend God's benevolent rule in all the world.[24] However, it is at least plausible that the description of the place of the human in the garden in Gen 2:15, "Then Yahweh Elohim took the human and put him into the garden of Eden to tend it and protect it,"[25] qualifies the mandate in chapter 1.[26] As such, it provides a basis for the redemptive narrative noted above.

If the transformation of creation into the temple is a motif in the redemptive narrative of the Old Testament, then a natural extension of this idea is to view the human image-bearers as the priests in this temple. This idea is strongly embedded in Eastern Orthodox thought and is a significant component for its liturgy, soteriology, and environmental ethic.[27] It is in the Eucharist that liturgy, soteriology, and environmental ethics come together. In it is imaged the human priest, offering up the world (embodied in the bread and wine) to God, who in turn sanctifies the world and gives it back to human beings.[28] Here human beings are involved in transforming some of the produce of the world into the elements of the Eucharist, working in and with the world to offer the world back to God in worship. God, in turn, accepts this offering of the world from the priests, and offers it back in the concrete act of eating the bread and drinking the wine. For the purposes of the present discussion, this Eucharistic act accomplishes two things. First, it sacramentally represents the benevolent subduing of the world—acts that increasingly claim the world as the temple of God. Secondly, it sacramentally represents God's giving back the world to human beings to be tended and protected as stated in Gen 2:15. The liturgical act of the Eucharist is a proclamation *in nuce* of the narrative of God's redemption of creation, with its call for the human image-bearers to care for creation in anticipation of its ultimate redemption.

How might this notion inform Pentecostal creation-care? Here current Pentecostals should heed the call of Chris Green to reclaim a ro-

23. Habel, "Playing God," 39; White, "Historical Roots," 1203–7.

24. Freitheim, *Genesis*, 346.

25. Translation from Richter, "Environmental Law," 376.

26. It may be that Gen 2:15 actually subverts the negative potential or even intent of Gen 1:26–28.

27. As seen in the collected environmental writings and addresses of the Ecumenical Patriarch Bartholomew, *On Earth as in Heaven*.

28. Zizioulas, *Eucharistic Communion*, 133–75.

bust theology and practice of the Eucharist as evidenced in the earliest stages of the Pentecostal movement.[29] Among other things, a renewed focus on the Eucharist would entail a renewed assessment on the place of creation in the redemptive drama of God in Christ. Eucharistic devotion would portray the hallowing of creation in doxology and call human beings to perform their priestly role of mediating God's redemption of creation in their ethical responsibility to tend and protect the garden and to expand this sense of garden into the whole world, reclaiming it as the place of God's dwelling. So in keeping with Tallman's refrain, Pentecostals would need to expand their understanding of the recipients of the sanctifying presence of God to include creation, as well as to enhance their Eucharistic devotion.

Creation declaring the glory of God

Some advocates of creation-care are uncomfortable with what they perceive to be an anthropocentric bias that leads to hermeneutical and theological conclusions that elevate the value of human beings at the expense of the other-than-human creation.[30] So the picture sketched in the previous section of this discussion is criticized for seeing a value posited to other-than-human creation only in terms of human mediation. While these critics do point out a potential danger in overestimating the place of human beings in the created order, it seems impossible to deny that the biblical metanarratives of creation and redemption place a significant emphasis on the role of human beings in bringing about God's purposes for the world.[31] Yet despite this heavy biblical emphasis on the place of

29. Green, *Lord's Supper*, esp. 252–53 and 257–58, where he draws a connection between the Eucharist and creation.

30. Northcott, *Environment and Christian Ethics*, 133–34; Habel, "Introducing Ecological Hermeneutics," 1–8.

31. Horrell, *Greening Paul*, 123–25, draws a couple of helpful distinctions that are pertinent in the present discussion. They argue that a distinction must be drawn between "anthropomonism" and "anthropocentrism" in the biblical texts. They claim that many biblical passages, though having anthropocentric interests, are not necessarily anthropomonistic, that is, having human beings as their sole focus. Moreover, noting that the Bible does indeed shape its discourse in anthropocentric terms, rather than seeing this as a "teleological anthropocentrism" that ascribes ultimate significance to human beings, they suggest seeing it as an "instrumental anthropocentrism" that acknowledges the unique position of human beings in the biblical story and their status as the intended audience of the Bible in order to call for ecological action in the world.

human beings in God's order, there are several passages that indicate that the other-than-human creation has intrinsic value of its own in God's sight. One need only look at the declarations in Gen 1 that these aspects of creation are good in God's sight, the statements in the Wisdom corpus that creation reflects the manifest wisdom of God (e.g., Prov 3:19, 8:22–31; Wis 7:22—8:1), or the affirmations of what I have elsewhere called "creational Christology" (John 1:10; 1 Cor 8:6; Col 1:16–17; Heb 1:2–3a; Rev 3:14) in which Christ is lauded as the agency and sustainer of the created order,[32] to see that even the other-than-human created order exhibits something of the nature and character of God in its being. Moreover, the panoramic sweeps of the created order in Ps 104 and Job 38—41 depict God's care for creation, evidenced in the detailed care with which God created the vast, diverse array of life in the cosmos and described in terms in which human beings are not central to their own being.[33] Perhaps a Rabbinic interpretation of the creation story in Gen 1 tempers an overly anthropocentric view: the reason human beings were created at the end of God's creative work just before the establishment of Sabbath is to teach them humility, for if their minds become too proud, "[they] may be reminded that even the gnat preceded [them] in the order of creation" (Sanhedrin 38a).

In light of the value God places on the other-than-human creation, one way in which the perspective of Jesus as Sanctifier may inform a Pentecostal creation-care is to examine the motif of the other-than-human creation as co-worshipers of God alongside human beings. This motif is best illustrated in the words of Ps 148:

---

32. Lamp, *Greening of Hebrews?*, 10.

33. Brown, *Seven Pillars*, 125–31, 158–59.

¹Praise the LORD!
Praise the LORD from the heavens;
praise him in the heights!
²Praise him, all his angels;
praise him, all his host!

³Praise him, sun and moon;
praise him, all you shining stars!
⁴Praise him, you highest heavens,
and you waters above the heavens!

⁵Let them praise the name of the LORD,
for he commanded and they were created.
⁶He established them forever and ever;
he fixed their bounds, which cannot be passed.

⁷Praise the LORD from the earth,
you sea monsters and all deeps,
⁸fire and hail, snow and frost,
stormy wind fulfilling his command!

⁹Mountains and all hills,
fruit trees and all cedars!
¹⁰Wild animals and all cattle,
creeping things and flying birds!

¹¹Kings of the earth and all peoples,
princes and all rulers of the earth!
¹²Young men and women alike,
old and young together!

¹³Let them praise the name of the LORD,
for his name alone is exalted;
his glory is above earth and heaven.

The psalm's progression is telling. The psalm divides into two major movements, with the other-than-human creation called to praise God in vv. 1–10 and the human component of creation called to praise in vv. 11–12. Within the other-than-human portion, heavenly beings are enjoined to praise in vv. 1–2, followed by celestial entities in vv. 3–6, and earthly entities including meteorological and biological entities in vv. 7–10. All of these are joined in praise of God by human beings of all ranks, genders, and ages in vv. 11–12, with v. 13 standing as a summary call to worship for all of creation to stand in unison in praise of the Lord whose name is exalted above all that God has created. Brown's words, describing Ps 104 originally, seem appropriate with respect to Ps 148: "[It is a] panoramic sweep of creation from the theological and the cosmological to the ecological and the biological, all bracketed by the doxological."[34] A similar scene where Christ is exalted by the whole creation is envisioned in Rev 5:13.

So how does the perspective of Jesus as Sanctifier help inform Pentecostal creation-care here? In its most basic sense, sanctification entails a setting apart for God, especially in terms of worship. Levitical legislation is concerned in part to establish protocols for ensuring that worshipers are properly prepared to worship God appropriately, having been set apart to approach God in holiness. Pentecostals are known, perhaps even caricatured, as a people of passionate worship, having been set apart as God's people by Christ and the Spirit. The biblical picture of the other-than-human creation worshiping God alongside God's people should challenge Pentecostals to expand their vision of that which is set apart to worship God. God values all of creation, and all of creation sings forth its gratitude in praise. Seeing creation in these terms hallows creation and establishes it as something that should be tended carefully.

"And God Will Be All in All"

N. T. Wright, in his book *Surprised by Hope*, speaks of the Christian hope in terms of the renewal of the entire cosmos in which resurrected human beings dwell in the united new heaven and new earth, a world filled by God's presence and love such that God will be all in all (1 Cor 15:28).[35] Numerous scholars, from both non-Pentecostal and Pentecostal circles, have adopted a construct similar to Wright's articulation, but speak of such a dynamic in terms of pneumatology.[36] For sake of space, the present discussion will look briefly at the articulation of one representative

34. Brown, *Seven Pillars*, 145.

35. Wright, *Surprised by Hope*, 101–4.

36. Representative of non-Pentecostals are Boff, *Cry of the Earth*, 271; and Moltmann, *God in Creation*, 12, 15–17. Representative of Pentecostals are Macchia, *Baptized in the Spirit*, 102–3; Pinnock, *Flame of Love*, 48–49; Studebaker, "Spirit in Creation," 943–60; Studebaker, "Creation Care," 248–63; Swoboda, "Eco-Glossolalia," 101–16.

Pentecostal scholar, Frank Macchia, in terms of how this perspective might help define Pentecostal creation-care.[37]

In *Baptized in the Spirit*, Macchia reconfigures the Pentecostal understanding of Spirit-baptism to conceptualize God's saving activity in the world, and thus the church's mission in the world, in terms of a robust pneumatological framework. The result is an account of Spirit-baptism that extends beyond individual experience of the Holy Spirit, so frequently caricatured in the Pentecostal focus on glossolalia, so that "the Spirit is seen as involved in the reach of life toward renewal in all things."[38] Put succinctly, Macchia's reappropriation of the Pentecostal metaphor of Spirit-baptism reframes the metaphor such that "Spirit baptism is a baptism into the love of God that sanctifies, renews, and empowers until Spirit baptism turns all of creation into the final dwelling place of God."[39]

Macchia makes much of the words of Gregory of Nyssa in his understanding of a more cosmically-scoped pneumatology: "The Spirit is a living and a substantial and distinctly subsisting kingdom with which the only begotten Christ is anointed and is king of all that is."[40] For Macchia, this means that it is in the Spirit that creation is transformed to participate in the kingdom's reign of life. It is also through the Spirit that the lordship of Christ is realized. The Spirit-endowed and resurrected Jesus in turn pours out the Spirit on all flesh in order to liberate creation from within history for new possibilities of eschatological life both in the present and for the future.[41] It is through the church, the Spirit-baptized people of the kingdom, that the cosmos-transforming ministry of the Spirit is enfleshed in witness of the eschatological transformation of the cosmos.[42]

It is at this point that the perspective of Jesus as Sanctifier helps define a Pentecostal practice of creation-care. Again, it will require an expansion of scope, particularly in terms of that which is sanctified in order for God to dwell. In a way analogous to the outpouring of the Spirit to create a people in which God dwells, so too is the Spirit poured out in all of creation in preparation for its ultimate destiny of becoming the dwell-

37. I have discussed this in more detail in Lamp, *Greening of Hebrews?*, 65–67; and Lamp, "New Heavens," forthcoming.

38. Macchia, *Baptized in the Spirit*, 41.

39. Ibid., 60.

40. Green, *On the Lord's Prayer*, 3. Quoted in Macchia, *Baptized in the Spirit*, 89.

41. Macchia, *Baptized in the Spirit*, 97.

42. Ibid., 155, 203–4.

ing place of God. But more than this, the Spirit-endowed people of God are also a conduit through which the Spirit works this transformation of all creation. Care for creation in anticipation of its final redemption becomes one avenue through which the Spirit witnesses of this redemption in the mission of the church in the world. Spirit-endowed believers work in concert with the Spirit in order to transform creation into the dwelling place of God. Wright calls this "building for the kingdom," a view that sees work done in the present in anticipation of the future kingdom as being mysteriously taken up and incorporated in that future kingdom.[43] Practicing creation-care serves as evidence of the kinds of work that the Spirit is doing leading to the hallowing of the cosmos necessary to prepare the cosmos to become the place of God's eternal dwelling.

Is five better than four?

So does the addition of the motif of Jesus as Sanctifier advance upon the fourfold model for Pentecostal creation-care proposed by Tallman? If so, how? To answer this, we return to the opening section of this essay, where we cited Archer to the effect that the understanding of Jesus as Sanctifier speaks to the ontological transformative reality at the core of Pentecostal soteriology and communal identity. It is this transformational element that is pertinent. To summarize, we identified three motifs descriptive of this emphasis on Jesus as Sanctifier: creation as sacred space in which the human vocation to serve and care for creation is understood as a priestly vocation; the biblical image of the created order as co-worshipers of God alongside human beings; and the fitting of creation to be the eschatological dwelling place of God. We further summarized these emphases under the rubric "doxological ecology" in keeping with Tallman's approach. Each of these motifs entailed viewing the other-than-human creation as set apart (the basic sense of the term "sanctify"), hallowed in God's estimation, created good and holy, and though presently corrupted by the effects of sin, destined for transformation and redemption along with God's human creation. Analogous to human beings, the other-than-human creation will experience a transformation in connection with the transformation of human beings leading to final redemption. Moreover, again analogous to human beings, the other-than-human creation is already experiencing its transformation in the present, seen in the priestly vocation to carry out

43. Wright, *Surprised by Hope*, 208.

the creational mandate to make creation into the dwelling place of God. And one more time, analogous to human beings, the other-than-human creation shows forth the glory of God and issues forth in praise of God for his goodness. A Pentecostal creation-care keeps in view the destiny of the whole created order and participates in the realization of that destiny in the present, viewed in terms of transformation best seen in the picture of Jesus as Sanctifier.

This picture of "doxological ecology" also helps bring the other four planks of Tallman's model into a more coherent whole by providing a *telos* for the other components of the model. Creation is currently experiencing, and will undergo, transformation in attainment of its destiny. The transformation envisioned by seeing Jesus as Sanctifier ecologically provides the substance of what will be attained under Tallman's heading of "soteriological ecology." The current priestly role of human beings in caring for creation in the process of creation becoming the dwelling place of God helps define the "ecological healing" advanced by Tallman. The contemporary focus of Pentecostal thinkers on seeing the Spirit as active through the church to shape creation to participate eternally as the dwelling place of God obviously speaks to the concerns of Tallman's "pneumatological ecology," but speaks equally as obviously to the category "eschatological ecology." Moreover, it also picks up the themes of "soteriological ecology" and "ecological healing" as well. Finally, all creation sings out in praise to God for this whole complex of themes, bringing to crescendo the notion of "doxological ecology" entailed in viewing Jesus as Sanctifier in ecological terms.

For those Pentecostals who adhere to a fivefold gospel position, inclusion of an ecological understanding of Jesus as Sanctifier provides a depth and coherence to a Pentecostal approach to creation-care that makes for a stronger rationale for Pentecostals to engage in care for God's creation.

BIBLIOGRAPHY

Archer, Kenneth J. "The Fivefold Gospel and the Mission of the Church: Ecclesiastical Implications and Opportunities." In *Toward a Pentecostal Ecclesiology: The Church and the Fivefold Gospel*, edited by John Christopher Thomas, 7–45. Cleveland, TN: CPT, 2010.

Bartholomew, Ecumenical Patriarch. *On Earth as in Heaven: Ecological Vision and Initiatives of Ecumenical Patriarch Bartholomew*. Orthodox Christianity and Contemporary Thought. Bronx, NY: Fordham University Press, 2011.

Beale, Gregory K. *The Temple and the Church's Mission: A Biblical Theology of the Dwelling Place of God*. Downers Grove, IL: InterVarsity, 2004.

Boff, Leonardo. *Cry of the Earth, Cry of the Poor*. Maryknoll, NY: Orbis, 1997.

Brown, William P. *The Seven Pillars of Creation: The Bible, Science, and the Ecology of Wisdom*. Oxford: Oxford University Press, 2010.

Dayton, Donald W. *Theological Roots of Pentecostalism*. Grand Rapids: Baker Academic, 1987.

Fretheim, Terence. *The Book of Genesis*. New Interpreter's Bible. Nashville: Abingdon, 1994.

Green, Chris E. W. *Toward a Pentecostal Theology of the Lord's Supper*. Cleveland, TN: CPT, 2012.

Habel, Norman C. "Introducing Ecological Hermeneutics." In *Exploring Ecological Hermeneutics*, edited by Norman C. Habel and Peter Trudinger, 1–8. SBL Symposium 46. Atlanta: SBL, 2008.

———. "Playing God or Playing Earth? An Ecological Reading of Genesis 1.26–28." In *"And God Saw That It Was Good." Essays on Creation and God in Honor of Terence Freitheim*, edited by Frederick Gaiser and Mark Throntveit, 33–41. Word and World Supplement 5. St. Paul, MN: [AQ]Word and World, Luther Seminary, 2006.

Hollenweger, Walter J. *The Pentecostals*. 2nd ed. Peabody, MA: Hendrickson, 1988.

———. "After Twenty Years' Research on Pentecostalism." *International Review of Mission* 75, no. 297 (1986) 3–12.

Horrell, David G., et al. *Greening Paul: Rereading the Apostle in a Time of Ecological Crisis*. Waco, TX: Baylor University Press, 2010.

Laansma, Jon. "Hidden Stories in Hebrews: Cosmology and Theology." In *A Cloud of Witnesses: The Theology of Hebrews in Its Ancient Contexts*, edited by Richard Bauckham et al., 9–18. London: T. & T. Clark, 2008.

Lamp, Jeffrey S. *The Greening of Hebrews? Ecological Readings in the Letter to the Hebrews*. Eugene, OR: Pickwick, 2012.

———. "New Heavens and New Earth: Early Pentecostal Soteriology as a Foundation for Creation-Care in the Present." *Pneuma*, forthcoming.

Land, Steven J. *Pentecostal Spirituality: A Passion for the Kingdom*. Journal of Pentecostal Theology Supplement 1. Sheffield: Sheffield Academic, 1993.

Macchia, Frank. *Baptized in the Spirit: A Global Pentecostal Theology*. Grand Rapids: Zondervan, 2006.

———. *Justified in the Spirit: Creation, Redemption, and the Triune God*. Grand Rapids: Eerdmans, 2010.

Middleton, J. Richard. *The Liberating Image: The* Imago Dei *in Genesis 1*. Grand Rapids: Brazos, 2005.

Moltmann, Jürgen. *God in Creation: A New Theology of Creation and the Spirit of God*. Translated by Margaret Kohl. Minneapolis: Fortress, 1993.

Northcott, Michael S. *The Environment and Christian Ethics*. New Studies in Christian Ethics. Cambridge: Cambridge University Press, 1996.

Pinnock, Clark. *Flame of Love: A Theology of the Holy Spirit*. Downers Grove, IL: InterVarsity, 1996.

Richter, Sandra L. "Environmental Law in Deuteronomy: One Lens on a Biblical Theology for Creation-care." *Bulletin for Biblical Research* 20 (2010) 355–76.

Studebaker, Steven M. "Creation-care as 'Keeping in Step with the Spirit.'" In *The Liberating Spirit: Pentecostals and Social Action in North America*, edited by Michael Wilkinson and Steven M. Studebaker, 248–63. Eugene, OR: Pickwick, 2010.

———. "The Spirit in Creation: A Unified Theology of Grace and Creation-Care." *Zygon* 43 (2008) 943–60.

Swoboda, A. J. "Eco-Glossolalia: Emerging Twenty-First Century Pentecostal and Charismatic Ecotheology." *Rural Theology* 9 (2011) 101–16.

Tallman, Matthew. "Pentecostal Ecology: A Theological Paradigm." In *The Spirit Renews the Face of the Earth: Pentecostal Forays in Science and Theology of Creation*, edited by Amos Yong, 135–54. Eugene, OR: Pickwick, 2009.

Thomas, John Christopher. *The Spirit of the New Testament*. Leiden: Deo, 2005.

Walton, John H. *Ancient Near Eastern Thought and the Old Testament: Introducing the Conceptual World of the Hebrew Bible*. Grand Rapids: Baker, 2006.

White, Lynn, Jr. "The Historical Roots of Our Ecologic Crisis." *Science* 155 (1967) 1203–7.

Wright, N. T. *Surprised by Hope: Rethinking Heaven, the Resurrection, and the Mission of the Church*. New York: HarperOne, 2008.

Yong, Amos. *In the Days of Caesar: Pentecostalism and Political Theology*. Grand Rapids: Eerdmans, 2010.

Zizioulas, John. *The Eucharistic Communion and the World*. Edited by Luke Ben Tallon. London: T. & T. Clark, 2011.

10

Sins of the Ancestors:
Generational Sin, Pentecostalism,
and the Ecological Crisis[1]

Michael J. Chan

Transgenerational judgment

It was a Saturday evening, sometime around 2001. The auditorium was full of young people in various postures of worship—hands raised, kneeling, slumped over in chairs. A pastor stood on the stage, accompanied by a worship band, which played soft, contemplative, background music. The pastor led the congregation through a series of prayers to break the chains of "generational sin." According to the pastor, sins inherited from our families were able to reach across generational divides and influence us negatively in the present, even predisposing us to sin in particular ways. In the fever of revival, we followed his lead, confessed our forbearers' sins, and cheered in victory when it was over. This was a great moment, the pastor insisted, for we were free from generational sin.

The anecdote above is from my own journey. Many of those who have spent time in Pentecostal-Charismatic (hereafter "PC") communities, however, can attest to similar experiences. The notion that the sins of the ancestors can negatively affect us has powerfully influenced many American PC churches. This perspective, moreover, has spread to other

---

1. I would like to dedicate this article to Chris Green (Pentecostal Theological Seminary)—a blazing light amid a new generation of Pentecostal theologians.

countries as well, following in the wake of PC growth.[2] Marilyn Hickey, one of the more well-known popular authors on the topic, defines generational sin ("generational cursing," in her language) as: "An uncleansed iniquity that increases in strength from one generation to the next, affecting the members of that family and all who come into relationship with that family."[3] Unaddressed iniquities are passed on to subsequent generations in the form of sinful *predispositions*. Such "curses" remain active until the believer chooses to deal with them by appropriating Christ's forgiveness.

Scripture is supremely important for Hickey. She often appeals to the Bible in support of her claims, especially Exod 20:5–6, 34:7, Num 14:18; and Deut 5:9–10. In another book co-authored with her daughter-in-law, Sarah Bowling, Hickey makes the following comments regarding Exodus 34:6–7:

> Here, in a few brief lines, is a picture of God's balanced justice. On the one hand, we have God's mercy, patience, and an abundance of goodness, truth, mercy, and forgiveness. On the other hand, God allows the iniquity of a person to be visited upon that person's heirs. The sins of the fathers are passed down because they have not been cleared. This is a vitally important concept for you to understand. The way we are set free from the iniquity of the fathers is God's merciful and generous forgiveness . . . We do not need to be trapped by the sins of those who have gone before us. We do not need to live out the predisposition for ungodly behavior placed within us. We can make a choice to seek God's forgiveness, and in so doing, we can reverse the curse of what has been planted in us.[4]

Hickey and Bowling seem to view the "iniquity of the fathers" in terms of transmitted sinful tendencies, which can be reversed through God's mercy.[5] She interprets God's visiting of the iniquities upon later genera-

2. See, e.g., Asamoah-Gyadu, "Healing, Deliverance, and Generation Curses in Ghanaian Pentecostalism," 389–406.

3. Hickey, *Breaking Generational Curses*, 13.

4. Hickey and Bowling, *Blessing the Next Generation*, Chapter 1 (e-version did not provide page numbers).

5. For other examples, see Rallo, *Breaking Generational Curses and Pulling down Strongholds*. A recent article in *Relevant* magazine featured the topic of generational sin: Gilligan, "Breaking Generational Sin," n.p., April 26, 2010, http://www.relevant-magazine.com/life/whole-life/features/21350-breaking-generational-sin (accessed July 21 2013). The well-known author, preacher, and radio show host Chuck Smith takes a

tions as a description of sinful predispositions finding their way into the lives of later generations.

Bob Larson, another popular writer on the topic of spiritual warfare, argues that there are two kinds of curses (implicit curses and explicit curses), both of which are hereditary, transgenerational, and (typically) involuntary. Like Hickey and Bowling, he grounds his claims about generational sin, at least in part, in a reading of Exodus 20:3–5 and 34:6–7:

> The third and fourth generations was not meant to be taken literally, except as a minimum. The writer indicates that a curse can follow a family or national line for at least four generations, but he doesn't put an end on it there. Essentially, he indicates that a curse remains active in perpetuity, although as I have already indicated, it may or may not remain activated.[6]

For Larson, curses are not automatically inherited. Apparently, "Something has to happen to activate both curses and blessings . . . If they do not have a reason to land on you, essentially they remain dormant and ineffective."[7] It is unclear where in either of these texts (Exod 20:3–5; 34:6–7) Larson sees the concept of cursing. None of the standard Hebrew words/roots for cursing (e.g., $\sqrt{}$ʾrr [Gen 12:3; 27:29; Mal 2:2]; $\sqrt{}$qbb [Lev

---

somewhat critical view of how generational sin is discussed in contemporary churches. In his comments on the topic, however, Smith does not clearly distinguish between the consequences of sin and the passing along of sinful tendencies, which makes his comments interesting but ultimately problematic for its lack of clarity. He writes, for instance, "Have you ever heard a sermon on the devastation caused by 'generational sin'? Preachers base their frightening comments on texts like Exodus 20:5 . . . Some people hear such a verse and say, 'God's not fair! Why should children suffer for their parents' sin?' Let's admit that the sins of parents often have terrible consequences upon their children . . . Of course, this doesn't mean that if you had unrighteous parents, then you must face the wrath of God for the rest of your life . . . While it may logically follow that a boy raised in an ungodly atmosphere is apt to grow up to be very ungodly himself, thank God for the love and grace of Jesus Christ. You can break any hurtful or wrong relationship with the past. Maybe your parents did not bring you up in the fear and admonition of the Lord; perhaps they set a very poor spiritual example. But thank God, that chain can be broken . . . You don't have to suffer because of your parents' hatred of God or because of their mistakes. You can break that curse." Smith, Love, 57–58. Reading this passage, it is not entirely clear what generational sin is to Smith. Is it facing the wrath of God for one's parents' sins, or is it living an ungodly life in response to the environment in which one grew up?

6. Larson, *Curse Breaking*, 22–23.

7. Ibid., 23.

24:11; Num 23:25]; √*qll* [Gen 27:12; Deut 28:15, 45; Judg 9:57]) are present. As far as I can tell, this gap in his exegesis is unexplained.

Also, the popular author and speaker, Beth Moore, teaches about "generational bondage." She writes,

> We need to examine areas of devastation or defeat that have been in our family lines for generations. Then we can explore resulting generational bonds that need breaking. Yokes can often be caused by severed relationships, lives left in ruins because of a loss or a tragedy, ancient family arguments and inheritances of hate, or generational debris scattered by a bomb that dropped and a life that refused repair.[8]

Moore strikes a slightly more pastoral tone, emphasizing that "tragedies" and brokenness can also create points of access for generational sin. In her view, generational bondage, moreover, often goes unnoticed because we think of it more in terms of "who we are rather than how we're bound."[9]

Few would disagree with Larson, Hickey, Bowling, Moore, et al that destructive behavioral and psychological tendencies often persist across generational lines. The adage, "Like father, like son" show itself to be true day after day, both for better and worse. But is this what the biblical texts—and especially those that speak of God visiting the iniquity of the fathers upon the third and fourth generation—are really concerned with?

Texts that make reference to the transgenerational formula, I submit, are less about the transference of sinful tendencies or harmful curses and more about "transgenerational judgment"—a concept in which the *consequences of one generation's sins wash up on the shore of the next generation.* Judgment, as it is understood in this essay, does not refer to arbitrary acts of divine intervention—Zeus capriciously hurling bolts of death at his human victims for instance—but rather to divinely mediated consequences of human sin. In Terence Fretheim's words, "That sins have consequences is judgment and that can be named an experience of the wrath of God."[10] To experience divine judgment in this way is to experience God's "understandable wrath"[11] in which God's fury is ensconced within

8. See Moore, *Breaking Free*, 84.

9. Ibid.

10. See Fretheim, "Theological Reflections on the Wrath of God in the Old Testament," 11.

11. Bayer, in his discussion of Luther's theology, makes a helpful distinction between God's "understandable wrath," which refers to the "sphere of actions that bring about consequences" and that divine wrath which cannot be connected to actions—

the outworking of the created moral order. "Understandable wrath" is the wrath that Jonah knows only too well: God rages in the storm (Jon 1:12).[12] Our world, however, is highly interconnected, making the process of judgment somewhat messy.[13] Add to this the fact that God frequently uses historical, even sinful, agents to bring about divine judgment (e.g., the Babylonians), which certainly contributes to the problem, since God does not perfect these agents before using them. Such a move entails, of course, a risk for God whose name and reputation become associated with the agents of judgment.[14] Transgenerational judgment, then, is not a special category of divine judgment, but rather, a different way of talking

---

God's "incomprehensible" wrath. This paper is expressly concerned with the former. See Bayer, *Martin Luther's Theology*, esp. 196.

12. Ibid., 196.

13. Fretheim helpfully refers to the present moral order as a "spider web" of a world, in which the sins of one may ripple out to other corners of creation. Fretheim, *God and World in the Old Testament*, 19. Innocent members of a family can be caught up in the judgment of a single person. One thinks, for instance, of the nameless child of David and Bathsheba, who dies over a matter of seven days because of David's indiscretion (2 Sam 12:14–15). This child is not the only one to suffer for David's sins, however. Nathan indicates that David's wives would be forced into having sex in broad daylight with an enemy of David—making them "trophy wives" in the worst possible sense of the term. Humanity's sin in Genesis 3, moreover, has a profoundly negative impact on the ground and its ability to produce edible plants (Gen 3:17–18). Perhaps the most dramatic example, however, is the killing of the Egyptian firstborns in Exodus 11–12 (see Exod 11:5; 12:12, 29). Shocking as it is, God does not even spare the firstborn of the marginalized or vulnerable: the child of the slave girl behind the millstone and the firstborn of the cattle will be struck down (see Exod 11:5). Human and non-human alike suffer in Egypt because of Pharaoh's unwillingness to bend.

14. As Fretheim notes, the agents of divine judgment are often described metaphorically as weapons in the hand of God. See Fretheim, "I Was Only a Little Angry," 365–75. Assyria, for instance, is referred to as the "rod of my anger" (Isa 10:5; see my "Rhetorical Reversal and Usurpation," 717–33). Jeremiah 50:25 refers to "the weapons of his [Yhwh's] wrath." Other texts refer to Yhwh's deliverance of Israel into the hands of her enemies. For instance, in 2 Kings 17, which provides a theological interpretation of the Northern Kingdom's fall, an important editorial speech claims, "So the LORD spurned all the offspring of Israel, and He afflicted them and delivered them into the hands of plunderers [*wayyitněm běyad šōsîm*], and finally He cast them out from His presence" (2 Kgs 17:20; cf. Jer 32:3). Jeremiah 27:8 depicts the Babylonians as divine weapons: "The nation or kingdom that does not serve him—Nebuchadnezzar king of Babylon—and does not submit its neck beneath the yoke of the king of Babylon, with the sword, famine, and pestilence, I will 'visit' that nation—says Yhwh—until I finish them off by his [Nebuchadnezzar's] hand." Needless to say, God makes use of historical agents to get things done in the world.

about the moral interconnectedness of the world, and more precisely the interconnectedness of generations.

The notion of transgenerational judgment, even in the de- and re-constructed form above, remains a useful concept for PC theology. In fact, it provides Pentecostals and Charismatics with a helpful evaluative heuristic, which can be applied to any number of complex, multi-generational situations.[15] As a way of demonstrating its usefulness to PC theology, I will argue that the current ecological crisis can be helpfully interpreted through the lens of "generational sin"—or, as I have renamed it above, "transgenerational judgment." Given the increased interest in global warming, the time is ripe to begin thinking theologically about the ecological crisis in terms that are familiar to Pentecostals and their Charismatic siblings.[16]

The essay proceeds as follows. I will discuss several of the key biblical texts cited above, and in particular those claiming that the guilt of the fathers is visited upon the third and fourth generations. It is argued that these texts have nothing to do with sinful tendencies (much less curses!) passing from one generation to the next. Rather, they concern how sin's *consequences* (i.e., judgment) can affect later generations. This interpretation of the texts becomes evident when one realizes that the transgenerational formula provided a theological lens through which to interpret the sixth century exile of Judah. On analogy with the exile, I argue that the

15. To take just one example, the history of Pentecostalism is unfortunately tainted with racism. These negative consequences—felt by the "third and fourth" generations—are helpfully labeled as "generational sin," or "trans-generational judgment" to use the nomenclature adopted here. Pentecostalism today suffers because of its racial fragmentation. For discussions of racism and Pentecostalism, see Lovett, "The Present," "Racism," and *Kingdom Beyond Color*; Robeck, "The Past"; Jacobsen, *Thinking in the Spirit*, see chap. 5 ("Theology and Race"), etc.

16. The ground has already been broken by a number of Evangelical, Charismatic, and Pentecostal forerunners. For example, The New Evangelical Partnership for the Common Good has a specific statement titled, "Creation Care." See "Creation Care," n.p., http://www.newevangelicalpartnership.org/ (accessed 4 October 2013). The Evangelical Climate Initiative (ECI) is another well-known organization that is pushing for climate change. Notably, they claim that "Christian moral convictions demand our response to the climate change problem." "ECI Statement," n.p., http://christiansand-climate.org/statement/ (accessed 4 October 2013). See also Merritt, *Green Like God*. See also the brief summary of evangelical efforts to address climate change in, Krakoff, "Parenting the Planet," 160–61. Tri Robinson of the Vineyard Boise in Idaho has become a leader in the Charismatic green movement. See, e.g., Robinson with Chatraw, *Saving God's Green Earth*. On the academic Pentecostal front, climate change has recently been addressed in Swoboda, *Tongues and Trees*.

current signs of ecological (di-)stress are the emerging consequences of generations of sinful human exploitation of the earth and its resources.[17] Due to the extended time over which these consequences will be realized, however, the generations responsible for setting the planet on its current course will be long gone by the time the worst arrives. For Christians, to understand the current climate crisis in exclusively empirical, economic or scientific terms is inadequate. The ecological crisis, with all its deleterious effects, is best understood as transgenerational judgment for humanity's failure to fulfill its vocation on this earth.[18]

Like troubled Jeremiah living in the decades prior to 587 BCE, eco-sensitive theologians have a responsibility to proclaim that divine judgment looms on the horizon. Given the apparently advanced nature of the crisis, we may be forced to take up the humble confession of an unnamed Assyrian monarch: "Who knows? God may relent and change his mind?" (Jon 3:9). Theologians, of course, are not lone voices crying out in the wilderness. Scientists, politicians, and world leaders have been sounding this alarm for decades. To our shame, we as theologians are arriving late to a very important party. But this does not make our voices irrelevant. We have a unique audience that may be largely inaccessible to other voices in the ecological movement, which makes our contributions all the more important: Scientists can call our spoilation of the environment irresponsible and uninformed. Politicians may call it unpatriotic. Only preachers can call it sin.

Our actions or inactions in response to the ecological crisis will help shape the nature and severity of that judgment, whether it is severe or mild, catastrophic or manageable. We must not respond as Jeremiah's misguided audience did—with a numbing and blinding trust that things would go on as usual (see Jeremiah 7). Rather—and on this point I agree with Moore, Hickey, and my college pastor—what transgenerational judgment requires is decisive, passionate, and resolute repentance.

---

17. At the time this essay was penned, the most recent climate change report was made by the UN-backed Intergovernmental Panel on Climate Change on September 27, 2013. See "UN Urges Global Response to Scientific Evidence that Climate Change is Human-Induced," http://www.un.org/apps/news/story.asp?NewsID=46069&Cr=clima te+change&Cr1=#.UkWtnYakrLU (accessed September, 27 2013).

18. For some helpful comments on the vocation of the human with respect to creation, see Davis, *Scripture, Culture, and Agriculture*, 53–65. For a review, see my "Review of Ellen Davis, Scripture, Culture, and Agriculture."

The guilt of the ancestors

At the center of many popular Christian books, sermons, and literature on generational sin are texts claiming that YHWH will "visit" (*pqd*) the "iniquity" or "guilt" (ʿwn) of the fathers upon the third and fourth generations (see, e.g., Exod 20:5–6; 34:6–7; Num 14:18; Deut 5:9–10; cf. Deut 28:45–46). In the following paragraphs, I will argue that these texts have nothing to do with the transference of sinful tendencies or curses to later generations, but rather with the spilling over of divine judgment to later generations. Even though the idiom itself (*pqd* + ʿwn) and its variants remain somewhat ambiguous,[19] what is clear is that this theological concept was used to explain the sixth century Neo-Babylonian exile, and more specifically to explain this disaster in terms of transgenerational judgment.[20] I begin with a discussion of the transgenerational formula in Exodus 20:5–6, and then proceed by examining exilic and post-exilic texts that interpret the exile according to the transgenerational formula.

As the first explicit canonical reference to transgenerational judgment, the Decalogue in Exodus 20 is a helpful starting point. The text reads as follows:

> You shall not bow down to them or serve them. For I the LORD your God am an impassioned God, visiting the guilt of the parents upon the children, upon the third and upon the fourth generations [of those who reject Me],[21] but showing kindness to the thousandth generation of those who love Me and keep My commandments (Exod 20:5–6, TNK)

Leaving aside the various ways in which the commandments are numbered, the threat of transgenerational judgment is clearly linked to the first prohibition: "You shall have no other *gods* before me." (Exod 20:3; italics mine) In point of fact, the only antecedent for "them" in v. 5 is found in v. 3 ("gods") and not v. 4, which is a later redactional inser-

---

19. See, e.g., the helpful discussion of these options in Widmer, *Moses, God, and the Dynamics of Intercessory Prayer*, 175–83.

20. Spieckermann, "Barmherzig und gnädig ist der Herr," 10.

21. *lĕśōnĕʾây* ("to those who hate me") is found in Deut 5:9 but is missing from Exod 34:6–7; Num 14:18; Jer 32:18. The most likely explanation is that the notion of transgenerational judgment was morally offensive to the editors of Exodus 20 (cf. Ezek 18:1–4, 20) and was, as a result, edited to reflect a more acceptable theological viewpoint. That is, by adding *lĕśōnĕʾây*, God's judgment is linked to the sins of the individual who "hates" God.

tion that clarifies and expands upon the meaning of "gods" to include manmade images. Clearly, the consequences of one generation's faithlessness to YHWH are quite serious: YHWH visits "the guilt of the parents" (*pqd ʿwn ʾbt*) upon later generations. Faithfulness, alternatively, carries its own, even greater, transgenerational reward ("showing kindness to the thousandth generation")—an heirloom gifted from ancestors to descendants. As Reinhard Feldmeier and Hermann Spieckermann note, the "glaring asymmetry" of YHWH's love and compassion underscores the gracious nature of YHWH.[22]

Jeremiah 32:18 clearly echoes the transgenerational formula found in Exodus 20:5–6; 34:6–7, etc. and uses it as a lens through which to view the Babylonian domination of Jerusalem. The text claims that:

> You [God] show kindness to the thousandth generation,
> but visit the guilt of the fathers upon their children after them
> (Jer 32:18, TNK)

The Jewish Publication Society's TNK translation unfortunately covers over the corporeal imagery in this verse. Rendered woodenly, v. 18 says that YHWH "repays the sin of the fathers into the lap of their children after them" (Jer 32:18). But what exactly does it mean that YHWH repays the "sin of the fathers" (ʿwn ʾbwt) into the lap of the children—or, in the words of the cultic formula, that God is one who "visits" (*pqd*) the sins of the fathers upon later generations? Attention to the literary context is helpful at this point. Verse 18 is part of a prayer that Jeremiah utters while sitting in prison, after having been consigned there by Zedekiah (see Jer 32:2–5). While there, Jeremiah's cousin, Hanamel, pays him a visit and asks him to buy land in Anathoth, which Jeremiah does (Jer 32:8–12). What seems like an unspectacular transaction, however, is in fact an opportunity for YHWH to speak. Jeremiah instructs his scribe Baruch to hide the legal documents related to the sale for a later time. This purchase was a prophetic "sign-act" or "symbolic sign"[23] with a hopeful message: "Houses, fields, and vineyard will again be purchased in this land" (Jer 32:15). Jeremiah then prays a prayer, which includes v. 18 above. In a

---

22. Feldmeier and Spieckermann, *God of the Living*, 133.

23. A "sign act" or "symbolic act" is a prophetic action that "functions as a dramatic means to symbolize YHWH's intentions or actions toward the people and to confirm the prophetic statement." The genre typically contains three elements: "(1) an instruction to perform a symbolic act; (2) the report that the act was performed; and (3) a statement that interprets the significance of the act." Sweeney, *Isaiah 1–39*, 536–37.

section of the prayer that recollects parts of Israel's history, the prayer links the sins of prior generations to the current judgment under the Babylonians:

> You gave them this land, which you swore to their fathers to give them—a land flowing with milk and honey, and they seized possession of it. But they did not obey your voice or follow your instruction. All that you commanded them to do they did not do. So you brought about *this entire disaster* (Jer 32:22–23, my translation)

What is important to notice here is that "this entire disaster" (i.e., the current siege of Jerusalem, see Jer 32:2) is the result of what "they [their fathers] did not do." Jeremiah's generation was reaping the consequences of sins committed by their forebears—recognizing, of course, that these sins continued on into Jeremiah's day. The main point, however, is that Jeremiah's prayer interprets the Babylonian subjugation of Jerusalem as the result of generations-old sins, the consequences of which have been placed in the "lap" of his generation.

The previous chapter (Jeremiah 31) also assumes the validity of transgenerational judgment, but it imagines a future in which such a reality no longer exists:[24]

> See, a time is coming—declares the LORD—when I will sow the House of Israel and the House of Judah with seed of men and seed of cattle; and just as I was watchful over them to uproot and to pull down, to overthrow and to destroy and to bring disaster, so I will be watchful over them to build and to plant—declares the LORD. In those days, they shall no longer say, "Parents have eaten sour grapes and children's teeth are blunted." But every one shall die for his own sins: whosoever eats sour grapes, his teeth shall be blunted (Jer 31:27–30, TNK).

This text divides history into moral dispensations, with the current age being one in which children's teeth may be "blunted" (*tiqhênāh*) by their parents' consumption of sour grapes. The experience of judgment at the hand of the Babylonians, of course, informs the viticultural metaphor. The future, however, consists of a very different moral economy, one in which personal accountability is emphasized. The fact that we continue to

---

24. Similarly, see Holladay, *Jeremiah*, 2, 197; Levinson, *Legal Revision and Religious Renewal in Ancient Israel*, 61; Schipper, "Hezekiah, Manasseh, and Dynastic or Transgenerational Punishment," 97.

see children suffering for the sins of their parents suggests that, whatever new age Jeremiah had in mind, we are not living in it yet.

The book of Jeremiah, however, is not the only text to interpret the Babylonian exile in terms of transgenerational judgment. As Bernard Levinson argues, Lamentations 5:7 interprets the fall of Jerusalem similarly:[25]

> Our fathers sinned (*ḥāṭĕʾû*) and are no more.
> and we must bear their guilt (*ʿăwōnōtêhem*) (TNK)

R.B. Salters rightly notes that the reference here to "fathers" is a reference to earlier generations, which sought refuge in Egypt and Assyria (see v. 6).[26] But Jerusalem's destruction left plenty of blame to go around. As v. 16 indicates, responsibility also fell on the shoulders of the current generation: "Woe to us that we have sinned!" (see Lam 5:16b). Even though guilt is shared by several Israelite generations, the negative consequences are felt most keenly by the generation that lives during and after the destruction of Jerusalem. In Adele Berlin's words, "The destruction did not result only from the present generation's sins, but from the long history of accumulated sin that God could no longer leave unpunished. Earlier generations escaped punishment, but this generation did not."[27] As Ulrich Berges notes, this dual horizon of culpability is not unique. Nehemiah 1:6, for instance, records a prayer saying , "Let Your ear be attentive and Your eyes open to receive the prayer of Your servant that I am praying to You now, day and night, on behalf of the Israelites, Your servants, confessing the sins that we Israelites have committed against You, sins that I and my father's house have committed (Neh 1:6 TNK)."[28]

Levinson further argues that the notion of transgenerational punishment informs the final chapters of the book of Kings, and especially the interpretation of Manasseh's reign. He writes,

> Ancient Israel endured a catastrophe in 587 B.C.E. when, following a two-year siege, the Babylonian army breached the walls of Jerusalem, burned the city, gutted the Temple, and deported

25. Levinson, *Legal Revision and Religious Renewal in Ancient Israel*, 57–88. See also Schipper, "Hezekiah, Manasseh, and Dynastic or Transgenerational Punishment," 97–98.

26. Salters, *Lamentations*, 350.

27. Berlin, *Lamentations*, 120.

28. See Berges, *Klagelieder*, 285.

the majority of the population to Babylon. The editor of the book of Kings, charged with narrating that history, explains the destruction as the result of divine punishment for the unprecedented iniquities committed not by the generation contemporary with the destruction but rather by King Manasseh (696–641 B.C.E.), who ruled three generations beforehand (2 Kgs 21:1–15; 23:26–27; 24:3–4; contrast 24:19–20).[29]

The key text to note in this regard is 2 Kings 21:11–13:

> Because King Manasseh of Judah has done these abhorrent things—he has outdone in wickedness all that the Amorites did before his time—and because he led Judah to sin with his fetishes, assuredly, thus said the LORD, the God of Israel: I am going to bring such a disaster on Jerusalem and Judah that both ears of everyone who hears about it will tingle. I will apply to Jerusalem the measuring line of Samaria and the weights of the House of Ahab; I will wipe Jerusalem clean as one wipes a dish and turns it upside down. (2 Kgs 21:11–13, TNK)

The divine threat of judgment, however, is not actualized during the reign of Manasseh. According to 2 Kgs 24:1-3, the word spoken against Manasseh is actually fulfilled in the reign of Jehoiakim (Amon son of Manasseh, Josiah son of Amon, Jehoahaz/Jehoaikim sons of Josiah).[30]

> In his days, King Nebuchadnezzar of Babylon came up, and Jehoiakim became his vassal for three years. Then he turned and rebelled against him. The LORD let loose against him the raiding bands of the Chaldeans, Arameans, Moabites, and Ammonites; He let them loose against Judah to destroy it, in accordance with the word that the LORD had spoken through His servants the prophets. *All this befell Judah at the command of the LORD, who banished them from His presence because of all the sins that Manasseh had committed, and also because of the blood of the innocent that he shed.* For he filled Jerusalem with the blood of the innocent, and the LORD would not forgive. (2Kgs 24:1-4 TNK, emphasis mine)

It is no accident that the deuteronomistic editors of Kings include a fulfillment formula in the reign of Jehoiakim, who is three generations after Manasseh. The horrific consequences of Manasseh's infidelity to YHWH

29. Levinson, *Legal Revision and Religious Renewal*, 56.
30. Ibid., 56n57.

were never in fact seen by Manasseh himself. A later generation paid the price for an earlier generation's sins.

The texts discussed here make it quite clear that the transgenerational judgment formula had a profound impact on how some Judahites interpreted the sixth century Babylonian exile. These texts interpret Babylonian aggression toward Jerusalem, at least in part, as judgment for sins committed by earlier Judahites and especially Judahite kings. The concept may sound strange to modern ears, but even a cursory glance at world history indicates all too clearly that the sins of former generations often have disastrous effects on later generations.

A Nehemiah Moment

One thing is obvious: the current ecological crisis is also a transgenerational phenomenon.[31] Responsibility for the creation's current and future wellbeing falls on the shoulders of generations past and present. The ecological crisis, as I see it, is helpfully interpreted in terms of transgenerational judgment.[32] Keep in mind that the term "judgment" here does not refer to God's intervention into the normal functioning of the world. Quite to the contrary, divine judgment refers to the *consequences of sin*, in, with, and under which God is at work. The current ecological crisis, like the sixth century exile of Judah, is the result of both present sins and the sins of former generations. It is an example of "generational sin."

PC theology is a theology of response: we respond to the Spirit, to the neighbor's needs, to the presence of God, and to calls of repentance. In Keith Warrington's words, PC theology is a "theology of the dynamic."[33] What the transgenerational ecological crisis needs at this very moment is a full-bore, pedal-and-face-to-the-floor, response, that recognizes that we are living in an age of judgment—an era of wrath, when God looks upon humanity's relationship to creation and sighs rather than smiles, regrets

31. For introductory works on climate change and its history, see, e.g., Maslin, *Global Warming*; Maslin, *Global Warming: A Very Short Introduction*; Weart, *The Discovery of Global Warming*; Eggleton, *A Short Introduction to Climate Change*.

32. Fretheim makes a similar point: "As a contemporary example, should the ecosystem be damaged by moral evil to the point where all creatures are adversely affected—that would be an experience of the wrath of God, to use biblical categories." See Fretheim, "Theological Reflections on the Wrath of God in the Old Testament," 12.

33. Warrington, *Pentecostal Theology*, 16.

rather than rejoices (cf. Gen 6:6-7). God's wrath is everywhere. We need only ask for eyes to see it.

Humanity's first "fall" resulted in damage to the creation. Even the precious soil (*hāʾădāmāh*) from which the first human (*ʾādām*) was fashioned is cursed as a result of human sin (Gen 3:17). The first couple's sins may have involved a personal decision to disobey, but the consequences were far from personal. All of creation suffered. The current ecological crisis is similar. Vulnerable soil, water, and species suffer because of generations of human sin and irresponsibility. The initiators of the ecological crisis are long dead and we are left either to continue their destructive behavior or else to combat it with technology, restraint, passion, and penitence. As it was in Jeremiah's time, the crisis is looming, the signs are all around us, but precious few Christians are paying heed. We are far too comfortable with our carbon footprints and too far removed from the depleting polar ice caps and snuffed out species to recognize the threat posed by climate change. What we need in this hour is for Christians—Pentecostal and Charismatic alike—to react as Nehemiah did—with tears, sorrow, and prayers of confession for our sins and for the sins of our ancestors (Neh 1:4-6).

BIBLIOGRAPHY

Asamoah-Gyadu, J. Kwabena. "Healing, Deliverance, and Generation Curses in Ghanaian Pentecostalism." *International Review of Mission* 93 (2004) 389–406.

Bayer, Oswald. *Martin Luther's Theology: A Contemporary Interpretation*. Grand Rapids: Eerdmans, 2008.

Berges, Ulrich. *Klagelieder. Herders Theologischer Kommentar zum Alten Testament*. Freiburg: Herder, 2002.

Berlin, Adele. *Lamentations*. Old Testament Library. Louisville: Westminster John Knox, 2002.

Chan, Michael J. Review of Ellen Davis, *Scripture, Culture, and Agriculture: An Agrarian Reading of the Bible*. *Word and World* 29 (2009) 304–5.

———. "Rhetorical Reversal and Usurpation: Isa 10:5–34 and the Use of Neo-Assyrian Royal Ideology in the Construction of an Anti-Assyrian Theology." *Journal of Biblical Literature* 128 (2009) 717–33.

"Creation Care." http://www.newevangelicalpartnership.org/ (accessed October 4, 2013).

Davis, Ellen. *Scripture, Culture, and Agriculture: An Agrarian Reading of the Bible*. Cambridge: Cambridge University Press, 2008.

Eggleton, Tony. *A Short Introduction to Climate Change*. Cambridge: Cambridge University Press, 2013.

"ECI Statement." http://christiansandclimate.org/statement/ (accessed October 4, 2013).

Feldmeier, Reinhard, and Hermann Spieckermann, *God of the Living: A Biblical Theology*. Translated by Mark E. Biddle. Waco: Baylor University Press, 2011.

Fretheim, Terence E. *God and World in the Old Testament*. Nashville: Abingdon, 2005.

———. "'I Was Only a Little Angry': Divine Violence in the Prophets." *Interpretation* 58 (2004) 365–75.

———. "Theological Reflections on the Wrath of God in the Old Testament." *Horizons in Biblical Theology* 24 (2002) 1–26.

Gilligan, Alyce. "Breaking Generational Sin: How to Recognize—and Deal With—Family Sins that Never Seem to Go Away." July 21 2013. http://www. relevantmagazine.com/life/whole-life/features/21350-breaking-generational-sin.

Hickey, Marilyn. *Breaking Generational Curses*. Tulsa: Harrison House, 2000.

Hickey, Marilyn, and Sarah Bowling, *Blessing the Next Generation: Creating a Lasting Family Legacy with the Help of a Loving God*. New York: Faith Words, 2008.

Holladay, William L. *Jeremiah*. 2 vols. Hermeneia. Minneapolis: Fortress, 1989.

Jacobsen, Douglas G. *Thinking in the Spirit: Theologies of the Early Pentecostal Movement*. Bloomington: Indiana University Press, 2003.

Krakoff, Sarah. "Parenting the Planet." In *The Ethics of Global Climate Change*, edited by Denis G. Arnold, 145–69. Cambridge: Cambridge University Press, 2011.

Larson, Bob. *Curse Breaking: Freedom from the Bondage of Generational Sins*. Shippensburg, PA: Destiny Image, 2013.

Leonard Lovett. *Kingdom Beyond Color: Re-examining the Phenomenon of Racism*. Orlando: Higher Standard, 2004.

———. "The Present: The Problem of Racism and Discrimination and Our Racial Division in the Pentecostal Movement." *Cyberjournal for Pentecostal-Charismatic Research* 14 (2005). http://www.pctii.org/cyberj/.

———. "Racism: Death of the Gods." In *The African Cultural Heritage Topical Bible*, edited by Derwin Stewart, 73–79. Bakersfield, CA: Pneuma Life, 1995.

Levinson, Bernard M. *Legal Revision and Religious Renewal in Ancient Israel*. Cambridge: Cambridge University Press, 2008.

Maslin, Mark. *Global Warming: A Very Short Introduction*. New York: Oxford University Press, 2004.

———. *Global Warming: Causes, Effects, and the Future*. Stillwater, MN: Voyageur, 2002.

Merritt, Jonathan. *Green Like God: Unlocking the Divine Plan for Our Planet*. New York: FaithWords, 2010.

Moore, Beth. *Breaking Free: Discover the Victory of Total Surrender*. Nashville: B. & H., 2000.

Rallo, Vito. *Breaking Generational Curses and Pulling down Strongholds*. Lake Mary, FL: Creation House, 2000.

Robeck, Cecil, Jr. "The Past: Historical Roots of Racial Unit and Division in American Pentecostalism." *Cyberjournal for Pentecostal-Charismatic Research* 14 (2005). http://www.pctii.org/cyberj/.

Robinson, Tri with Jason Chatraw. *Saving God's Green Earth*. Norcross, GA: Ampelon, 2006.

Salters, R. B. *Lamentations*. International Critical Commentary. London: T. & T. Clark, 2010.

Schipper, Jeremy. "Hezekiah, Manasseh, and Dynastic or Transgenerational Punishment." In *Soundings in Kings: Perspectives and Methods in Contemporary Scholarship*, edited by Mark Leuchter and Klaus Peter Adam, 81–108. Minneapolis: Fortress, 2010.

Smith, Chuck. *Love: The More Excellent Way*. Costa Mesa, CA: Word for Today, 2008.

Spieckermann, Hermann. "Barmherzig und gnädig ist der Herr." *Zeitschrift für die alttestamentliche Wissenschaft* 102 (1990) 1–18.

Sweeney, Marvin. *Isaiah 1–39*. Forms of the Old Testament Literature. Grand Rapids: Eerdmans, 1996.

Swoboda, A. J. *Tongues and Trees: Toward a Pentecostal Ecological Theology*. Journal of Pentecostal Theology Supplement 40. Blandford Forum, UK: Deo, 2013.

"UN Urges Global Response to Scientific Evidence that Climate Change is Human-Induced." September 27, 2013. http://www.un.org/apps/news/story.asp?NewsID=46069&Cr=climate+change&Cr1=#.UkWtnYakrLU.

Warrington, Keith. *Pentecostal Theology: A Theology of Encounter*. London: T. & T. Clark, 2008.

Weart, Spencer R. *The Discovery of Global Warming*. Cambridge, MA: Harvard University Press, 2003.

Widmer, Michael. *Moses, God, and the Dynamics of Intercessory Prayer: A Study of Exodus 32–34*. Forschungen zum Alten Testament 2.8. Tübingen: Mohr/Siebeck, 2004.

PART THREE

Contemporary Practice

11

Healing for a Sick World: Models of Pentecostal Environmentalism in Africa

Matthew Tallman

Introduction

One of the more memorable scenes ever featured in an animated film opens with a panoramic view of the African Sahel and a musical score espousing an environmental philosophy entitled *The Circle of Life*.[1] In real life, you do not have to go far from this scene to observe the same "circle of life" vividly demonstrated in the Masai Mara during the Great Migration. Millions of wildebeest from Tanzania's Serengeti cross the Mara River, thousands of predators depend upon these creatures as a source of food, thousands more scavengers depend upon what the lions and crocodiles leave behind, and the remaining carcasses help fertilize the soil that grows the abundant grassland that the wildebeest feed on as they migrate North. *The Lion King* is also remembered for a famous melody titled *Hakuna Matata* which most people remember as a Swahili phrase meaning "no worries."[2] This popular song reflects the "worry-free philosophy" of a highly relational culture found in much of Africa today. Ironically, while the "circle of life" can still be found in certain preserved natural segments of Africa, there is great cause for worry and concern for

1. Disney, *The Lion King*.
2. Rice and John, "Hakuna Matata."

the environmental challenges currently facing Africa and the rest of the world.

This essay will look at just a few of these challenges, some of the opportunities that exist, and the hope that Pentecostal Christianity can bring to a vulnerable continent in a world sickened by humanity's harmful intervention in creation. This harmful intervention originates from sinful acts and a sinful nature that attempts to ignore or even destroy what God has created. Finally, this essay looks specifically at both the challenges and hopes facing Africa. This is largely due to my own experience living in and visiting Africa for much of the past decade. Additionally, the emphasis on Africa is due to the dramatic growth of Pentecostal Christianity in Africa where Charismatic expressions of worship and pneumatological emphasis affect every Christian denomination and where Christianity of the Pentecostal and/or Charismatic persuasion has become the dominant form of religion in most of sub-Saharan Africa.[3]

While the pneumatic emphasis of Pentecostalism is an obvious foundation upon which to build a theology of Pentecostal environmentalism, the healing praxis of most Pentecostal groups is sometimes overlooked in developing a theology of environmentalism. The possibilities for creating models of environmental healing in Pentecostal Christian communities are almost limitless. For example, one of the more popular current healing movements in modern North American Pentecostal Christianity is healing homes or rooms modeled after the original healing room of Pentecostal pioneer John G. Lake when he lived in Spokane, Washington. Pentecostal Christians involved in this healing movement today can and should expand their healing prayers beyond humanity to all of creation.

Interestingly, while John G. Lake's healing rooms had significant influence upon communities like Spokane, Washington and Portland, Oregon where he founded such rooms, perhaps his greatest legacy to Pentecostal Christianity occurred during his residency in South Africa, where he led crusades, established churches, and founded the Apostolic Faith Mission of South Africa, representing over a million constituents and producing ecumenical leaders such as David du Plessis, a pioneer of the modern Charismatic Movement. This same early Pentecostal movement helped initiate many of the AIC denominations (African Initiated Churches) and also eventually influenced the creation of innovative theological movements such as the AAEC (Association of

---

3. Barrett and Johnson, *World Christian Atlas*, 13, 20.

African Earthkeeping Churches) that have successfully melded a fusion of Pentecostal theology and environmentalism into a variety of groups practicing and preaching healing and hope for Zimbabwe, South Africa, and other African nations.

In Zimbabwe, tree planting "Eucharist" services have helped reverse deforestation as mostly Pentecostal AIC churches have integrated environmentalism into church praxis, church prayers, church theology, and church worship.[4] In Zambia, the Heritage of the Mission organization has also encouraged reforestation and small scale agriculture.[5] In South Africa, the Faith and Earthkeeping Project encourages religious engagement in ecological and developmental arenas through research, awareness, and mobilization.[6] Abalimi Bezekhoya (Planters of the Home) promotes urban agriculture in South Africa, and through an auxiliary organization called the Cape Flats Tree Project, promotes the greening of local neighborhoods.[7]

This essay will focus on Christian environmentalism in three African nations: Rwanda, Kenya, and Zimbabwe. Environmentalism in Rwanda is mentioned because of my own experience visiting that nation on several occasions and because of Rwanda's leadership in environmental causes. Kenya is mentioned because of my broader experience living in that nation and also because of Kenya's environmental challenges and promising opportunities that represent much of what the entire continent is facing today. Finally, Zimbabwe is mentioned because of the work of M.L. Daneel in galvanizing an integrative and creative approach for Pentecostal environmentalism.

Rwanda

My own experience briefly living in Rwanda demonstrated a great deal of promise for environmental healing both in Christian communities and on a national scale. While most of Rwanda's Christian community is Roman Catholic, it is heavily influenced by the Charismatic Movement, and the Pentecostal community represents a vibrant and significant minority of the densely populated nation. More importantly for the pur-

4. Comradie et al., "Seeking Eco-Justice in the South African Context," 151–52.

5. Ibid, 152.

6. Ibid, 148.

7. Ibid, 149.

poses of this paper is how the nation of Rwanda as a whole has responded and rebounded from the depths of a horrific genocide in 1994 to emphasize models of healing both for human society and all of creation. Through the practice of *gacaca*, victims of genocide meet face-to-face with the criminals and facilitators of Rwandan genocide, with the hope of healing and reconciliation for all of Rwandan society.[8] When I first visited Rwanda in 2005, I expected a nation still traumatized and paralyzed by the aftermath of mass execution, but I experienced and encountered people transformed by God's grace and living lives filled with forgiveness towards others in contrast to the bloodlust and vengeful vendettas of a decade earlier. Others have had similar observations as they see Rwanda rapidly becoming a model of reconciliation and unity even though they are surrounded by tribalistic factions and factors in Kenya, Congo, Uganda, Sudan, and much of the rest of Africa.[9]

Another fascinating reflection of Rwanda's resurgence after their genocide is their society's emphasis upon good citizenship to benefit creation. When I first visited Rwanda in 2005, I noticed it was the cleanest country I had ever visited in Africa—perhaps one of the cleanest countries I have ever visited in the world. After spending a few weeks there, I quickly realized why. President Paul Kagame regularly proclaims a national cleanup day that all Rwandan citizens join.[10] In addition, while progressive cities in North America (such as Portland, Oregon in early 2013) have only recently instituted a comprehensive ban on plastic bags, Rwanda instituted a national ban nearly a decade earlier in 2004.[11] In 2005, I noticed that some hotels I stayed in had removed all plastic rubbish bins, but they had not yet replaced them with any other type of rubbish container such as a wicker basket container found in some more upscale hotels I could not afford. While this practice was unnerving at first, I found that I was much more conscious of any paper waste I produced, and consequently, I significantly reduced any waste that I left behind in Rwanda. For ordinary Rwandan citizens, some of these adjustments have been significant, as they are all required to participate in monthly

8. Kinzer, *A Thousand Hills*, 257, 264–67. Also see my presentation on "Genocide, Tribalism, and the Hope of Reconciliation" at the SPS convention in 2011 in Memphis, Tennessee.

9. See for example Kinzer's comments in *A Thousand Hills*, 2.

10. Wen, "Two for the Road," in *The New York Times*, June 15, 2007, para. 2.

11. "Rwanda Gets Tough on Plastic Bags," *BBC News*, January 17, 2006, para. 11–13.

national clean up days. Because our organization once unfortunately planned a pastor's training conference during one of these national clean up days, four hundred pastors in our conference had to submit written permission to the national government in Kigali to temporarily excuse themselves from a national cleanup day and promise to "volunteer" on an alternate day or face severe penalties. Of course "volunteering" for National Cleanup Day in Rwanda is somewhat ironic since Paul Kagame often leads his country like a benevolent dictator. Nevertheless, to his credit, Kagame also leads by example, and participates in almost every National Cleanup Day alongside ordinary Rwandans.

Kenya

While Kenyan Pentecostal environmental praxis does not appear as impressive or progressive as Rwandan environmental stewardship, my living in a Kenyan village for a year afforded the opportunity to observe both the promises and pitfalls of Pentecostal Christian stewardship in East Africa.[12] My initial impressions centered around four things: minimal waste and recycling; minimal energy requirements; deforestation and afforestation; and human encroachment, corruption, and wildlife endangerment.

In Kenya, I noticed that at our office in Eldoret, at our feeding program in Kambi Teso (a slum of Eldoret), and at our children's village and school in Mlango, I saw very little waste. Very few things were pre-packaged, all food and food waste was eaten either by humans or fed to the goats and chickens at our village, and the desire for material goods among our children was relatively simple. During family prayer time I would never hear them ask for God to give them the latest Nintendo game, a new computer, or the latest Western toy, even though every home at the village had a computer and access to Western material goods. Instead their prayers were selfless and frequently interjected with pleas for God to protect their friends they left behind in the slums of Eldoret to live at our village. We also had a relatively good recycling program at our

12. My wife and I had the opportunity to serve as missionaries with Open Arms International in Eldoret, Kenya from 2009–2010 and help start a children's village in Mlango, Kenya, near Eldoret. We have continued to visit the village frequently and I serve on their board of directors. For more information about our work in Kenya or about Open Arms International please refer to their web site at www.openarmsinternational.com.

village, with buckets at each house that divided waste into food waste, burnable waste, and non-burnable waste. The food waste was all fed to the chickens, goats, and sheep at our village. The burnable waste was used to supplement the cooking fuel for each home. The non-burnable waste for the entire village, which serviced approximately six hundred people on a daily basis, accumulated the amount of waste two to three average Western families of four gathered on a daily basis.[13] While normal Kenyan families do not typically have this type of recycling program, all of the *shambas* or local farms in our community utilize all of their food waste and from my own casual observations, accumulated even less non-burnable waste than our own village.[14]

While there is no formal recycling program of any kind in Eldoret, and very little formal recycling occurring in Nairobi, Kenya, it is interesting to see what Kenyans and Kenyan children in our community have done with non-burnable solid waste. I was always amazed to see children at our village converting old waste into creative toys, makeshift toy vehicles, and a wide assortment of balls and play materials. Of course, wherever I went in East Africa, children were constantly playing soccer with the ubiquitous "rag balls" made out of old, bundled plastic bags. However, recycling is still a challenge, especially when one observes the problems with solid waste that larger African cities like Nairobi face on a regular basis. While fifty percent of all solid waste is recycled in my home state of Oregon, the city of Nairobi, with approximately the same population as the state of Oregon, recycles only five percent of its solid waste, and only twenty seven percent of all solid waste ever makes it to the city's main landfill.[15] In addition, this problem is exacerbated by Nairobi's high density population with very few urban gardens, farms, or *shambas*. Sixty five percent of the city's refuse comes from bio-waste which would have normally been used in a more rural setting.[16] Nevertheless, while these are dismal figures for Nairobi's recycling program, Nairobi

13. This is entirely an estimate, but the amount of burnable waste gathered at the village on a daily basis was approximately ten to fifteen gallons of solid waste of which as much as half of this same waste came from Western staff and visitors at the village.

14. Since the shambas or farms surrounding our village had virtually no Western visitors or influence, it can be surmised that our Western guests, per capita, added significantly to the amount of non-burnable waste our village accumulated.

15. Kamunyori, "Can recycling help Nairobi?," para. 2–3; and Oregon D.E.Q., "2010 Oregon Material Recovery and Waste Generation Report," 2.

16. Kamunyori, "Can recycling help?," para. 6.

should be applauded for its minimal amount of total solid waste: 3,121 tons annually, in comparison to Oregon's total accumulated annual waste of 4,340,486 tons![17]

One other notable feature I observed while living in Kenya was the minimal energy use of most of its citizens. In fact, Kenya's total installed capacity for electrical production is 1600 megawatts, while my own state of residence, Oregon, with less than ten percent of the total population of Kenya, has an installed capacity of nearly 15,000 megawatts.[18] To be fair, these figures could be misleading since most Kenyans do not have regular access to electricity and the Kenyan utilities are making very little effort to create more access except in urban areas.[19] For most Kenyans, the only universal need for electricity seems to be the desire to recharge their cellular phones. As a result, some unusual niche marketing has started in various cities where small kiosks allow users to recharge their cellular phones for a small amount of money. Nevertheless, those who do have access to electricity generally use very little of it in comparison to Western consumption. I have never seen a dryer for laundry sold in any retail store in Kenya. Power tools, appliances, and refrigerators are not commonplace. Finally, while consumption and capacity are low in Kenya, most of Kenya's electrical power grid is supplied by somewhat "green" sources such as hydroelectric dams, solar power, and geothermal energy.[20]

Another aspect of Kenya's minimal "carbon footprint" is its low percentage of private automobile usage. Per capita, only twenty four out of every 1000 Kenyans own an automobile as compared to 797 out of every 1000 U.S. citizens.[21] Hundreds of Kenyans, out of necessity, can be seen riding their bicycles on the tarmac in front of our village, laden with piles

17. Ibid., para. 2–3; and Oregon D.E.Q., "2010 Oregon Waste Report," 2. According to these figures, the state of Oregon produces nearly 1,400 times the amount of solid waste that the city of Nairobi does.

18. Ombok, "Kenya Electricity," para. 7; and Clean Edge, Inc., "Oregon's Clean Energy Economy," 5.

19. Ombok, "Kenya Electricity" para. 9. One informal conversation I had with a regional supervisor for Kenya Power in Eldoret suggested that only about 20 percent of the Kenyan population had regular access to electricity. Another online source ("Access to Electricity," para. 1) confirms that less than 17 percent of the Kenyan population has access to electricity.

20. Ombok, "Kenya Electricity," para. 2, 4, and 11.

21. "Motor Vehicles," The World Bank, para. 1.

of firewood, jugs of milk, and large bags of charcoal. Most Kenyans avail themselves of the tens of thousands of *matatu* drivers throughout Kenya who load small mini-vans with twenty people or more when the seating capacity often only warrants half that amount. One wonders, however, if Kenya's economy grows at a rate similar to what has happened in China in the last three decades, if the consumption of fossil fuels will rise exponentially and wiser use of resources and technology will be needed to avoid a similar scenario to China's rapidly degrading air quality.[22]

Deforestation has been one of the most egregious ecological crises on the continent of Africa over the past century. For the past several decades, eleven million hectares of African forest have been destroyed annually.[23] One anecdotal reference to deforestation comes from Robert Clobus' own experience, growing up in Accra, Ghana. "I have been walking the countryside for a good twenty years and previously could go from village to village under a canopy of trees. Now I can look two or three miles ahead and see the rusty tin roofs of the neighboring village surrounded by coconut palms."[24] Clobus cites several different causes for the rapid deforestation of Ghana. He mentions that the rapid population growth of Accra, from 20,000 in 1911, to over one million inhabitants in the early 1990s has been a significant factor.[25] He lists other related causes including the timber and mining industries, but "food farming was and still is the greatest single cause of deforestation."[26]

In Kenya, Wangari Maathai became a national hero and the first African woman to win the Nobel Peace Prize for her efforts in establishing the Green Belt Movement and mobilizing 30,000 women to plant over fifty million trees in the past thirty five years.[27] Her efforts have gal-

22. Economy, "The Great Leap," 2. When I first visited China in 1984, an automobile was very rare in the country, but as their economy has grown from the eighth highest ranked GDP in 1984, to the second highest ranked GDP in 2013, their automobiles per capita, and especially their sulfur dioxide air pollution from unfiltered coal fueled power plants has grown exponentially. Most disturbing is how Kenya is now planning to add coal fired power plants to its energy arsenal (most likely ones retrofitted without air scrubbers because of the economic cost of adding them) and add an extra 2400 Megawatts of electrical energy by 2030 through this source alone ("National Energy Policy," 16–17).

23. World Commission, *Our Common Future*, 2.

24. Clobus, "Ecofarming and Land-ownership in Ghana," 65.

25. Ibid, 66.

26. Ibid, 68.

27. For more information about her movement and her contributions to environ-

vanized other groups throughout the country to organize tree planting ceremonies in their communities. When I first arrived in Eldoret, Kenya in 2005, I witnessed one of these ceremonies as the service began with a Christian prayer, a community speech, and the tribal chief inviting honored guests, including myself, to join him in planting dozens of trees in his community. In 2012, our village sponsored a larger tree planting ceremony where we invited fifty guests to assist our village children in planting over 2500 indigenous trees in our community. We began with prayer and extended worship before going to plant trees for the day.

Nevertheless, these efforts are mostly negated by the massive consumption of trees for cooking fuel in East Africa. Improved technology with the widely used Kenya Ceramic Jiko has helped curb some of the deforestation in East Africa, but Kenyans still consume seventy percent of their energy needs by using wood fuel or wood charcoal as cooking fuel.[28] While a ban on harvesting trees in public forests was enacted by the Kenyan government in 2002, its enforcement seems rather lax at times.[29] In 2010, my wife and I stayed overnight at Menengai Crater, the second largest surviving volcanic crater in the world, surrounded by a natural reserve overlooking Nakuru and Lake Nakuru National Park. While Lake Nakuru National Park is surrounded by an electric fence to keep the large mammals in and the poachers out, the reserve surrounding the crater cannot afford such a luxury. While looking inside the crater, I observed smoke filling the air above the crater from dozens of large piles of wood burning underneath mounds of earth to create charcoal. Many proposals have been offered to help curb deforestation, but the most promising appear to be continued afforestation through community efforts, better management of woodland, adopting more efficient wood burning technologies, and looking at other alternative forms of biomass.[30]

Perhaps the most vocal and visible efforts towards environmentalism in Africa have been centered on the preservation of large mammal populations, many of which are facing endangerment or extinction. Only 7,000 to 10,000 cheetahs remain in Africa and their population continues to dwindle as humans encroach on the wide-open grasslands

---

mentalism in East Africa, see Maathai, *The Green Belt Movement*.

28. Githiomi and Oduor, "Strategies for Wood fuel in Kenya," 22.

29. Ibid.

30. See Githiomi's article "Strategies for Wood fuel in Kenya," 23–25, for a full list of proposed viable strategies.

these amazing creatures prefer to hunt in.[31] White Rhinoceros have been endangered for several decades in Africa, and while Black Rhinoceros were once the most numerous species of rhinoceros in Africa, their numbers have fluctuated in the past decade to as low as 2,410 with regional extinction occurring in West Africa.[32] While African Elephants are not considered endangered because their current population ranges between 500,000 and 600,000 in Africa, it is estimated that twelve percent of their total population was killed by ivory poachers in 2012 alone.[33] In China, 83% of the rapidly growing middle class population intends to purchase ivory, and with the rapidly expanding ivory market, it is estimated that African Elephants could become critically endangered or extinct in the next decade.[34] While Kenya's notable act of burning a large stockpile of twelve tons of ivory in 1989 led to a global ban on ivory trade in 1990, and a subsequent increase in the elephant population of Africa, loosening of this ban in the past decade has led to a significant decrease in the population of elephants in the past few years.[35]

Zimbabwe

M.L. Daneel's work in organizing and writing about the Association of African Earthkeeping Churches (AAEC) has been widely recognized as one of the inspirational success stories for global Pentecostal environmentalism. In the early 1990s, he recognized the potential of African Independent Churches (AIC) in his region of Africa to initiate a grassroots Christian environmental movement. Members of this movement began confessing ecological sins in their prayer meetings, and churches started including a tree planting ceremony as part of their Eucharist services.[36] Many of these neo-Pentecostal churches expressed a close affinity with God's creation in their worship and practice. Bishop Kindiam Wapendama, leader of the Signs of the Apostles Church, and a member of the AAEC, offers this prayer as part of their liturgy which incorporates both Eucharist and a tree planting ceremony: "Indeed, there were forests,

31. "Cheetah," National Geographic, para. 3.
32. "Diceros bicornis," The IUCN Red List, para. 1–2.
33. "Battle for the Elephants," PBS documentary.
34. Ibid.
35. Ibid.
36. Daneel, "African Traditional Religions," 107.

abundance of rain. But in our ignorance and greed we left the land naked. Like a person in shame, our country is shy in its nakedness. Our planting of trees today is a sign of harmony between us and creation. We are reconciled with creation through the body and blood of Jesus"[37]

While some may find African AIC theology comingling Christian and animistic thought, African churches do not easily separate Christian thought into simple categories of systematic theology. In African theology and thought, "the relationship between humanity and nature is harmonious—one of relationship rather than one of exploitation."[38] This is in sharp contrast to the words of Henry Spence; an early twentieth century missionary to what is now Zaire, who, while helping to build his missionary compound stated: "It was wonderful to see the forest coming down on all sides. I could feel the power of Satan receding as every tree fell."[39]

The practical goals of the AAEC include afforestation, wildlife conservation, and the protection of water resources.[40] Within a few short years, the movement had garnered two million members and planted millions more trees in certain regions of Zimbabwe[41] However, Daneel has not written much about this movement lately, and one wonders if the political and socio-economic challenges that Zimbabwe has recently faced under Robert Mugabe's leadership has also forced this movement to curtail their environmental efforts.

What can the rest of christianity and the world learn from Africa?

First of all, African Christian environmentalism offers an example of how putting Christianity and environmentalism in the same phrase is not oxymoronic. While many groups have often suggested that Christianity and environmentalism are antithetical movements, much of African Christianity offers an integrative and holistic approach to environmental healing and praxis.[42] In the history of modern Christianity and the

37. Daneel, "African Independent Churches," 258.

38. McMinn, *Walking Gently on the Earth*, 31.

39. As quoted by Colin Turnbull in *The Lonely African*, 114–15.

40 Daneel, "African Independent Churches," 249.

41. Ibid.

42. Some scholars would refute this point stating by suggesting that African indigenous religions, and not African Christianity, represent a pro-environmental stance

era of African colonialism sometimes Christianity and environmentalism have pushed towards opposing goals. Nevertheless, indigenous
Christian movements such as the AAEC in Zimbabwe have demonstrated that Pentecostal environmentalism can work—and is working—in
South Africa.

Second, while recycling programs are not very common in much of
Africa and recycling rates in cities such as Nairobi are abysmal compared
to most major cities in the First World, the state of Oregon, with one
of the best recycling programs in the United States, still puts nearly 700
times more waste in its landfills than the city of Nairobi.[43] The developing
nations of Africa can remind the developed world that their simplicity
and lack of waste trumps the best efforts of recycling in the face of massive consumption and waste.

Third, as demonstrated in Rwanda, good leadership is crucial for the
future of Africa and the world. The changes taking place in Rwanda are
quite remarkable considering what they went through only two decades
ago in the Rwandan Genocide of 1994. However, this type of leadership is
often scarce in places like Somalia, Sudan, Congo, and even in Zimbabwe
where Robert Mugabe's corruptive regime often negates the best efforts of
M.L. Daneel and the AAEC. Many of the challenges facing African leadership are rooted in the endemic corruption at every level of government
that overlooks environmental pollution, toxic waste, and animal endangerment. With a quick bribe or a payoff, policemen, security agents, and
government officials overlook these violations.[44] Of course, no country is

---

in their theology and practice. For an example, see Mpanya, "Impacts of a Church
Project," 106–7. While I would agree that both religions are environmentally friendly,
the examples that these scholars cite are typically Western missionary endeavors in
Africa and not indigenous African Christian groups.

43. Kamunyori, "Can recycling help?," para. 2–3; Oregon D.E.Q., "2010 Oregon
Waste Report," 2.

44. Anyone travelling throughout much of Africa can witness the policemen on
the side of the road pulling vehicles over for bribes and government officials stalling
conservation efforts at the behest of certain industries or black market ivory traders.
Kenya, where I lived, ranks 139th out of 176 countries surveyed by Transparency
International. Somalia is tied for last place with North Korea and Afghanistan. Sudan
is one spot above last place. Rwanda is the second highest African nation ranked at
fifty and Botswana, at thirty, is ranked highest (there are two island nations off the
continent of Africa that are ranked higher than Rwanda). I witnessed policemen in
Kenya collecting bribes on the side of the road every day but I never observed the same
occurrence in Rwanda.

immune from corruption, but good leadership is crucial for the ecological status of our world.[45]

Just as good leadership can make a massive difference in any country, some of the creative and innovative grassroots efforts of poor African nations like Rwanda, organizations like the AAEC in Zimbabwe, and simple communities like Open Arms Village in Kenya have proven that good innovative environmental technology and ecological progress does not always depend upon a nation's GDP. Unfortunately, sometimes certain authors and leaders have submitted to the status quo or the fatalism of defeat when N. Boegman and C.J. Els suggest that sulfur dioxide emissions in South Africa cannot be reversed since "any of the present technologically acceptable methods of abatement would raise the cost of electricity beyond the means of users."[46] However, they do not consider the alternative forms of power already being utilized effectively in other parts of Africa including solar, geothermal, and hydroelectric energy. Worse yet, they question whether we should be concerned about the dangers of air pollution in Africa "which will only become significant after sixty years, if the normal life expectancy in your community is only forty years?"[47] In their conclusion, Boegman and Els suggest that "air pollution is one of the penalties paid for progress."[48] This same fatalism and lack of vision has led China, with its rapid economic expansion in the past three decades, to become the largest polluter of greenhouse gases in the world, in addition to having sixteen of the twenty most polluted major cities in the world.[49]

Finally, the confession of our own sinful complicity in harming and destroying God's creation is a good starting point for Pentecostal

45. Using the same source at www.transparency.org,, the United States ranks nineteenth, and Russia probably ranks the lowest among more developed nations at 133rd. Denmark currently has the best ranking.

46. Boegman and Els, "Air Pollution," 93. They are correct in asserting that abatement methods for coal fired power plants currently are too expensive for any reasonable power grid in a third world or developing nation. The cost of installing the average air scrubber in North American coal fired power plants is about $300 million with over $30 billion invested in 110 plants in the last four years (Power Engineering, "US coal-fired power plants"). While this has successfully reduced sulfur dioxide emissions in the US 68 percent over the past two decades, sulfur dioxide emissions in developing nations have increased exponentially in the past two decades.

47. Boegman and Els, "Air Pollution," 97.

48. Ibid, 98.

49. Economy, "The Great Leap Backward," 2.

Christian worship and environmental praxis. From this point of recognizing our own guilt, prayers of healing can be offered for the environment and prayers of reconciliation can be offered for all of creation
that has been fractured by humanity's sin. Consider a section of Bishop
Wapendama's sermon to the AAEC during a tree planting ceremony in
1993: "We are the followers of Jesus and have to continue with his healing
ministry. You are the believers who will see his miracles in this afflicted
world. So, let us all fight, clothing the earth with trees!"[50]

Conclusion

It is often said that "big things have small beginnings." In spite of their
poverty, lack of resources, lack of technology, and sometimes because of
these factors, many African nations and communities are offering creative, innovative, and sometimes very significant examples of environmental leadership. Paul wrote to a charismatic, Spirit-filled Corinthian
church that "God chose the weak things of the world to shame the
strong."[51] With this preference of God's Spirit, the face of Christianity has
expanded globally to the poorest parts of the world, and sometimes in
the most unexpected places, God has also inspired Pentecostal communities to offer healing to an environment sickened by humanity's sinful
destruction of nature.

Sometimes it is the smallest efforts that make the biggest differences.
The innovation of a Kenyan Ceramic Jiko stove has started to make a difference in the deforestation of East Africa. In addition, one of the newest
innovative trends in global Christian missions has been the implementa-
tion of hydroponic projects or other related cyclical projects that utilize
or implement entire ecosystems in small communities in impoverished
areas of Africa.[52] These small projects make a massive difference in the
economic and ecological status of these communities. Perhaps as other
communities in more developed nations begin to replicate these models

50. Daneel, "African Independent Churches," 252.

51. 1 Cor 1:27 (NIV).

52. See Gustafson, "Integrated Holistic Development," 134–36, for a great cyclical
model that is being successfully used in Thailand. Also see a very successful project
developed by teenagers in Swaziland at Wall, "Teens Win $50,000 with Hydroponics,"
June 7, 2012. In addition, staff at Open Arms Village in Mlango, Kenya, has developed
a very successful and sustainable greenhouse model for growing tomatoes for widows
in the community.

of healing, we will once again see the "circle of life" replicated not only on the African Sahel, but throughout the world.

BIBLIOGRAPHY

"Access to Electricity (% of Population) in Kenya." *Trading Economics*, http://www. tradingeconomics.com/kenya/access-to-electricity-percent-of-population-wb-data.html (accessed September 23, 2013).

Antonio, Edward P. "Letting People Decide: Towards an Ethic of Ecological Survival in Africa." In *Ecotheology: Voices from South and North*, edited by David G. Hallman, 227–34. Geneva: World Council of Churches, 1994.

Bakken, Peter W., et al, eds. *Ecology, Justice, and Christian Faith: A Critical Guide to the Literature*. Westport, CT: Greenwood, 1995.

Barrett, David B., et al, eds. *World Christian Encyclopedia: A Comparative Survey of Churches and Religions in the Modern World*. Vol. 1. New York: Oxford University Press, 2001.

Berhane-Selassie, Tsehai. "Ecology and Ethiopian Orthodox Theology." In *Ecotheology: Voices from South and North*, edited by David G. Hallman, 155–74. Geneva: World Council of Churches, 1994.

Boegman, N., and C. J. Els. "Air Pollution: Is it Serious?" In *Are We Killing God's Earth: Ecology and Theology*, edited by W. S. Vorster, 89–99. Pretoria: University of South Africa, 1987.

"Cheetah." *National Geographic*, http://animals.nationalgeographic.com/animals/mammals/cheetah/ (accessed September 20, 2013)

Clean Edge, Inc. "Oregon's Clean Energy Economy: A Clean Edge State Clean Energy Leadership Index Report." 2011. http://sites.ieee.org/sustech/files/2012/05/Oregon-Clean-Energy-Economy2011.pdf (accessed January, 2012).

Clobus, Robert. "Ecofarming and Landownership in Ghana." In *Missionary Earthkeeping*, edited by Calvin B. DeWitt and Ghillean T. Prance, 63–90. Macon, GA: Mercer University Press, 1992.

Comradie, Ernst, et al. "Seeking Eco-Justice in the South African Context." In *Earth Habitat: Eco-Justice and the Church's Response*, edited by Dieter Hessel and Larry Rasmussen, 135–58. Minneapolis: Fortress, 2001.

"Corruption by Country." *Transparency International*, http://cpi.transparency.org/cpi2012/results/ (accessed September 21, 2013).

Daneel, M. L. "African Independent Churches Face the Challenge of Environmental Ethics." In *Ecotheology: Voices from South and North*, edited by David G. Hallman, 247–63. Geneva: World Council of Churches, 1994.

———. "The Liberation of Creation: African Traditional Religious and Independent Church Perspectives." *Missionalia* 19, no. 2 (1991) 99–121.

"Diceros bicornis." *The IUCN Red List of Threatened Species*, http://www.iucnredlist.org/details/6557/0 (accessed September 20, 2013).

Economy, Elizabeth C. "The Great Leap Backward." *Foreign Affairs* 86, no. 5 (2007) 1–13.

Fowler, Robert Booth. *The Greening of Protestant Thought*. Chapel Hill: University of North Carolina Press, 1995.

Gustafson. "Integrated Holistic Development and the World Mission of the Church." In *Missionary Earthkeeping*, edited by Calvin B. DeWitt and Ghillean T. Prance, 111–47. Macon, GA: Mercer University Press, 1992.

Githiomi, J. K., and N. Oduor. "Strategies for Sustainable Wood fuel Production in Kenya." *International Journal of Applied Science and Technology* 2, no. 10 (2012) 22–25.

Hallman, David G. "Climate Change and Ecumenical Work for Sustainable Community." In *Earth Habitat: Eco-Justice and the Church's Response*, edited by Dieter Hessel and Larry Rasmussen, 125–34. Minneapolis: Fortress, 2001.

———. "Ethics and Sustainable Development." In *Ecotheology: Voices from South and North*, edited by David G. Hallman, 264–83. Geneva: World Council of Churches, 1994.

Kamunyori, Sheila. "Can recycling help Nairobi cut its waste?" *Urban Africa: News and Information about Cities in Africa*. http://urbanafrica.net/news/2013/06/10/can-recycling-help-nairobi-cut-its-waste (accessed September 18, 2013).

Kinzer, Stephen. *A Thousand Hills: Rwanda's Rebirth and the Man Who Dreamed It*. Hoboken, NJ: Wiley and Sons, 2008.

Kritzinger, J. J. "Mission, Development, and Ecology." *Missionalia* 19, no. 1 (1991) 4–19.

Le Roux, P. J. "Environment Conservation: Why and How?" In *Are We Killing God's Earth? Ecology and Theology*, edited by W. S. Vorster, 29–44. Pretoria: University of South Africa, 1987.

Maathai, Wangari. *The Green Belt Movement: Sharing the Approach and the Experience*. New York: Lantern, 2006.

McMinn, Lisa Graham, and Megan Anna Neff. *Walking Gently on the Earth: Making Faithful Choices about Food, Energy, Shelter, and More*. Downers Grove, IL: InverVarsity, 2010.

Ministry of Energy, Republic of Kenya. "National Energy Policy." May 11, 2012. Nairobi, Kenya. http://www.energy.go.ke/index.php/universal-access/download/finish/3-ministerial-documents/6-national-energy-policy-third-draft-may-11-2012

Moltmann, Jürgen. *God in Creation: A New Theology of Creation and the Spirit of God*. Translated by Margaret Kohl. San Francisco: Harper & Row, 1985. "

———. "God's Covenant and Our Responsibility." In *The Care of Creation: Focusing Concern and Action*, edited by R. J. Berry, 107–13. Leicester, UK: Intervarsity, 2000.

———. "Pentecost and the Theology of Life." In *Pentecostal Movements as an Ecumenical Challenge*, edited by Jürgen Moltmann and Karl-Josef Kuschel, 123–34. London: SCM, 1996.

———. *The Spirit of Life: A Universal Affirmation*. Translated by Margaret Kohl. Minneapolis: Fortress, 1992.

"Motor vehicles (per 1000 people)." *The World Bank*, http://data.worldbank.org/indicator/IS.VEH.NVEH.P3 (accessed September 18, 2013).

Mpanya, Mutombo. "The Environmental Impacts of a Church Project: A Zairian Village Case Study." In *Missionary Earthkeeping*, edited by Calvin B. DeWitt and Ghillean T. Prance, 91–110. Macon, GA: Mercer University Press, 1992.

National Geographic. "Battle for the Elephants." PBS Documentary, televised February 27, 2013.

Northcott, Michael S. *A Moral Climate: The Ethics of Global Warming*. Maryknoll, NY: Orbis, 2007.

Nürnberger, K. "Ecology and Christian ethics in a semi-industrialised and polarised society." In *Are We Killing God's Earth? Ecology and Theology*, edited by W. S. Vorster, 45–67. Pretoria: University of South Africa, 1987.

Ombok, Eric. "Kenya Electricity Hydro-Power Generation to Fall to 45% in 2014." *Bloomberg*, November 15, 2012. http://www.bloomberg.com/news/2012-11-16/kenya-electricity-hydro-power-generation-to-fall-to-45-in-2014.html.

Oregon Department of Environmental Quality; Land Quality Division, Solid Waste Policy and Program Development. "2010 Oregon Material Recovery and Waste Generation Rates Report." Salem, Oregon, October, 2011. http://www.deq.state.or.us/lq/pubs/docs/sw/2010MRWGRatesReport.pdf.

Pratney, Winkie. *Healing the Land: A Supernatural View of Ecology*. Grand Rapids: Chosen, 1993.

Rice, Tim, and Elton John. "Hakuna Matata." In *The Lion King* as performed by Nathan Lane et al. Walt Disney Pictures, 1994.

Ruether, Rosemary Radford. *Gaia and God: An Ecofeminist Theology of Earth Healing*. San Francisco: HarperCollins, 1992.

"Rwanda gets tough on plastic bags." *BBC News*. January 17, 2006. http://news.bbc.co.uk/2/hi/africa/4619748.stm (accessed September 20, 2013)

Sorrell, Roger D. *St. Francis of Assisi and Nature: Tradition and Innovation in Western Christian Attitudes toward the Environment*. New York: Oxford University Press, 1988.

Sowumi, M. Adebisi. "Giver of Life—'Sustain Your Creation.'" In *Ecotheology: Voices from South and North*, edited by David G. Hallman, 149–54. Geneva: World Council of Churches, 1994.

Tallman, Matthew. "Genocide, Tribalism, and the Hope of Reconciliation in East Africa." Paper presented at the Society for Pentecostal Studies meeting, Memphis, Tennessee, March 18, 2011.

———. Interview with Peter Illyn, founder of Restoring Eden. Vancouver, Washington, June 3, 2013.

———. "Pentecostal Ecology: A Theological Paradigm for Pentecostal Environmentalism." In *The Spirit Renews the Face of the Earth: Pentecostal Forays in Science and Theology of Creation*, edited by Amos Yong, 135–54. Eugene, OR: Wipf & Stock, 2009.

Testerman, Dennis E. "Missionary Earthkeeping: Glimpses of the Past, Visions of the Future." In *Missionary Earthkeeping*, edited by Calvin B. DeWitt and Ghillean T. Prance, 11–44. Macon, GA: Mercer University Press, 1992.

Turnbull, Colin. *The Lonely African*. New York: Simon and Schuster, 1962.

"US coal-fired power plants invested more than $30bn on scrubbers in last four years." *Power Engineering*. March 25, 2013. http://www.power-eng.com/articles/2013/03/us-coal-fired-power-plants-invested-more-than-30bn-on-scrubbers-.html (accessed September 20, 2013).

Van Dyke, Fred, et al. *Redeeming Creation: The Biblical Basis for Environmental Stewardship*. Downers Grove, IL: Intervarsity, 1996.

Wall, Tim. "Teens Win $50,000 with Hydroponics." *Discovery Communications*, June 7, 2012. http://news.discovery.com/human/teens-win-by-fighting-hunger-with-hydroponics-120607.htm.

Walt Disney Pictures. *The Lion King*. DVD. 1994.

Wen, Leana. "Rwanda, Past and Present." *The New York Times*, June 15, 2007. http://twofortheroad.blogs.nytimes.com/2007/06/15/rwanda-past-and-present/.

World Commission of Environment and Development. *Our Common Future*. Oxford: Oxford University Press, 1987.

12

River from the Temple: The Spirit, City Earthkeeping and Healing Urban Land

Paul Ede

Introduction

Contemporary cities face complex questions of environmental sustainability including land ownership, pollution, consumption and environmental quality.[1] How might Pentecostal and Charismatic (hereafter, PC) churches respond? What biblical resources exist to help undergird such mission? We begin by turning to a case study: a charismatic church's contemporary response to the urban environmental crisis faced in post-industrial Glasgow, Scotland.

Within days of moving into the Glaswegian[2] community of Possilpark to lead an incarnational church-planting team, a flyer appeared on the doorstep of my new home. It advertised a type of community event that I had not encountered before: turning a derelict plot a few hundred yards down the road into a wildflower meadow.[3] A first-time visitor to Possil is struck by how much vacant and derelict land exists, the irony being that Possil*park* has no land worthy of being called such. Abandoned, once productive brownfield land, previously set aside for industrial use, scars the community geographically and psychologically. We discerned that

1. Toly, "Cities and the Global Environment," 47–68.

2. Glasgow, Scotland.

3. Run by CHIP, the Children's Inclusion Partnership, a local charity based in Possilpark.

205

behind the flyer might be an invitation from the Holy Spirit to explore transformative work that he was establishing. This encounter began a long journey of collaboration with local people to see unproductive land in our community rehabilitated.

Pathologies of the land in abandoned places of empire

"Derelict and Vacant Land in Possilpark" © Paul Ede

Later, in reflecting on our journey, the following passage had fresh meaning:

> The people of the city [Jericho] said to Elisha, 'Look, our lord, this town is well situated, as you can see, but the water is bad and

the land is unproductive.' 'Bring me a new bowl,' he said, 'and put salt in it.' So they brought it to him. Then he went out to the spring and threw the salt into it, saying, 'this is what the LORD says: 'I have healed this water. Never again will it cause death or make the land unproductive.' And the water has remained pure to this day, according to the word Elisha had spoken. (2 Kgs 2:19–22, NIV).

Similar to Jericho, residents in Possil had articulated a pressing need to rehabilitate unproductive land, in part as a means to tackle the social consequences associated with it. On almost every index of population health, from drug and alcohol abuse to levels of breast-feeding and suicide, Possil fares significantly, in some cases shockingly, worse than the national average.[4] Social and environmental pathologies mutually reinforce one another. While no one has died in Possil because of poisoned drinking water, the degraded environment of Possil is part and parcel of the "death" that people confront here.

Urban earthkeeping as practiced by clay community church (CCC)

Since 2007, various forms of urban earthkeeping have become core to our church mission. Reflecting on the Elisha-Jericho narrative in light of Matthew 5:13, we have wondered whether (among other things) Jesus had in mind the healing of the land at Jericho when he described those who follow him as the "salt of the earth."[5] The church has initiated small scale actions such as Guerilla Gardening, seed-bombing, garden makeovers, and working alongside local initiatives such as Friends of Possilpark Greenspace.[6] These include securing Local Nature Reserve status for a ten hectare brownfield site with high biodiversity known as the "Clay Pit,"[7] and supporting the development of two other areas of brownfield scrubland at the heart of the community.[8] In this process we have developed a

4. Glasgow Centre for Population Health, *A Community Health and Wellbeing Profile for North Glasgow*, 36–37.

5. Kreider, "Salty Discipleship." Salt is a common fertilizer to stimulate land productivity.

6. Friends of Possilpark Greenspace, "Friends of Possilpark Greenspace."

7. Friends of Possilpark Greenspace, "Clay Pit."

8. Friends of Possilpark Greenspace, "Possil Meadow;" "Brothers Path."

contextualized approach to Spirit-led empowerment through brownfield regeneration.[9]

"The Clay Pit, a 10 hectare site in Possil soon to become a Local
Nature Reserve." © Thomas McGrory

We have reconstructed our ecclesiology and liturgical calendar around creative new approaches to reflect our commitment to urban earth-keeping This includes an Easter Sunday tree-planting Eucharist with a scriptural liturgy celebrating the anthropological and cosmological significance of Christ's resurrection, and an outdoor celebration of the Feast of Tabernacles in autumn.[10] Additionally, we have created space for gospel proclamation and personal testimony in light of our ecological *praxis*. Healing the land is seen as complementing a more traditional charismatic emphasis on the spiritual and physical healing of the human body.[11] In this regard we are expanding the charismatic understanding of what

9. Ede, "Earth-keeping in the City," 284–303.

10. A copy of the Eucharist itself can be downloaded from http://www.academia. edu/1917882/Tree-planting_Eucharist_booklet. For more information about this and how we have gone about the other activities listed above, please see Ede, *Urban Eco-mission*.

11. If a degraded environment has a damaging effect on our bodies, why would we only focus on healing the symptoms rather than the cause? Similarly, it is a natural step from enacting land healing alongside our neighbours to offering prayer for their physical healing.

Miroslav Volf has characterized as the "materiality of salvation," in light of his engagement with liberation theology.[12] How can such experience and practice be understood in light of Pentecostal-Charismatic theology?

Land and city: the judgment of sodom

Walter Brueggemann has identified three land pathologies in Scripture: *enclosure* (unjustly preventing the poor from owning land that is rightly theirs), *covetousness* (willfully monopolizing land ownership out of greed and a desire for commercial gain), and *defilement* (polluting the land in moral or physical ways so that it becomes unproductive).[13] Taken together, enclosure, covetousness and defilement can be collectively defined as anti-creational sins, to use Terence Fretheim's terminology. Fretheim develops this term while reflecting on the plague narratives of Exodus, and uses the term to describe actions that run counter to God's call for creation to "be fruitful" (Gen 1:22, 28). Pointing towards the "pervasive usage of the word *eres* ('earth, or land') in every plague story—over fifty times,"[14] Fretheim argues that the Exodus plagues,

> . . . are the effect of Pharaoh's anti-creational sins, the function-
> ing of which may be described as divine judgment. At the same
> time, they are *signs* (italics mine) pointing beyond themselves to
> unmitigated historical disaster.[15]

The land in Possilpark has paid witness to a long history of oppressive practices being greatly affected by all of Fretheim's anti-creational sins. The estate where Walter MacFarlane built Saracen Iron Foundry was constructed through a system of enclosures during the agricultural revolution. The land was polluted not just physically by industrial practices but morally by the social pathologies that have resulted from the economic collapse of these industries. And the remaining land has more recently been subject to structural covetousness with the transfer of public land assets to City Property, an arm's length enterprise organization which exists to resell this land to private interests for development.

---

12. Volf, "Materiality of Salvation," 447–68.

13. Brueggemann, *The Land*, 195.

14. Fretheim, "The Plagues as Ecological Signs of Historical Disaster," 392.

15. Ibid., 386.

Anti-creational practices, the land, and ancient urbicide

The biblical narrative reveals that these anti-creational practices frequently recur in urban contexts: Pharaoh's anti-creational sins in Exodus are perpetrated in the name of, and enabled by, his urban ambitions. Having said this, the subtle, nuanced portrayal of city life, citizen and creation in Scripture resists facile attempts to lock-down the metropolis as either causal of, or caused by, sin. That cities are the result and cause of anti-creational practices with regard to the land *can be* the case (and often is), but does not have to be. The pattern emerges that cities and citizens which work against the life-giving agency of the Holy Spirit economically, socially and ecologically are ultimately brought to their knees by that same Spirit. The great hope is our Creator's commitment to the resurrection of cities (see section 2.1.2).

The story of Sodom's destruction remains today as a stark example of the failure of the urban dream.[16] Sustained reflection on it, and other stories in Scripture, is critical as we face urban crises today. In fact, Scripture leads us to understand that God intended Sodom's story to be remembered by future generations in just this way (Gen 18:17–19). Sodom's destruction can be seen as a recapitulation of Babel's urban failure and a foreshadowing of both the judgment on the urbanizing empire of Egypt during the Exodus and the plague narrative of the city of Ashdod in 1 Sam 4—5.[17] In addition, the devastation that comes upon Jerusalem around 587 BCE is often attributed by biblical authors to be the direct result of God applying similar judgment on the chosen people and their city (e.g. Ezek 16:44–52). Thus all these situations are in fact negative exemplars revealing how Yahweh expects humanity and urban civilization to act rightly towards creation, towards itself, and towards God.

The usual PC response to the question "what was the sin of Sodom?" is to focus on the sexual sins of the Genesis narrative.[18] In Brueggemann's schema this would result in land *defilement*. Indeed, Scripture emphasizes God's judgment not only on the city of Sodom but also on

---

16. Brueggemann, *The Land*, 3.

17. The judgment plagues against Ashdod (1 Sam 5:6–10) are a recapitulation of God's judgment against Empire-driven anti-creational practices, promulgated in an urban context. The oppression of the Israelites is here symbolized by the stealing of the Ark of the Covenant and the idolization of Dagon. In 1 Sam 5:12 we read that: "Those who did not die were afflicted with tumors, and the outcry of the city went up to heaven."

18. See also Jude 7.

the land itself: "the LORD rained down burning sulfur on Sodom and Gomorrah—from the LORD out of the heavens. Thus he *overthrew* those cities and *the entire plain*, destroying all those living in the cities—*and also the vegetation in the land*." (Gen 19:24–25, italics mine). This points toward a need to cleanse the land itself, not just arrest the anti-creational social forces endemic to Sodom. But less well known is the passage where Ezekiel describes Sodom's sin in the following way: "Now this was the sin of your sister Sodom: She and her daughters were arrogant, overfed and unconcerned; they did not help the poor and needy." (Ezek 16:49). This is suggestive of land pathologies of both *enclosure* and *covetousness*. John Goldingay suggests that the outcry raised to God over Sodom relates "to Sodom's oppressive relationship with the countryside around; the city is often a parasite on the countryside."[19] Together, all these sins describe anti-creational practices with regard to the three critical relationships of God, humanity and land. The judgment of the Creator God must come against such anti-creational practices. Through it all we are invited to discern the agency of the Holy Spirit sustaining and protecting creation by preventing anti-creational sin. The Holy Spirit is necessarily destructive in creation in order to ultimately cause its *ongoing sustenance*.[20] In most readings of the story of Sodom, the judgment of fire is assumed to be where its story ends. But is that actually the case?

The apokatastasis of the polis.

A close examination of the prophecies of Ezekiel suggests that fiery judgment is not the end for Sodom. The prophet holds up Sodom and Samaria as Jerusalem's sister cities (Ezek 16:46). This links the sinfulness of Jerusalem and the sin of other cities explaining why Israel has been put into exile. Ezekiel speaks of the two sister cities themselves having

19. Goldingay, *Genesis for Everyone Part 2*, 28.

20. Wallace's understanding of the "dark side of the Spirit" can be helpful here. Swoboda discusses this in the following way: "Wallace reminds us that a biblically informed pneumatology must and should go beyond imagining solely the Spirit's life-giving role. As well, the biblical Spirit must be understood similarly in its judgmental and destructive character within the creation schemata . . . Wallace refers to this as "the dark side" of the Spirit, exemplified in the judgment of Ananias and Sapphira in the book of Acts and the Spirit's power and strength giving role with the Judges of Israel in destroying Israel's enemies . . . Therefore, eco-pneumatology must have two eyes: the creative eye and the destructive eye. As the Holy Spirit broods over creation, it likewise ushers in the storm, the typhoon, and the earthquake in similar fashion. The Spirit therefore judges all false forms of separation." Swoboda, *Tongues and Trees*, 136.

daughters, which may in context refer to the inhabitants of the cities, or possibly the outlying villages and hinterlands that they dominated. In fact, Ezekiel goes even further and suggests that the sin of Jerusalem actually outstripped Sodom (the exemplar of the failure of the urban promise) making it "seem righteous" by contrast (Ezek 16:47–8, 51–2).

What follows is the prophecy: "I will restore the fortunes of Sodom and her daughters and Samaria and her daughters, and your [Jerusalem's] fortunes along with them . . . Sodom with her daughters and Samaria with her daughters, will return to what they were before (Ezek 16:53, 55)."[21] Yahweh is committed to resurrecting the fortunes of these two Gentile cities as well as Israel. We are reminded of the psalmist's eschatological prophecy about Gentile cities and civilizations: "I will record Rahab and Babylon among those who acknowledge me; Philistia too, and Tyre, along with Cush—and will say, 'This one was born in Zion' . . . As they make music they will sing, 'All my fountains are in you.'" (Ps 87).[22]

The vision of Sodom's future restoration is reinforced by the prophecy in the first half of Ezekiel 47. Here we see wondrous images of the Dead Sea being transformed from salt to fresh water. A healing stream flows down Jordan River, southwards through the Arabah and into the basin of the Dead Sea. The source of the new stream is the Temple Mount of Jerusalem. The revivification affects fish, fisherman, vegetation, water and land. It is a picture of restoration of the fortunes of the region, and the healing of the land. Indeed, where most translations speak of the water "being made fresh," the Hebrew word that is used is *rapha*, which means 'to heal.'

---

21. The Hebrew root word for the word "restore" in the phrase "restore the fortunes" is *shoob*. Block writes that: "[T]he clearest indication of the common meaning of the idiom is provided by Job 42:10. Here shoob involves the restoration of Job's original good fortune, including the return of his standing in the community, his wealth, and his family. Jeremiah, who uses the phrase most frequently, offers the fullest information on its prophetic force. The idiom appears for the first time in Jer 29:14, but its eight occurrences in chapters 30–33 suggest that these chapters represent an exposition of the idiom. Here, as in Ezek 39:25 [it] identifies a model of restoration according to which Yahweh reverses his judgment and restores a condition of well-being, which often includes a correction of the causes that led to the judgment." Block, *The Book of Ezekiel: 1-24*, 513. Block makes the point that however we read *shoob* with regards to Sodom and Samaria, we need to sustain consistency with how it is used in other similar prophecies for Jerusalem. It would appear, then, that Ezekiel is actually prophesying a material future restoration, similar to the land promise for exile in Israel, for the city of Sodom.

22. For a fuller exploration of this idea, see Ede, "Waste Land," 73.

We begin to move towards the full import of this prophecy when we enquire into the geographical location of Sodom. In biblical geography, the location of Sodom and the location of the Dead Sea are in fact one and the same. Lot travelled east into the Jordan valley and pitched his tents near Sodom (Gen 13:12). The Dead Sea was therefore understood to be the result of the firestorm of judgment that later followed—the story explaining the smell of sulfur and pillars of salt found in the area. Ezekiel 47, from the perspective of creation theology, can therefore be seen as a picture of how God intends to restore creation, even when anti-creational urban activities lay waste to the earth and oppress humankind on the land. Where God had once overthrown even "the vegetation in the land" (Gen 19:25b) because of its defilement, the same vegetation now flourishes and the land is productive. In a reversal of what is usually the case in contemporary urban experience, the city of Zion (wherein the Temple is located) *restores* rather than *exploits* the ecology of its surrounding hinterland by the power of the Spirit. In light of a) the promise of urban restoration in Psalm 87 and b) the suggestion in Revelation 21–22 that urban culture will be part of a wider resurrection of creation, it can be understood that the story of Sodom is paradigmatic of God's ultimate plan to restore even cities that have defiled the land, and establish a sustainable equilibrium with creation. The Scriptures portray a hopeful narrative of eschatological judgment and restoration, death and resurrection for the land and the city, as well as humankind: a post-judgment new creation (*apokatastasis*) of both the city (*polis*) and the land (*ktema, chora*).[23]

---

23. To be clear, contra the caution of Moey, I do not understand such an interpretation of Ezekiel to be a "literal" interpretation of the text. I am not saying that I believe an actual river will flow from the Temple. Rather, such an interpretation takes seriously the fact that this metaphorical passage is taken up in John's apocalyptic imagery (Rev 22) to point toward a material transformation that will come to pass in the New Creation: a material healing of the created order that has been inaugurated by the resurrection of Christ and will be completed at his return. See Bauckham, *Bible and Ecology*, 177. To take seriously the material healing of the land that this prophecy points to is to take this text no more "literally" than to say that the prophecy of Revelation 22 points to a coming material transformation. With regards to his concern to emphasize the now-and-not-yet of inaugurated eschatology, I can affirm that I am suggesting that the church's call is to anticipate this through practical care of the environment, mindful always that the full healing of the land will only happen in the new creation. Eschatologically, I hold to an interpretation of Revelation that emphasizes *transformatio-mundi* rather than *annihilatio-mundi*, as held by, e.g., Wright and well articulated in Moo, "Eschatology and Environmental Ethics," 23–43. Lastly, I am not seeking to deny other more anthropocentric interpretations (e.g., worship- or baptism-oriented), but rather to expand

Temple and city

How does Scripture discuss the way that the restoration of city and land will come about? First, some background is required. Urban historian Joel Kotkin in his classic *The City: A Global History*, asserts that "since their earliest origins, urban areas have performed three separate critical functions – the creation of sacred space, the provision of basic security, and the host for a commercial market."[24] He posits that while contemporary Majority world cities face most threat in the areas of commerce and security, the greatest threat facing contemporary Western cities is of spirituality, or a common moral bond.[25] Ecological degradation has the potential to destabilize all these aspects of city life. Returning to the issue of "spirituality," it can be seen historically that these shared belief systems have usually been provided by religion. In antiquity, such city-wide belief systems were symbolized and embodied by the temple system created in each specific context.

To the ancient mind, therefore, temple and city were intimately connected. Right worship and right governance were inseparable. This was embodied by the Israelites in their vision of Zion as the holy city-temple of God (Heb 12:22–24).[26] The right integration of Jerusalem and the Israelite people with the cosmos was symbolized by the cosmological imagery which adorned every aspect of the walls of the first Temple. The seven-pronged candlestick (Menorah) was a rich symbol of the tree of life from the Garden of Eden,[27] and the traditional colors of the Temple (white, blue, red and purple) were symbolic of the four elements. It was the latest iteration of the same trope in a long scriptural tradition.

First, as the place where Adam walked with God, Eden should be seen as "the first archetypal temple in which the first man worshipped

---

their purview and embed (rather than subsume) them in the wider, cosmological implications of the resurrection. My conscious goal is to subvert the often exclusively anthropocentric readings of Pentecostals and charismatics to fill out a more biblical, cosmological interpretation. See Moey "Response to Paul Ede," 65.

24. Kotkin, *The City*, xiv.

25. Ibid., xv.

26. "It is difficult, perhaps, to imagine in our current secular era the degree to which religion played a central role during much of urban history . . . Given the primacy of the priestly class, it is not surprising that temples celebrating the gods dominated the earliest primitive skyline . . . The high temple, suggests Mercia Eliade, constituted a cosmic mountain connected directly to the cosmos." Kotkin, *The City*, 4–5.

27. Beale, *The Temple and the Church's Mission*, 25.

God."[28] Second, in his wanderings through Canaan, Abraham sets up altars, often in the vicinity of large trees, such as at Mamre and elsewhere. A rich symbolism is resident in these moments: raising an altar near a tree is intended to recall Eden's great Tree of Life.[29] Third, the amazing dream of Jacob at Bethel (Gen 28:10–22) is a significant part of the iterative journey of the Temple tradition. His vision of the angels "ascending and descending from heaven" is clearly a moment pointing towards the idea of the possibility of heaven and earth reconnecting. This reality is later attributed to the First Temple. Fourth, we have the tradition of the Tabernacle in the wilderness and the embodiment (at this time while the Israelites were still nomadic) of the whole concept of God coming to dwell in the midst of his people during a time when they dwelt in a nomadic city.[30] It is from the patterns and traditions of the wilderness Tabernacle not only that the designs for Solomon's Temple were conceptualized but also the tradition of the Feast of the Tabernacles (Booths) derived. Fifth, in 1 Samuel 6, we see the connection being made between the Philistines at Ashdod re-establishing right worship in the Temple (by returning the Ark of the Covenant) and the promise that God will heal them of their plagues. Sixth, we have the decision of David and his son to establish the Temple in the heart of mount Zion, the Holy City of Jerusalem: the declaration of a settled people which symbolically draws together themes of Temple, the promised land and the city of peace. This mirrors the established tradition of ancient people discussed by Kotkin while also seeking to redeem that paradigm through monotheistic culture.

Turning from how the first Temple subsumed within itself the existing traditions of Israel in terms God's dwelling place, we now look to see how this summation was itself developed in the tradition that followed. First, the powerful imagery of the fountain of living water springing from the Temple in Ezekiel 47, read as a new creation text, makes richer connections than ever before between the Temple and the restoration of

28. Ibid., 66.

29. What seems so ironic is that, despite Abraham's practice, the later tradition of Torah specifically banned Israelites from worshiping near trees on high places, for fear of syncretism with the Canaanite tradition of worshiping Asherah poles. This prohibition is reversed in Revelation with the return of the Tree of Life to the heart of the temple-city .

30. It is from the patterns and traditions of the wilderness Tabernacle not only that the designs for Solomon's temple were conceptualized but also the tradition of the Feast of the Tabernacles (Booths) derived.

the city and its hinterlands. Second, the final verse of Psalm 87—"all our fountains are in you"—suggests that even pagan cities will experience the monotheistic Temple hope of having a fountain of living water at their heart. Third, as with so much of the prophetic tradition, John's Revelation subsumes both these images into the picture of the New Jerusalem, with a fountain of living water at its heart, in which God's presence is so pervasive that the Temple is no more needed. City, Temple and Creation are integrated in symbolic representation of the whole created order. Indeed the detail of Ezekiel 47 "facilitates our recognition of the ecological character of the water of life and the trees of life in Revelation."[31] The imagery of the new creation is of a city, fulfilling Ezekiel's vision, that is integrated with nature rather than being parasitic upon it: in the new creation the destroyers of the earth will have been themselves destroyed (Rev 11:18). As Richard Bauckham affirms, "the city that both includes paradise unspoiled (Rev 22:1–2) and is adorned with the beauty of paradise (Rev 21:19) points to that harmony of nature and human culture to which ancient cities once aspired but which modern cities have increasingly betrayed."[32]

In all of this, what can be seen is that the tropes of Temple and City increasingly interact in the trajectory of Scripture. The rich cosmological symbolism of the Temple and its implications for ecological mission, especially in urban contexts, is under-developed in Western Christianity and PC theology. By excavating the neglected Temple-City meta-narrative of the Bible we find a foundation for a sacred vision for the ecological transformation of the modern metropolis. This is only reinforced by a study of how the theme of the Temple also interacts with the theme of the Land.

Temple and land

In *Towards Cosmopolis*, urbanist Leonie Sandercock profiles a number of grassroots initiatives pioneered by minority groups and women that have had a significant impact on urban land and environmental issues,

31. Bauckham, *Bible and Ecology*, 175.

32. Bauckham, *The Theology of the Book of Revelation*, 135. Additionally, while John's vision is one of the whole created order rather than a city per se, if we also take into account Psalm 87 and the declaration that "This one and that one [cities] were born in her," we can understand the new creation as containing within it a whole range of "resurrected" cities patterned (in their own unique way) after this vision of integration.

demonstrating that they utilize diverse epistemologies that nevertheless need to be recognized and validated.[33] Respecting and dialoguing with these new approaches opens up the possibility of approaches to urban ecological transformation informed by faith perspectives. David Smith, reflecting on her work, states that "perhaps the most remarkable aspect of Sandercock's vision for the future [of the city] relates to the return of the sacred, which she regards as essential if a way is to be found to prevent total environmental degradation."[34] The relationship that Sandercock intuits between urban environmental questions and the religious or sacred vision is captured in the biblical story by in the linked themes of Temple and Land.[35] Nowhere in Scripture is this link made more clearly than at the high point of the dedication of the first Temple, when the Lord appears to Solomon at night and declares:

> When I shut up the heavens so that there is no rain, or command locusts to devour the land or send a plague among my people, if my people, who are called by my name, will humble themselves and pray and seek my face and turn from their wicked ways, then I will hear from heaven, and I will forgive their sin and will heal their land. (2 Chr 7:13–14).

Here we see an invocation of Israel's cultural memory of the judgment plagues that can come upon city-empires which live un-righteously, resisting God. A direct link is made between right worship through the Temple system and the possibility of reversing such a curse brought upon the land.

One PC interpretation of this passage focuses on the need for intercessory prayer against the principalities and powers, with representational confession[36] moving God to transform the structural systems of a city or nation. In such a view, "land" (*eres*), is often viewed as a metaphor for the institutional system. This tendency points to the PC tradition's syncretistic tendencies with regard to modernity and urbanization. It leads to a devaluation of the creational perspective, a point I have argued

33. Sandercock, *Towards Cosmopolis*, 147

34. Smith, *Seeking a City with Foundations*, 95

35. Smith, reflecting on her work, states that "perhaps the most remarkable aspect of Sandercock's vision for the future [of the city] relates to the return of the sacred, which she regards as essential if a way is to be found to prevent total environmental degradation." Smith, *Seeking a City with Foundations*, 95.

36. Petrie, *Releasing Heaven on Earth*.

elsewhere.[37] But in context, given the environmental effects of judgment that are being described, surely an ecological reading is more appropriate. Land here refers to the earth itself rather than just being a metaphor: the possibility of its healing, a restoration to the natural order and productivity and fruitfulness.

From a PC perspective, what remains interesting in 2 Chr 7:13–14 is the connection of the Temple promise to *land* healing, the key word being the Hebrew *rapha* also used in this regard in Ezekiel 47. This is exactly the same word used in the Old Testament to describe moments when God physically heals humans (e.g. Gen 20:17), but here it is applied to the land itself. It begs the question as to whether the gift of Pentecostalism to the church (the rediscovery of pneumatological healing), has been unwittingly truncated along anthropocentric lines.

How may we understand the ways in which God might "heal the land?" Here we return to the themes of enclosure, covetousness, and defilement previously discussed. What healing does Scripture offer for these scenarios, according to Brueggemann? To heal enclosure, Scripture speaks of *inalienable patrimony*, or the idea that heritable land rights remain in place no matter what (unjust) legal provisions are later put in place (Jer 32:1–15). Healing land covetousness involves *land redistribution*, which relates to the practice of Jubilee, and can be seen in the vision of Ezekiel 48 in which the land will be reapportioned fairly after the return from Exile. Lastly, healing defilement we have the idea of *restored fertility* (Hos 2:21–23), in which land polluted by a) sin or b) physical contamination comes into productivity once more. The stories of Cain and Abel (Gen 4) can be seen to exemplify (a), while the Elisha-Jericho passage can be seen as an example of (b).[38]

New creation: the temple and land-healing in eschatological perspective

Eschatologically, it can be said that the new creation will be witness to a reality of shalom in which the land restored to fertility is justly redis-

37. Ede, " Waste Land," 63–77.

38. Beyond this, we also need to acknowledge that land pathologies exist that have everything to do with the fallenness of creation itself, and no discernible direct link to human action. Of course, Paul later locates the groaning of creation to the fall of Adam and Eve (Rom 8), implying that there is a moral root to all situations of disharmony between humanity and creation. But it seems not all situations of environmental degradation can be linked to specific sins.

tributed by breaking down the inequalities of enclosure in light of the Creator's inalienable patrimony freely offered to all, as He apportions. All of this flows from the throne of God established through Christ, worshipped by all of creation in heaven and on earth. This is precisely the vision that is placed in view in the penultimate and final chapter of the prophecies of Ezekiel, contextually a vision of the forthcoming return from exile, but quarried by John in Revelation 21 and 22. The first half of Ezekiel chapter 47 is an outworking of the promise of 2 Chronicles 7:14, resulting in restored fertility. The often overlooked second half of chapter 47 and chapter 48 portrays the subsequent redistribution of land for the people of God. In a new departure, an area will be set aside for the common use of the city, including pasture land designated to provide food for all its workers, who derive from all the tribes of Israel. This is an insurance against the exploitative practices that had occurred in pre-exilic days and had resulted in exile (Ezekiel 16). Moreover, special provision is to be made for outsiders and aliens. In the new creation, not only will the land be healed of pollution, but enclosure will also be subverted: the meek really will inherit the earth.

For PCs to arrive at this interpretation requires what for them is a subversive reading of the text. The question "where does the river flow *to?*" re-orientates us towards a spatial, new creation interpretation, expanded beyond the anthropocentric.[39] This opens the door to an inaugurated pneumatology of *creation* not just humanity. It is, in fact, just as much the Spirit's work to sustain and redeem the wider created order.

The tendency to neglect land as central theme of Ezekiel 47 and 48 should cause us to enquire as to the extent to which Pentecostalism has colluded with the darker side of both modernity and Christendom in choosing to be strait-jacketed by eschatological positions that de-emphasize land-restoration and cosmological new creation.[40] Why has

39. Pentecostals often apply Ezekiel 47 in something like the following way: "How deep have you gone in the river? Are you ankle-deep, knee-deep, or swimming in the river of the Spirit?" This focuses on the experience of spiritual gifts and fruits, and the presence of the Spirit in the individual life of the believer. It emphasizes a despatialized, metaphorical, anthropocentric reading. Brueggemann suggests that "an inordinate stress on covenant to the neglect of land is a peculiarly Christian temptation and yields to a space/time antithesis." Brueggemann, *The Land*, 200. In tending to stress this kind of reading of Ezekiel 47, Pentecostalism can be seen to have syncretized itself as much as wider Western Christian thought under modernity with regard to deemphasizing the land.

40. It should nevertheless be noted that Lamp has done some interesting research

Pentecostalism so readily accepted these presuppositions, given its roots among the land*less*? I would argue that a subversive reading of Ezekiel 47 that embeds an anthropocentric interpretation in the wider context of land healing rather than ignoring the latter completely, is actually more congruent with the history of the Pentecostal movement. It enables a resistance to co-option by Christendom thought and suggests a very fruitful addition to the growing yearning among Pentecostal Christians to develop a robust social (and environmental) ethic of justice. Ezekiel 47 and 48 taken together decisively affirm God's promise to Solomon at the inauguration of the Temple as to the intended connectedness between Temple and Land, right worship and land justice, the presence of God and restored ecological fertility.

Bringing it all together: The spirit
of god and pc praxis for healing urban land

We have sketched the broad biblical outlines of a theology of Temple, City and Land. Now we need to draw all of these insights together to develop a specifically PC theology for ecological mission in the City. Recalling the Jericho-Elisha story from the introduction, the word *rapha* ("to heal, restore") is used to describe the miracle Elisha works in restoring the land of the town of Jericho to productivity. We can now view Elisha's miracle as a *Land text* in the sense of being an anticipation of God's future promise to "heal" the land of the Arabah once defiled by Sodom (geographically, Jericho is situated in the region of the Arabah near the Dead Sea). We can see the same story as a *City text* in the sense of it being an anticipation of the wider story of the resurrection of cities, symbolized by the advent of the New Jerusalem. And we can read it as a *Temple text*, being a partial fulfillment of God's promise at the founding of Solomon's Temple to "heal their land" if His people will "humble themselves and pray" (2 Chr 7:14).

How are we to connect the Holy Spirit to the intertwined themes of Land, Temple and City? Earlier, we discovered the importance of the symbolism of the Feast of Tabernacles in evoking for the Israelites the themes of God's presence as part of the over-arching Temple tradition.

---

in which he uncovers evidence that the idea of "transformatio mundi" rather than "annihilatio mundi" is in fact not foreign to the early Pentecostal tradition. As he explains of certain early Pentecostal writers, "The new heavens and earth are not replacements for the current versions; rather, they are in continuity with and recognizable forms of the current versions." Lamp, "New heavens and new earth," 7.

By Jesus' day, this third of the three great Jewish festivals had accrued to itself many different meanings: in particular it was a feast that fore-grounded the hope of the coming of the Messiah through the East Gate of the temple. Significantly for our topic, one particular part of the ritual celebrations in Jerusalem, the heart of the city and temple traditions of Israel, had developed as an acted parable of the prophecy of Ezekiel 47. At a certain moment, a water libation ceremony was enacted at the altar in the Temple precinct: water was poured out over the altar so that it flowed towards the East Gate.[41] This was intended to evoke the flow of water from the Temple in Ezekiel's prophecy. The event occurred at the height of the celebrations on the last day of the festival. John recounts that:

> On the last and greatest day of the festival, Jesus stood and said in a loud voice, 'Let anyone who is thirsty come to me and drink. Whoever believes in me, as Scripture has said, rivers of living water will flow from within them.' By this he meant the Spirit, whom those who believed in him were later to receive. (John 7:37–39).

In so doing, Christ identified himself to be the true source of living wa-ter in Ezekiel's prophecy, located himself once more as the fulfillment of the Temple tradition (John 1:51; 2:19), and effectively declared himself Messiah in fulfillment of the hope that the feast pointed towards. Here is the Christological consummation of our themes of City, Land and Temple, and the foundation for the Spirit-powered new-creation escha-tology of land healing and restoration, also in relation to urban contexts. It follows that Christ also identifies himself as the ultimate source of the land healing at Jericho in 2 Kings 2:22, the fulfillment of the promise of land healing of 2 Chronicles 7:14, and the fountain of the water of life for the resurrected city of Zion (and all who are in her) in Psalm 87 and Revelation 22. It is in Christ through the Spirit that cities which live according to the pattern of Sodom with regards to anti-creational prac-tices will be both destroyed as "destroyers of the earth" (Rev 11:18) and then resurrected in a renewed and sustainable pattern, after the image of the New Jerusalem.

Developing the implications for the church's mission, in Ephesians 2:11–22, Paul expounds the teaching that the church should understand itself as the new Temple: "In him the whole building is joined together

---

41. Wright, *John for Everyone Part 1*, 104–5.

and rises to become a holy Temple in the Lord. And in him you too are being built together to become a dwelling in which God lives by his Spirit." (v.21–22). N.T. Wright observes, "The church, as it stands, is thus already the new Temple, and the spirit that dwells within is the new *Shekinah*. In second-Temple Jewish terms, there could not be a higher Pneumatology than this."[42] In this way, the fulfillment of the prophecy of Ezekiel 47 taken up by Christ is then appropriated by his followers, the church, upon which he has sent his Spirit (Acts 2). We can therefore understand that one goal of the Spirit's anointing on the church is the inauguration (though not fulfillment) in the present of the eschatological healing of (urban) land. The church as the New Temple is called to apply itself to pro-creational practices with regard to (urban) land healing: working against unjust land enclosure, land covetousness, and land defilement.

Concluding remarks

The Spirit acts to arrest and judge anti-creational practices, which often converge with selfish habits promulgated in and exacerbated by urban contexts. The same Spirit calls us to pro-creational action with regards to the land. Rereading scriptural passages beloved by the PC tradition (2 Chr 7:14; Ezek 16; 47–48) subverts the anthropocentricity of received interpretations, freeing them from collusion with anti-creational eschatologies, demonstrating the rich potential of a legitimately broadened PC pneumatology to inform a missiology for creation-care and sustainable cities. There is an urgent need for Christian theology and especially Pentecostal theology to engage with urban ecology, because the direst urban consequences of the environmental crisis will hit those locations where global Pentecostalism is most strong: the slums of the cities of the Majority world.[43] Faithful discipleship that walks in the step with the Spirit in our urban centers must lead to an awakened sense of the import of the type of urban environmental mission modeled in Glasgow by Clay Community Church. And these but scratch the surface of a host of other creative possibilities by which the river of the Spirit could flow through the churches of our cities to heal the land, as Ezekiel's prophecy foretold.

42. Wright, *Paul and the Faithfulness of God.*
43. See Lamp, "New Heavens and New Earth," 14.

BIBLIOGRAPHY

Bauckham, Richard. *Bible and Ecology: Rediscovering the Community of Creation.* London: Darton Longman and Todd, 2010.

———. *The Theology of the Book of Revelation.* Edinburgh: Cambridge University Press, 2001.

Beale, G. K. *The Temple and the Church's Mission: A Biblical Theology of the Dwelling Place of God.* New Studies in Biblical Theology. Downers Grove, IL: InverVarsity, 2004.

Block, Daniel I. *The Book of Ezekiel: 1–24.* Grand Rapids: Eerdmans, 1997.

Brueggemann, Walter. *The Land: Place as Gift, Promise, and Challenge in Biblical Faith.* Overtures to Biblical Theology. Rev. ed. Minneapolis: Fortress, 2002.

Donne, A. Le. 2013. "The Improper Temple Offering of Ananias and Sapphira." *New Testament Studies* 59 (2013) 346–64.

Ede, Paul. "Earthkeeping in the City: Faithful Empowerment through Brownfield Rehabilitation." *Practical Theology* 6 (2013) 284–303.

———. *Tree-planting Eucharist: Booklet.* 2012. http://www.academia.edu/1917882/Tree-planting_Eucharist_booklet.

———. *Urban Eco-mission: Healing the Land in the Post-industrial City.* Cambridge: Grove, 2013. http://www.grovebooks.co.uk

———. "Waste Land: Theological Reflection on Brownfield Rehabilitation." *Theology in Scotland* 19 (2012) 63–77.

Fretheim, Terence E. "The Plagues as Ecological Signs of Historical Disaster." *Journal of Biblical Literature* 110 (1991) 385–96.

Friends of Possilpark Greenspace. "Friends of Possilpark Greenspace." http://sites.google.com/site/possilgreenspace/ (accessed July 12, 2013).

———. "Clay Pit." http://sites.google.com/site/possilgreenspace/local-work/clay-pit. (accessed July 12, 2013).

———. "Possil Meadow." http://sites.google.com/site/possilgreenspace/local-work/possil-meadow. (accessed July 12, 2013).

———. "Brothers Path." http://sites.google.com/site/possilgreenspace/local-work/brothers-bar—rear. (accessed July 12, 2013).

Glasgow Centre for Population Health. "A Community Health and Wellbeing Profile for North Glasgow." February 2008. http://www.gcph.co.uk/assets/0000/0625/NorthGlasgow.pdf.

Goldingay, John. *Genesis for Everyone Part 2: Chapters 17–50.* Edinburgh: SPCK, 2010.

Kotkin, Joel. *City: A Global History.* London: Weidenfeld & Nicolson, 2005.

Kreider, Alan. "Salty Discipleship: Bringing New Worlds to Life." http://www.anabaptistnetwork.com/node/291 (accessed July 13, 2013)

Lamp, J. S. "New Heavens and New Earth: Early Pentecostal Soteriology as a Foundation for Creation Care in the Present." Biblical Studies Interest Group paper, presented at the 41st Annual Meeting of the Society for Pentecostal Studies, 2012, 1–16.

Marshall, I. Howard. *Acts of the Apostles: an Introduction and Commentary.* Leicester, UK: InterVarsity, 1980.

Moey, M. "Response to Paul Ede: Theological Reflections on Brownfield Rehabilitation." *New Urban World* 3 (2013) 65–66.

Moo, Douglas. "Eschatology and Environmental Ethics" In *Keeping God's Earth: The Global Environment in Biblical Perspective*, edited by D. I. Block and N. J. Toly, 23–46. Downers Grove, IL: InterVarsity, 2010.

Moltmann, Jürgen. *God in Creation*. Translated by Margaret Kohl. London: SCM, 1985.

Sandercock, L. *Towards Cosmopolis: Planning for Multicultural Cities*. Chichester: Wiley & Sons, 1997.

Smith, D. W. *Seeking a City with Foundations*. Nottingham, UK: InterVarsity, 2011.

Swoboda, A. J. *Tongues and Trees: Toward a Pentecostal Ecological Theology*. Journal of Pentecostal Theology Supplement 40. Blandford Forum, UK: Deo, 2013.

Toly, Noah. "Cities and the Global Environment." In *Keeping God's Earth: The Global Environment in Biblical Perspective*, edited by D. I. Block and N. J. Toly, 47–68. Downers Grove, IL: InverVarsity, 2010.

Volf, Miroslav. "Materiality of Salvation: an Investigation in the Soteriologies of Liberation and Pentecostal Theologies." *Journal of Ecumenical Studies* 26 (1989) 447–68.

Wright, N. T. *John for Everyone: Part 1: Chapters 1–10*. London: SPCK, 2002.

———. *Paul and the Faithfulness of God*. Vol. 4 of *Christian Origins and the Question of God*. London: SPCK, 2013. Cited with permission prior to publication.

13

Spirit of Creation, Spirit of Pentecost: Reflections on Ecotheology and Mission in Latin American Pentecostalism

Richard E. Waldrop

When I love God I love the beauty of bodies, the rhythm of movements, the shining of eyes, the embraces, the feelings, the scents, the
sounds of all this protean creation . . . The experience of God deepens
the experiences of life . . . It awakens the unconditional Yes to life . . .
Life in God's Spirit is 'life against death' . . . .To say 'yes' to life means
saying 'no' to war and its devastations, To say 'yes' to life means saying
'no' to poverty and its humiliations. There is no genuine affirmation of
life in this world without the struggle against life's negations.

—JÜRGEN MOLTMANN[1]

Vitality and desolation in a beautiful land

Whether listening to the dawn chorus of birds along a remote jungle trail
in an Amazonian rainforest or enjoying the breathtaking beauty of a ma-
jestic Andean Condor soaring above the fragile alpine tundra, how can
one not sense that the Spirit of Life, the same Spirit of Creation, continues
to brood over the cosmos? And if these experiences of the Spirit are true,

1. Moltmann, *The Spirit of Life*, 97–98.

what are the ecological implications for a full-orbed Pentecostal understanding of mission?

My experience of over forty years as an environmentalist and amateur ornithologist—and as a Pentecostal missionary in Latin America—has taken me back, again and again, to these questions and has raised many others regarding the relationship between the Spirit of God in Creation,[2] the Spirit poured out on all flesh,[3] and the Spirit given specifically to the followers of Jesus on the day of Pentecost.[4] In these reflections, I attempt to answer, in part, some of these considerations.

Particular inspiration for the writing of these reflections came through two sources. First, the teaching of a seminary course on "Ecotheology and Mission" with missionary colleague Andrew Hudson and interactions with students at the *Seminario Sudamericano* (a Church of God—Cleveland, Tennessee affiliated seminary) in Quito, Ecuador. Secondly, additional clarity was received during a recent four-day immersion experience in the tropical rainforest of Northwestern Ecuador at the Playa de Oro Lodge, a community-operated ecotourism project.

Unfortunately, the diabolical forces of environmental and human destruction have been working overtime in Latin America for many centuries. The European conquest brought much pain, suffering and desolation to the peoples and the land of this continent during the past five hundred-plus years (1492–1992). More recently, the breathtaking Amazonian jungles of Ecuador have been ravaged by Western oil companies, leaving devastation and toxic pollution in their wake with untold damage done to the soil, to the myriad species of plants and animals and to the aboriginal peoples inhabiting their own ancestral lands.[5] In Peru, multinational mining corporations have been stripping the land and spewing toxic chemicals into the air to the detriment of all living beings.[6] In Central America, the international fruit companies and other commercial interests have wreaked violence upon the land and the people in the name of development and international trade. Extensive deforestation has been practiced throughout the region leaving all but the highest

2. Gen 1:2

3. Joel 2:28

4. Acts 2:1–4

5. See the excellent video documentary, *Texaco Toxico*, at www.texacotoxico.org.

6. See Quirynen, *Cerro de Pasco: Mining, Red Lakes, and Piles of Waste*, on the www. upsidedownworld.org website, *Covering Activism and Politics in Latin America*.

mountain elevations untouched and exposing the land to erosion and depletion. This pillage has left women and children—now working in subhuman conditions on huge coffee and banana plantations—to forage for firewood in the small patches of woodland that remain. Here it is very important to show the direct relationship between environmental destruction, institutionalized political and commercial violence, and human misery, poverty and oppression.

All of this destruction has been and continues to be done under the profit motivation of Western Capitalism and economic globalization, in collusion with political, commercial and religious interests in Latin America and the Global North.[7] As one case in point, the C.I.A., anti-governmental forces and the United Fruit Company worked together in 1954 to oust the democratically-elected but reform-minded President Jacobo Arbenz of Guatemala who ran for office on a platform of agrarian reform.[8] He was assassinated and replaced by the military dictator Carlos Enríquez Díaz de Leon. These tragic events then gave rise to a chain of military rulers, and additional social unrest which led to the creation of several revolutionary guerilla fronts and a civil war that lasted over thirty years resulting in the loss of over 200,000 lives, millions of internal and external refugees, and scorched earth military attacks leaving untold ecological damage. And to add insult to injury, the height of the violence and human rights violations on the part of the government in the civil war in Guatemala came during the short reign of terror of the infamous "born-again dictator," General Efrain Rios Montt, an ordained elder in the neo-Pentecostal Verbo Church who came to power as a result of yet another military coup.[9] Unfortunately, similar scenarios were repeated in El Salvador and Nicaragua with the same devastating consequences.

Pentecostal antecedents

Where have Pentecostals been in places like Guatemala during these tragic political and environmental developments? As far as we can tell, with all but a very few exceptions, Pentecostals were on the fringes of any direct concern for these situations even though many were person-

7. For historical analysis, see Galeano, *The Open Veins of Latin America.*

8. Schlesinger and Kinzer, *Bitter Fruit.* See also the political ornithology and travelogue, Maslow, *Bird of Life, Bird of Death.*

9. See Garrard-Burrnett, *Terror in the Land of the Holy Spirit.*

ally impacted by the violence—as many as fifty Church of God pastors were assassinated during the period and many additional church and family members murdered. Evidently, the oxymoronic Fundamentalist/ Dispensationalist version of Pentecostalism taken to Latin America by paternalistic North American missionaries and mission agencies during the first and middle periods of the twentieth century prevented the emerging national Pentecostal churches from fully developing their own theologies. Is it possible that a movement that began at the turn of the twentieth century in North America among the racially marginalized African-Americans, disenfranchised Mexican-Americans and impoverished Appalachian Euro-Americans could so quickly turn into an ally of Neo-Colonialism in Latin American and elsewhere in the majority world? It seems so.

To an even deeper level, however, goes this question: to what extent have modern Western Pentecostals been capable of a broader understanding and appreciation of the environmental and cosmic role of the Spirit in which they claim to be baptized individually? Even though there is documented evidence of at least one Pentecostal believer's prominent role in environmental concerns as the founder of International Earth Day,[10] there is little evidence that other North American Pentecostals have followed this example in the later years of the movement, outside of a narrow circle of Pentecostal academics.[11] On the contrary, most Western classical Pentecostals have shown outright antipathy, or indifference at best, to issues regarding the environment or creation-care and most of the academics addressing these issues are still considered to be on the fringes of the movement by their own denominational hierarchies. Only recently have some younger or more progressive Pentecostals scholars begun to push beyond the confines of the modernist Enlightenment

10. See Sparks and Rodgers, "John McConnell, Jr. and the Pentecostal Origins of Earth Day"; McConnell, *Earth Day: Vision for Peace, Justice and Earth Care, My Life and Thought at Age 96*; Weir, *Peace, Justice, Care of Earth*.

11. For example, Cheryl Bridges Johns, Professor of Discipleship and Christian Formation at the Pentecostal Theological Seminary (Cleveland, Tennessee) has participated in the Scientists and Evangelicals Initiative on the Care of Creation that produced the document/press release "An Urgent Call to Action: Scientists and Evangelicals Unite to Protect Creation," National Press Club, Washington, DC, January 17, 2007. See also her article "The Sanctity of Life," in the *Church of God Evangel* (January, 2009) 20–21, that raises issues related to environmental stewardship.

paradigm toward a more complete understanding of the work of the Spirit in the cosmos.

Unfortunately, as a result of the earlier, more fundamentalist theology of North American Pentecostals, similar views have been adopted by Pentecostal churches and ministers on all continents where missionaries have taken this particular brand of Christianity. In some places where Western missionary influence has been rejected however, some Pentecostal-type churches have developed their own, more indigenous approaches to earthkeeping as part of their self-identity. Perhaps the best documented cases of this differently understood identity comes from the African Initiated Churches (AICs).[12]

In Latin America the old paradigms are also beginning to give way to the new. There are some advantages for the development of this new paradigm in Latin America since indigenous worldviews still have significant influence, directly or indirectly, on the lives of millions of people across the continent and in every country, but especially in regions with predominant indigenous influence as in Ecuador, Peru, Bolivia, Guatemala and parts of Mexico.

Contributions of indigenous cosmologies in latin america

Is there a place in Pentecostal theology and spirituality for embracing the pre-historic, historic, and eschatological presence of the Spirit among the native peoples of the Americas, or must that necessarily be pejoratively labeled as syncretism? Was the Spirit domesticated in the West and taken to the rest—the many indigenous tribes and peoples groups—by mostly white, North American missionaries? In other words, have Western Pentecostal missionaries primarily understood ourselves as *following the Spirit of God* in the *missio dei* or do we rather *take the Spirit with us* to the "mission field?" If the former is true, then we must understand that the Spirit of Life has been present among the people of the millenarian cultures of Abya Yala from time immemorial.[13] That same Spirit

12. See Daneel, *African Earthkeepers*.

13. Abya Yala is from the Kuna (Panamá) language, meaning "continent of life" or "continent of full maturity." This term was adopted by representatives of 120 indigenous groups in Quito, Ecuador in 1992 at the First Continental Summit on Five Hundred Years of Indigenous Resistance and is widely used by many indigenous leaders as an alternative to "North and South America".

has imparted collective wisdom to these cultures and has given them a deep respect for and understanding of the undivided "natural" and "supernatural" worlds.

The Spirit would be understood by these Andean, Aymara, Maya and Aztec people to be the giver and sustainer of life in all of its manifestations: personal, communal, human, animal vegetable, earthly and heavenly. In the Peruvian and Bolivian Aymara cultures, it is the *Pachamama*, or Mother-Earth, whom is venerated in belief and ritual since she gives birth to life and interacts with feminine and masculine elements to sustain it. In indigenous cosmology, there is little to no separation between human beings, the earth and other living things. Ethics is also understood holistically in the multiple ecological, cosmic, human and spiritual dimensions of existence.[14]

Many Pentecostal churches now established among these peoples continue to hold to something of this broader understanding of the Spirit as the animator of all life, at least to a greater degree than their non-indigenous and non-Pentecostal counterparts that have been more severely impacted by modernity through Western government and religious ideologies. A major contributing factor to this openness to the activity of the Spirit beyond the narrow confines of church and individual believers is the Pentecostal distinctive of contact with the supernatural elements of life through Spirit-baptism, ecstatic utterances, dreams, visions and other spiritual manifestations.

In North America, there are Pentecostal indigenous voices and theologies that are now showing the way toward a more holistic understanding of the Spirit in creation as well.[15] Even among non-native Christians with strong ties to the land and nature, something of this indigenous spirituality can be perceived in many cultures. My own father, with strong Choctaw Indian roots, has often reflected on a special sense of "closeness to God" especially while fishing or hunting alone in the woods or on the bayous and lakes of Northeastern Louisiana.[16] So, in sum, a well-developed Pentecostal spirituality that takes the call to earth-care seriously, as

14. Irarrázaval, *Un Cristianismo Andino*, 226. In English, see Irarrázal's *Inculturation*.

15. See Woodley, *Shalom and the Community of Creation*; and Twiss, *One Church, Many Tribes*. Also see non-indigenous interpreters of the indigenous contextualization movement, Alexander, *Native American Pentecost*; and Waldrop and Alexander, "Salvation History and the Mission of God."

16. From conversations with my father, William Durwood Waldrop, of Monroe, Louisiana.

an important component of mission, must reconnect to the cosmologies of our ancestors and learn from the indigenous cultures that hold to a high view of the Spirit's ongoing work in creation.

Contributions of other christian
voices in latin america

Although indigenous influences are key in the development of a Pentecostal ecotheology and corresponding eco-mission, there are a variety of additional voices that are being added to the chorus. For example, Latin America has been blessed to have the prolific voice of Brazilian theologian Leonardo Boff, a former Roman Catholic priest, silenced by the Vatican, who now continues to use the pen as an instrument of choice in the struggle for ecojustice and liberation.[17] Boff's predilection for Francis of Assisi, with his love for all things created, adds a historical and pietistic dimension to his ecological and theological arguments.[18]

Similarly, it is no coincidence that the new Roman Catholic Pope, from Argentina, has taken the name Francis. There are other ecumenical and feminist voices from Latin America now forging their own new paths into the new mission paradigm for ecojustice.[19] Prominent Evangelical/ Protestant progressive voices are coming primarily from those associated with the *Fraternidad Teológica Latinoamericana* (Latin American Theological Fraternity). Included are mission theologians such as C. René Padilla, Juan B. Stam, Pedro Arana, Darío López and Ruth Padilla Deborst.[20] Perhaps the greatest non-Latin influence upon growing theological and ecological awareness is that of Jürgen Moltmann, many of whose works (*The Spirit of Life* and *God in Creation*)[21] are available in Spanish and widely used in Latin American theological seminaries.

17. See Boff, *Cry of the Earth, Cry of the Poor*; and *Ecology and Liberation*.

18. See Boff, *Francis of Assisi*.

19. See Ress, *Ecofeminism in Latin America*, and the Spanish review *Con-spirando: Revista latinoamericana de ecofeminismo, espiritualidad y teología*.

20. See Padilla, *El Cuidado de la Creación y el Calentamiento Global*. Also, Stam, *Las Buenas Nuevas de la Creación*. For a very helpful Wesleyan perspective in English, see Snyder and Scandrett, *Salvation Means Creation Healed*.

21. In Spanish, *El Espíritu Santo y la teología de la vida*, Ediciones Sígueme, 2000; and *Dios en la creación*, Ediciones Sígueme, 1987. Most recently, in English, see Moltmann, *Sun of Righteousness, ARISE!*

Nationalist Pentecostals are not left entirely out of the picture either. As far back as 1992, Pentecostals in Latin America were beginning to reflect upon the significance of Scripture for ecological concern. In the November, 1992 meeting of the Latin American Pentecostal Encounter (EPLA) in São Paulo, Brazil, under the auspices of the Latin American Evangelical Pentecostal Commission (CEPLA), the theme of the meeting and papers presented reflected these concerns.[22] Again, as in the missionary context of Africa, it should be emphasized that the Pentecostal churches and leaders represented in these meetings were mostly those of non-missionary aligned national churches with no restrictions imposed from the North in regards to theological concerns or agendas. More recently, other progressive Pentecostal leaders are beginning to address ecological subjects. For example, Church of God National Bishop, Darío López, of Peru speaks of "holistic care of creation" in a paper presented to an international (U.S. and Latin American) gathering of leaders in Quito, Ecuador in 2008, and further elaborates in a more recently published work.[23]

A way forward: the integration of contributions

So, what is the future for Pentecostal ecological concern in Latin America and beyond? Certainly we are living in a time of changing perspectives and paradigms and that should give hope to those of us who take our ecological responsibility seriously. In addition to the foundation of ancient reverence for life and nature bequeathed to us by the indigenous peoples of Abya Yala, we have the richness of our own Pentecostal theological tradition to draw upon. As we broaden our understanding and experience of the role of the Spirit of Life from the personal and social into the environmental and cosmic dimensions of life, our mission praxis must

---

22. The theme of the meeting was "Acción del Espíritu en la Iglesia y en la creación para la liberación de su esclavitud de corrupción: Romanos 8:16–23" (The Action of the Spirit in Church and Creation for its Liberation from the Slavery of Corruption: Romans 8:16–23). Also, see the conference paper presented by Ricardo Waldrop, "Profundización bíblico-teológica," Encuentro Pentecostal Latinoamericano, Comisión Evangélica Pentecostal Latinoamericana, São Paulo, Brasil, 1992.

23 See López, "El cuidado integral de la creación," a paper presented at the Church of God Care Conference in Quito, Ecuador, October, 2008. It is certain that Lopez's address to the "Care Conference" did not coincide directly with the ideas regarding "care" conceived by the organizers of the event from the U.S. since their concerns were mainly related to relief work and social assistance. Also see López, *Pentecostalismo y misión integral*.

also change. For certainly it is good to do research and write theological treatises, but that alone is not sufficient. Our research and writing must be accompanied by reflection leading to praxis.

Thankfully, as pointed out earlier, younger Western scholars and practitioners in the Pentecostal movement are showing the way forward and in Latin America we are also seeing hopeful signs of an awakening in this regard.[24] In the recent course offered on "Eco-theology and Mission," students were enthusiastic about the practical implications of our study. Some students have developed ecological projects to be implemented in local congregations, calling for the use of recycled material for Sunday School curricula and for other personal and commercial uses such as wristbands, necklaces, dolls, flowerpots and waste containers.[25] We also now have excellent contextualized printed and internet materials available for reflection and action, including a new "EcoBíblia" sponsored by the United Bible Society and the Latin American Theological Fraternity.[26] Another very helpful resource is the manual, *Iglesia verde: Guía para una misión por el planeta y la humanidad* (*Green Church: A Mission Guide for the Planet and for Humanity*).[27] Across the continent, among younger Pentecostal, postmodern, and post-Pentecostal pastors and leaders, there is growing concern for the practice of mission that is spiritual, contextual, social, political, and ecological. We are beginning to listen to and learn from our indigenous elders and from voices coming from other Christian traditions. We are learning to read the "Book of Nature" and practice a hermeneutics of creation along with our growing re-visioning of Scripture.[28] We are also in the process of recovering the radical roots of our own Pentecostal tradition. Hopefully, we will continue to learn together to discern the spirits, and as we are attentive to the Spirit of creation, the Spirit of Life, and the Spirit of Pentecost poured out on all flesh

24. See Yong's excellent chapter, "The Heavens Above and the Earth Below," in *The Spirit Poured Out on All Flesh*. See also the recent publication of Swoboda, *Tongues and Trees*.

25. My students Nataly Asencios, Jonathan Chasipanta, and Rufino Ávalos, in a final project presented for the Eco-theology and Mission course at the Seminario Sudamericano, Quito, Ecuador, June, 2013.

26. EcoBiblia, Sociedades Bíblicas Unidas, 2011.

27. Elaborated by Montesdeoca, Iglesia Verde.

28. Early and medieval theologians believed that the "Book of Nature" was a source of God's revelation to humanity and should be read alongside Scripture. For more on this subject, see Moltmann, *Sun of Righteousness, ARISE!*, 189–94.

234 RICHARD E. WALDROP

and in all of the cosmos, will respond in ways that will honor and protect both the Creation and human beings created in God's image.

BIBLIOGRAPHY

Boff, Leonardo. *Ecology and Liberation: A New Paradigm.* New York: Orbis, 1998.

———. *Francis of Assisi: A Model for Human Liberation.* New York: Orbis, 1982.

———. *Cry of the Earth, Cry of the Poor.* New York: Orbis, 1995.

Daneel, M. L. *African Earthkeepers.* 2 vols. Pretoria: Unisa, 1998.

Galeano, Eduardo. *Open Veins of Latin America: Five Centuries of the Pillage of a Continent.* New York: Monthly Review, 1997.

Irarrázaval, Diego. *Inculturation: New Dawn of the Church in Latin America.* New York: Orbis, 2000.

Maslow, Jonathan. *Bird of Life, Bird of Death: A Political Ornithology of Central America.* Manchester, NH: Laurel, 1987.

McConnell, John, Jr., and John C. Munday. *Earth Day: Vision for Peace, Justice, and Earth Care: My Life and Thought at Age 96.* Eugene, OR: Resource, 2011.

Moltmann, Jürgen. *God in Creation: A New Theology of Creation and the Spirit of God.* Translated by Margaret Kohl. Minneapolis: Fortress, 1993.

———. *The Spirit of Life: A Universal Affirmation.* Translated by Margaret Kohl. Minneapolis: Fortress, 1993.

———. *Sun of Righteousness, ARISE!: God's Future for Humanity and the Earth.* Translated by Margaret Kohl. Minneapolis: Fortress, 2010.

Ress, Mary Judith. *Ecofeminism in Latin America: Women from the Margins.* New York: Orbis, 2006.

Schlesinger, Stephen, and Stephen Kinzer. *Bitter Fruit: The Story of the American Coup in Guatemala.* Cambridge, MA: Harvard University Press, 2005.

Snyder, Howard, with Joel Scandrett. *Salvation Means Creation Healed: The Ecology of Sin and Grace.* Eugene, OR: Cascade, 2011.

Swoboda, A. J. *Tongues and Trees: Toward a Pentecostal Ecological Theology.* Journal of Pentecostal Theology Supplement 40. Blandford Forum, UK: Deo, 2013.

Woodley, Randy. *Shalom and the Community of Creation: An Indigenous Vision.* Grand Rapids: Eerdmans, 2012.

Yong, Amos, ed. *Remembering Jamestown: Hard Questions about Christian Mission.* Eugene, OR: Wipf & Stock, 2008.

———. *The Spirit Poured Out upon All Flesh: Pentecostalism and the Possibility of Global Theology.* Grand Rapids: Baker Academic, 2005.